Fiscal Governance in Europe

This book presents a theoretical framework to discuss how governments coordinate budgeting decisions. There are two modes of fiscal governance conducive to greater fiscal discipline, a mode of delegation and a mode of contracts. These modes contrast with a fiefdom form of governance, in which the decision-making process is decentralized. An important insight is that the effectiveness of a given form of fiscal governance depends crucially on the underlying political system. Delegation functions well when there are few, or no, ideological differences among government parties, whereas contracts are effective when there are many such differences.

Based on original research, the book classifies European Union countries from 1985 to 2004. Empirically, delegation and contract states perform better than fiefdom states if they match the underlying political system. In addition, chapters consider why countries have the fiscal institutions that they do, fiscal governance in Central and Eastern Europe, and the role of such institutions in the European Union.

Mark Hallerberg is professor of public management and political economy at the Hertie School of Governance. He also maintains an affiliation with the Political Science Department at Emory University in Atlanta, Georgia. He has published widely on fiscal governance, tax competition, exchange rate choice, and European politics. He has previously held academic positions at Emory University, the University of Pittsburgh, and the Georgia Institute of Technology. He has also served as a visiting scholar at the University of Amsterdam, University of Bonn, University of Mannheim, and University of Munich (all in economics departments). He has done consulting work for the Dutch Ministry of Finance, Ernst & Young Poland, the European Central Bank, the International Monetary Fund, the Organisation for Economic Cooperation and Development, and the World Bank.

Rolf Rainer Strauch is Adviser in the Directorate General Economics at the European Central Bank in Frankfurt, Germany. He previously worked at the Deutsche Bundesbank. He has been a consultant to the OECD, the European Commission, and the Dutch Ministry of Finance. He has also published widely in the area of public economics and European integration.

Jürgen von Hagen is professor of economics at the University of Bonn, Germany. He previously taught at the University of Mannheim and at Indiana University, where he maintains an affiliation with the Kelley School of Business. Von Hagen is a Research Fellow of CEPR, London, and a member of the Academic Advisory Council of the Federal Ministry of Economics and Technology in Germany, and he served as a member of the French Comité Economique de la Nation. He has been a consultant to the IMF, the World Bank, the Federal Reserve Board, the European Commission, the ECB, and numerous governments in Europe and beyond. Von Hagen has published widely in the areas of macroeconomics and public economics.

Cambridge Studies in Comparative Politics

General Editor
Margaret Levi *University of Washington, Seattle*

Assistant General Editor
Stephen Hanson *University of Washington, Seattle*

Associate Editors
Robert H. Bates *Harvard University*
Torben Iversen *Harvard University*
Stathis Kalyvas *Yale University*
Peter Lange *Duke University*
Helen Milner *Columbia University*
Frances Rosenbluth *Yale University*
Susan Stokes *University of Chicago*
Kathleen Thelen *Northwestern University*
Erik Wibbels, *Duke University*

Other Books in the Series

Continued after the Index

Fiscal Governance in Europe

MARK HALLERBERG

Hertie School of Governance and Emory University

ROLF RAINER STRAUCH

European Central Bank

JÜRGEN VON HAGEN

Rheinische Friedrich-Wilhelms-University Bonn

CAMBRIDGE
UNIVERSITY PRESS

CAMBRIDGE UNIVERSITY PRESS
Cambridge, New York, Melbourne, Madrid, Cape Town, Singapore, São Paulo, Delhi

Cambridge University Press
32 Avenue of the Americas, New York, NY 10013-2473, USA

www.cambridge.org
Information on this title: www.cambridge.org/9780521857468

First published 2009

Printed in the United States of America

A catalog record for this publication is available from the British Library.

Library of Congress Cataloging in Publication Data

Hallerberg, Mark.
Fiscal governance in Europe / Mark Hallerberg, Rolf Rainer Strauch, Jürgen von Hagen.
   p.   cm. – (Cambridge studies in comparative politics)
Includes bibliographical references and index.
ISBN 978-0-521-85746-8 (hardback)
1. Fiscal policy – European Union countries. 2. Finance, Public – European
Union countries. 3. Budget – European Union countries. 4. Fiscal policy – Europe.
5. Finance, Public – Europe. 6. Budget – Europe. I. Strauch, Rolf. II. Hagen,
Jürgen von. III. Title. IV. Series.
HJ1000.H352 2009
339.5′2094 – dc22   2008047220

ISBN 978-0-521-85746-8 hardback

Contents

Acknowledgments

This book has benefited from the gracious help of many people. We could not have completed it without the anonymous comments of relevant actors at finance ministries, central banks, and parliamentary budget committees in European Union countries who answered our surveys, phone calls, and faxes and who graciously made themselves available for in-person interviews where needed. Their willingness to respond to our queries over a fifteen-year period was essential to make this book possible. The book reflects numerous discussions and collaboration with colleagues in the academic and policymaking institutions over the years during which we have been working on studies on fiscal governance.

However, we would like to thank particularly several persons and institutions which directly supported the book project.

Stefania Fabrizio provided invaluable comments on the empirical sections, and her suggestions on the coding of some variables resolved some nagging problems.

Holger Gleich's work on Central and East European countries in the period prior to 2003 was especially welcome as background material for the examination of fiscal governance in these countries in Chapter 6. The institutional proposal for a Sustainability Council for Europe, elaborated in Chapter 7, draws on joint work with Antonio Fatás, Andrew Hughes Hallett, and Anne Sibert. Similarly, some tables and text in that chapter appeared in Jürgen von Hagen 2006, "Fiscal Rules and Fiscal Performance in the European Union and Japan," *Monetary and Economic Studies*, Vol. 24, No. 1 (March), Institute for Monetary and Economic Studies, Bank of Japan, and is reproduced with permission from the Bank of Japan.

We would like to thank participants at seminars at the following institutions for their suggestions to improve the argument and the book: Bank of Finland, Columbia University, Duke University, European Central Bank, European Commission, London School of Economics, Nuffield College at Oxford University, University of California at Davis, University of Essex, University of Kentucky, University of Virginia, and University of Zürich. Individuals who deserve particular thanks include David Bearce, Clifford Carrubba, William Roberts Clark, Henrik Enderlein, Robert Franzese, Matt Gabel, Herbert Kitschelt, Ashoka Mody, Christiane Nickel, Thomas Plümper, Eric Reinhardt, Philipp Rother, Alberta Sbragia, Holli Semetko, Ad van Riet, Joachim Wehner, Guido Wolswijk, and Sami Yläoutinen.

Andrew Kirkpatrick, Angelika Behlen, and Dayna Sadow provided research assistance and helped with editing issues.

The Dutch Finance Ministry generously provided funding for the second set of surveys and for follow-up interviews. Program Sprawne Państwo at Ernst & Young Poland supported research on Poland. The Program on Governance at Emory University's Halle Institute covered travel for coauthors and established a forum to bring together experts working on political economy issues to discuss parts of this book.

The publication process at Cambridge University Press has been remarkably easy. Margaret Levi has provided prompt and thoughtful feedback, while Lew Bateman has remained an important backer of the project.

The views that are expressed in this book are those of the authors and do not necessarily reflect the views of the European Central Bank.

Finally, books like these do not get written without the support of understanding spouses and families at home. Our biggest thanks go to Sabine, Carolina, Ilse, and our kids.

1

Introduction

In the early 1990s, the most pressing public policy problem in Europe was mounting debt. The average general government debt ratio as a percentage of GDP almost doubled in a little more than a decade, from almost 38% in 1980 to 73% in 1993 (AMECO 2005). These aggregates even conceal the full extent of the problem – in countries like Belgium, Ireland, and Italy the debt ratio moved above 100% of GDP. With these problems evident, the heads of state and government agreed to the road map to a single currency in the form of the Maastricht Treaty in December 1991. The designers of Economic and Monetary Union expected that governments would get their economies in shape before they adopted the new currency, the euro. Member states were consequently supposed to meet five "Maastricht" criteria. The most contentious of the five criteria concerned fiscal policy. States were expected to have general government budget deficits no greater than 3% of GDP and debts no larger than 60% or on a declining path. While the debt level ultimately was not critical, the deficit level was, and in the immediate years after the signing of the Maastricht Treaty in February 1992 it looked as if the euro would not get off the ground because of widespread deficit problems. In 1994, only Ireland and Luxembourg had deficits below 3%. A eurozone without big countries like France and especially Germany would never have been created in the first place.

By 1997, however, all countries but Greece had managed to get their deficits below 3% of GDP, and the Greeks seemingly pushed their deficits below this benchmark to qualify as well in 2000. In 2000 more generally, fiscal policy was healthy. Nine of fifteen European Union countries had budget surpluses. Only Portugal and, as it emerged later, Greece were either near or above the 3% level.[1]

It turned out that this fiscal performance was the calm before the storm. Figures were healthy, but it was not difficult to perform well as the European economies were especially strong. Large sums from the sale of mobile phone frequencies also boosted the revenues of some countries, making fiscal positions seem even stronger than they actually were. A recession hit the European Union countries beginning in 2001. Budget balances dropped from an average of 1.3% of GDP in 2000 to –1.8% by 2003. Five of the twelve countries in the eurozone had deficits above 3% (AMECO 2007).

The European Union had procedures to deal with this situation. The European Commission could recommend that the Union send "early warnings" to member states that would have deficits above 3% in the future. Once member states exceeded this reference value, it could also recommend that countries had "excessive deficits," starting the excessive deficit procedure for such countries. They would then be given deadlines to take measures to correct their deficits. If no action was taken, it was possible under the rules to fine a state.[2] Each step of the process required a Commission recommendation and the approval of a qualified majority of ECOFIN, the gathering of Economic and Finance Ministers. Portugal was found to have an "excessive deficit" in 2001, France and Germany in 2002, and Greece and the Netherlands in 2003. Yet despite these actions the deficits in France and Germany in particular did not improve. When it became clear that France would have a deficit above 3% again in 2004, the third year in a row, the European Commission recommended that ECOFIN place "notices" on France and Germany, a procedure which was one step away from formal sanctions (Morris, Ongena, and Schuknecht 2006, 17). The proposal failed to receive the backing of a qualified majority of member states. The European Commission then took the Council of Ministers to the European Court of Justice on the issue. While the Court did ultimately rule that the Council should not have suspended the punishment mechanism, it also noted that the Council more generally does have discretion (European Commission 2004; *Financial Times*, January 13, 2004). France and Germany ultimately ran "excessive" deficits for another two years, and the member states changed

---

[1] The Greeks were not as successful as first thought; revised figures a few years later put the deficit at above 4% of GDP in 2000 (AMECO 2007).

[2] An excellent review of the procedures is found in Morris et al. 2006.

the rules through a reform of the Stability and Growth Pact in March 2005.[3]

The discussion of the clash at the European Union level suggests that the European Union–level rules were not effective in maintaining deficits below 3%. At the same time, this is not the whole story. While all countries experienced the same recession in general, some had difficulties while others did not. The puzzle here is why some countries had larger fiscal deteriorations than others. To answer this question, we need to examine the fiscal institutions at the national level and then put them in the European context. How are budgets made in practice? Are some fiscal institutions, norms, and procedures more effective than others? Moreover, how does the overall political environment affect the effectiveness of those very fiscal institutions?

Our Approach

This book makes at least three contributions to the current literature when answering these questions. First, we provide a new theoretical explanation for differences in fiscal performance in Europe. Second, we take seriously the source of fiscal institutions and we endogenize them in our analysis. Finally, we present a new dataset on fiscal institutions, norms, and procedures over a twenty-year period for the fifteen European Union countries that were member states when the euro was introduced in 1999.

In terms of our theoretical argument, we begin with the premise that the way in which governments make budgets has a substantial impact on what those budgets look like, both when they are proposed and when they are executed. Procedures for determining the budget are so important because they affect the overall level of centralization of the budget process. A fundamental characteristic of modern public finances is that governments spend money drawn from a general tax fund on policies targeting specific groups in society. The fact that the group of those who pay for such policies (the general taxpayers) is larger than the group of those who benefit from them implies a divergence between the net benefits accruing to the targeted groups and the net benefits for society as a whole. This incongruity is called the *common pool problem of public finances* (von Hagen and Harden 1996). It causes the targeted groups and the politicians representing them to demand more spending on such policies than is optimal for society as a whole. Thus, the common pool

---

[3] Both countries managed to get their deficits below 3% of GDP in 2006.

problem leads to excessive levels of public spending. Putting the argument into a dynamic context, one can show that it also leads to excessive deficits and government debts (Velasco 2000; von Hagen and Harden 1996; Chapter 2).

This tendency for excessive spending, deficits, and debt increases with the number of politicians drawing on the same general tax fund, a point empirically confirmed by Perotti and Kontopoulos (1999). Ideological and ethnic divisions or ethnolinguistic and religious fractionalizations of societies increase the tendency of people on one side to neglect the tax burden falling on the other side, making the common pool problem more severe. Thus, empirical studies showing that such schisms result in higher spending levels, deficits, and debt confirm the importance of this problem (e.g., Roubini and Sachs 1989; Alesina and Perotti 1995; Annett 2000). The common pool problem also looms large behind vertical fiscal relations within countries. Transfers from the central to local governments imply that residents in one region benefit from taxes paid by residents in other regions. Bailouts of overindebted local governments are a special form of such transfers.

At the heart of the common pool problem of public finances is the externality that results from using general tax funds to finance targeted public policies. Individual politicians perceive that an increase in spending on targeted policies will provide their constituencies with more public services at only a fraction of the total cost. The resulting spending and deficit biases can be reduced if politicians can be made to take a more comprehensive view of the costs and benefits of their decisions. This is the main role of the budget process. The budget process consists of the formal and informal rules governing budgetary decisions of the executive and legislative branches of government. A centralized budget process contains elements that induce decision makers to internalize the common pool externality by taking a comprehensive view of their decisions. A fragmented budget process fails to do that.

We are interested in what we refer to as "forms of fiscal governance" that determine the level of centralization. The term "governance" connotes a broad perspective on the institutions, that is, the system of procedures (or fiscal institutions) in place to make budgets. It is tempting to focus on one procedure or rule only, and to proclaim that the adoption of that rule will "fix" the system. Our contention is that one needs to consider the entire system. Centralization of the process when the cabinet makes a decision may not yield a centralized outcome if parliament can add back in all of the spending that a finance minister excised months earlier. Similarly, a centralized procedure in parliament may have little effect if the common pool problem is rife in the budget the government proposes.

In this book, we develop two alternative roads to greater centralization. *Delegation* involves vesting the finance minister with significant decision-making powers over public monies. The finance minister both plays a dominant role within the cabinet during the proposal stage of the budget process and is responsible for monitoring the execution of the budget and making any necessary changes during the budget's implementation. In contrast, under *contracts* a group of agents with similar decision-making rights (usually political parties) enter an agreement to commit themselves strictly to targets for budget aggregates set for one or more years. These modes contrast with a *fiefdom* form of governance, where the decision-making process is fragmented, ministers dictate their own budgets, and fiscal discipline is consequently lax.

An important insight is that the effectiveness of a given form of fiscal governance depends crucially upon the underlying political system. If parties disagree on basic policy issues about how much should be spent where or on how much a given group in society should be taxed, they are unlikely to allow a finance minister to make decisions on the budget for all of them. Similarly, parties are less likely to delegate powers to one ministry if they expect to compete with one another in future elections. Finance ministers in this situation could use their position to advance their own party's interests at the expense of other parties. This discussion suggests that strengthening the formal powers of a finance minister where there are great ideological differences among the policymakers who are needed to approve the budget will have little practical effect, while a similar strengthening of the finance minister should have a large effect where there is little ideological discord in government, so long as the party or parties are running together in the next election. Alternatively, contracts should work well in places where ideological differences are large and/or where coalition parties are strong competitors for votes. Contracts make explicit the terms of the budgetary agreement, so there is little reason to worry about the motives of the finance minister, whose role is reduced to enforcing the preexisting contract. Because the parties that negotiate contracts consider the full tax burden, they internalize the common pool externality, so the level of centralization is the same as under a strong and effective finance minister.

We use our analytical framework to classify European Union countries during the period 1985–2004. On the basis of our own detailed surveys of finance ministry and central bank officials and members of parliament in

1991, 2000, and 2004 in the fifteen members of the European Union before the May 2004 enlargement, we construct a database describing the prevailing modes of fiscal governance during the twenty-year period. This database allows us to consider whether differences in fiscal institutions lead to differences in fiscal performance. Empirically, we find that countries that should be either *delegation* or *contract* states perform better the more fiscal institutions they adopt that are consistent with their predicted approach.

This discussion has important policy and theoretical implications. On the policy side, one can imagine a situation where a given form of fiscal governance is in place but where the underlying political environment changes. For example, the German government had closely aligned coalition governments under Chancellor Helmut Kohl. The move to a coalition under Chancellor Gerhard Schröder, characterized by policy differences between the Social Democrats and the Greens, and then to the grand coalition government between the Christian and Social Democrats, made the ideological differences larger. Our argument implies that the same set of fiscal institutions that worked well under Kohl should be less effective under Chancellors Schröder and Merkel. Indeed, as indicated before, the Schröder government had serious difficulties with fiscal discipline, which became fully visible in the recession of the early 2000s. The Merkel government enjoyed the double benefits of a tax hike and a strong global economy in its early years, but the verdict is still out on what it actually achieved to improve Germany's long-term fiscal health. We provide further strong empirical evidence that institutional effectiveness varies both across countries and within them depending upon the relevant underlying policy differences.

On the theoretical side, the comparative politics literature has increasingly focused on how different types of institutions interact and even reinforce one another, with one prominent approach focused on political system institutions and another on actors in the economy. Lijphart (1999) proposes two ideal types of systems, majoritarian and consensual. The former group of states have institutions that reinforce the power of a majority in a given country to enact legislation. They therefore usually have plurality electoral systems and two parties in the legislature, which, in turn, elect one-party majority governments. Consensual systems, in contrast, have political systems designed to require the assent of several groups in society, not just a simple majority, for there to be policy change. Such countries usually have proportional representation systems, many parties in the legislature, and multiparty coalition governments.

Rather than focusing on the characteristics of the political system, the varieties-of-capitalism approach (e.g., Hall and Soskice 2001) is actor-centered and discusses especially the requirements of firms. Firms face a series of coordination problems, be they industrial relations, vocational education and training, corporate governance and financing, or interfirm relations. There are two ideal sets of institutions to resolve these problems, which, in turn, lead to the ideal types of liberal market economies and coordinated market economies. In the former, institutions provide coordination through competitive market arrangements. Firms in the former economies receive market financing, support fluid labor markets, and expect employees to have general skills so that there is an emphasis on in-house training. Firms regard competition with each other as zero-sum, and there is little or no cooperation on research and development. Their counterparts in coordinated market economies, in contrast, receive some financing from more patient capital, such as banks; support more rigid labor markets; and expect employees to have more specialized skills that all firms in an industry have helped develop. There is some cooperation on research and development.

While we will explore some of the implications of this book for the respective literatures in more detail in the concluding chapter, we would like to emphasize at the outset that our work has important links with both of them. Like Lijphart, we consider the effects of electoral and party systems. Yet we add an important, and so far neglected, piece to the puzzle, namely, how these systemic variables affect the way governments organize themselves to produce policy. Moreover, we identify which parts of Lijphart's framework matter most. One would expect delegation to a strong finance minister in one of Lijphart's majoritarian systems, for example, but the reasoning in our case is that there is a one-party majority government in office. If the form of government shifts to a multiparty coalition, fiscal contracts would then be expected.

There are similar linkages with the varieties-of-capitalism literature. The solutions that firms reach for their coordination problems are achieved in the context of certain policy institutions or request some policy intervention. They are linked to the decision-making mechanisms of the set of actors who appear in government. Rather than firms, it is the set of political parties or government actors that have to reach agreements that are positive-sum. The varieties-of-capitalism approach has argued that government structures, and in particular the constellation of parties in government, have implications for the investment structure and for the relationship with employer and workers' associations. Much in line with the basic idea advanced in our approach for fiscal policies, coalition governments facilitate coordination with social partners because they may find it more difficult to change the policy stance, which renders trust in policy stability. By comparison, policy positions of powerful single-party governments – as in the United Kingdom – may be perceived as too changeable to generate trust and coordination (Hall and Soskice 2001). Therefore, the correspondence between the different types of institutions, that is, fiscal institutions in our case and firm-based institutions under the varieties-of-capitalism approach, is more than a coincidence. Countries we predict in our book should have long periods of fiscal contracts, such as Belgium, Finland, and the Netherlands, are all classified as coordinated market economies. However, the concrete assessment may also differ, because different institutional characteristics are taken into account. Most notably, while a delegation state would be suitable both for the United Kingdom and for Germany, the varieties-of-capitalism approach classifies them as different types of economies with contrasting forms of government-business coordination. We will explore further the possible relationship between the two in the Conclusion.

Outline of the Rest of the Book

The rest of the book proceeds as follows. Chapter 2 discusses the work done in political economy to date on fiscal institutions and fiscal performance. One strand of the literature, including landmark works like Roubini and Sachs (1989) and Persson and Tabellini (2000, 2004), considers how political institutions affect fiscal performance. Another strand, including most notably Wildavsky's early work, looks only at fiscal rules. Our book integrates both strands by considering packages of fiscal rules as forms of fiscal governance. All governments face a common pool resource (CPR) problem because policymakers potentially do not consider the full tax implications of their spending decisions. One form of governance is fiefdom, which arises when the budget process is decentralized. Fiscal discipline should be lax under fiefdom. Two alternative forms of governance, delegation and contracts, represent solutions to the CPR problem. These forms of fiscal governance differ in their functionality for the prevailing type of government in EU member states. Electoral systems shape the type of government and the inherent principal-agent problem for fiscal governance. *Contracts* are appropriate for countries with a proportionality rule, which tends to produce coalition governments. *Delegation* is the choice for countries with plurality rule or other systems that produce single-party governments (or the functional equivalent – governments where the same parties run together as a bloc in election after election, as in France and Germany).

Chapter 3 uses the theoretical framework to classify countries according to the forms of fiscal governance over the period 1985–2004. It presents a novel dataset to develop indices to consider how closely a given country fits either the "delegation" or "contracts" ideal. It finds that there has been a general improvement in the centralization of the budget process in most countries, but also that there remain significant differences between countries.

Chapter 4 explores whether these differences have real effects on budgetary performance. We consider in particular how forms of fiscal governance affect budget deficits, debts, expenditures, and forecasting errors. It finds that *delegation* and *contract* states are equally adept at maintaining fiscal discipline, while *fiefdom* leads to higher deficits, debt levels, and expenditure growth. Governments with elements of contracting in place are generally more conservative in economic forecasts than governments under either *delegation* or *fiefdom* forms of governance.

Chapter 5 then addresses the endogeneity question, namely: Why does a country adopt a given set of fiscal institutions, and why do these institutions sometimes approach one of the theoretical ideals we provide (delegation or contracts) and sometimes not? We suppose that populations face the same common pool problem that their representatives face. Why should they support politicians who are in favor of centralizing the budget process? We consider the role that fiscal crises play in informing populations and politicians alike about the consequences of decentralized political institutions. We find that countries with histories of fiscal crises have adopted more robust fiscal institutions. The expected form of fiscal governance matters as well. Countries make changes consistent with the form of governance that should perform best given the underlying political conditions. A brief case study of the Netherlands after 2000 provides more detail about how and why governments change their fiscal institutions when they do.

Chapter 6 considers the development of fiscal institutions in the accession countries in Central and Eastern Europe. These countries generally had to introduce new fiscal systems after the initiation of democracy and the move from a planned to a market economy in the early 1990s. Unlike in the countries analyzed in Chapter 5, the development of fiscal institutions is not burdened to the same extent by history and tradition. What sort of fiscal institutions did they adopt, and why did they choose some institutions and not others? We present fiscal institutional data from these countries. We find that experience with fiscal crises in the formative years of the new democracy as well as greater levels of ethnic fragmentation lead to more centralized fiscal institutions. At the same time, our argument would predict that fiscal contracts would be appropriate in all countries but Hungary and (maybe) Bulgaria, and no country has a form of fiscal governance that approaches contracts. More reforms of fiscal institutions in these countries are needed. The chapter concludes with a case study of the evolution of Polish fiscal governance.

Chapter 7 expands the focus to the European Union. It considers the interplay between national and European Union institutions. The delegation approach hinges on the delegation of power to the minister of finance to overcome the coordination problem inherent in budgetary decision making; the contract approach instead relies on preestablished budgetary targets and rules. The European Union rules reinforce the use of targets at the national level, but they do little to strengthen finance ministers. The contract approach, therefore, seems to be much more compatible with the European fiscal framework than the delegation approach. We propose the creation of a Sustainability Council for Europe that would provide additional support for domestic fiscal institutions.

The Conclusion discusses fruitful avenues for future work. The policy implications of our research are clear. The design of fiscal institutions for a given country depends critically upon the underlying political structure. All countries do need to centralize their budget processes, but there is no one-size-fits-all prescription on how best to do it. On the theoretical side, our work builds on the existing comparative political literature in several ways. The relative stability of delegation or fiscal contracts may depend on the variables the broader literature has identified, such as party systems. At the same time, our work provides a new framework to consider how party systems affect institutional choices and how these institutions that structure how governments make decisions have real policy consequences. On this account, the comparative perspective in this book complements and expands the insights from the literature in the field in two respects. First, our argument is truly comparative in the sense that it explains the variation of politics across countries. In Tilly's (1984) classification of comparative work, our approach is variation-finding, although the basic mechanism is derived from a general political economy argument. In this respect, this book complements much of the existing political economy and American politics literature on budgetary institutions, which lacks this dimension. Second, it shows the value and complementarity of different methods to analyze politics and the role of institutions. In our earlier work, we have made use of case studies, nonparametric statistical approaches, as well as more high-powered econometrics to advance the empirical evidence on the role of budgetary institutions. A preceding book (Hallerberg 2004) followed a process-tracing approach and used detailed comparative case studies. In this book, we pick up the argument advanced there on the interaction between government constellations and institutions, refine and formalize it, and again employ a "large-n" econometric approach to validate it. Nevertheless, short case studies are reported to clarify and illustrate the argument, but from a methodological perspective they do not carry the same burden of proof. Indeed, we hope that the compilation of evidence in our book helps the reader as a methodological guidepost on how to combine different analytical approaches to advance our knowledge in comparative politics.

2

Electoral and Fiscal Institutions and Forms of Fiscal Governance

For much of the post–World War II period, budgets remained roughly in balance over the economic cycle in industrialized countries. There were exceptions, such as in Fourth Republic France, but most countries performed well. The Bretton Woods system played an important role in keeping fiscal policies in line. European countries were pegged to the U.S. dollar and under the supervision of the International Monetary Fund. With strong and effective capital controls in place, weak finances meant that a country would have to borrow from the Fund.

Once Bretton Woods collapsed in the early 1970s, however, many countries liberalized their capital accounts and the IMF ended its role as a fiscal supervisor. There were two oil shocks, and one would have expected some increase in deficits and debts resulting from macroeconomic stabilization policies. Yet what one observes are high, and rising, levels of public debts and deficits in many countries through a much later period, or the early 1990s. The general government debt figures as a percentage of GDP are particularly revealing – while the average debt level for the European Union-15, the United States, and Japan was only about 28% of GDP in 1973, it increased in virtually every year to a high of 73% of GDP in 1996.[1] The average then dropped to about 65% by 2000 and stabilized at that level through 2004. These figures, however, mask a divergence in budgetary performance. While the United Kingdom had a debt burden 15% higher than Italy's 51.3% of GDP in 1973 at 64.9%, by 2004 the British debt burden was 64% lower than Italy's (or 41.6% versus 105.8%). Von Hagen (1992) indicates that this diversity is not due to differences in the economic

[1] Only from 1988 to 1989 was there a drop in the average debt to GDP ratio, from 59.7% to 58.1%. In every other year from 1973 to 1996 there was an increase in the average.

12

shocks the countries experienced. As Alesina and Perotti (1995) suggest, the challenge is to explain these differences in performance.

This chapter reviews three types of arguments put forward to explain the divergence in fiscal performance. The first set is from the macroeconomic literature. While such arguments may fit the pre-1973 world, they do not explain the divergence in fiscal performance. The second set focuses on underlying political variables, such as the electoral system or the stability of the government, that are characteristics of national governments. The third set considers fiscal rules that structure the budget process. The focus is on procedures that centralize the way policymakers plan, decide, and execute the annual budget.

We are sympathetic to the political and fiscal institutional arguments, but we argue in the second section of the chapter that they are inherently inter-related. Electoral systems in particular precondition the type of fiscal rules that are most effective at centralizing the budget process. There are two ideal forms of fiscal governance, delegation and contracts, which establish the appropriate package of fiscal rules. Delegation involves vesting the finance minister with significant decision-making powers over public monies. Under contracts a group of agents with similar decision-making rights enters an agreement to commit themselves strictly to budgetary norms, that is, targets for budget aggregates set for one or several years in the form of a fiscal contract.

Other underlying political institutions determine which form of fiscal governance is most appropriate for a given country. Countries with plurality systems or with proportional representation with high thresholds for parties to enter parliament encourage one-party majority governments or coalition governments with parties that are close to one another ideologically. Delegation to a strong finance minister works well in such settings. Proportional representation systems with low thresholds usually result in coalition governments where there are large differences in ideology among the parties. Such parties are not willing to delegate fiscal powers to a strong finance minister in this case, and fiscal contracts instead can provide the needed centralization of the budget process.

Explanations from Economics

For a number of reasons, fiscal developments since 1973 are difficult to explain on the basis of conventional economics alone. According to Keynesian economics, fiscal policy is an important tool to control the level of aggregate demand in the economy. Governments should run deficits in times of recessions and surpluses in times of prosperity to stabilize the economy. The incipient deficits during the oil crises of the 1970s fit this prescription, but their persistence after the end of the oil crises does not. Neoclassical economics, in contrast, denies the stabilizing potential of fiscal policy. According to this theory, taxes cause distortions in the labor market, and the welfare costs of these distortions increase when tax rates are changed frequently. Governments faced with an unavoidable, yet temporary, rise in spending, such as the response to a natural disaster or the outbreak of war, should engage in tax smoothing. Governments should raise tax rates only by a small amount and run deficits until the need for extraordinary spending has disappeared. They would then run surpluses in normal times to repay their debts (Barro 1979). Again, the persistence of the observed deficits does not fit this prescription; nor do large deficits in peacetime fit this view that tax smoothing should be applied only in times of national emergencies.[2]

One might argue that the increase in government debt during the 1970s was a response to low real interest rates, hence a low cost of borrowing. But the extent to which governments base their borrowing decisions on the level of real interest rates in practice is much in doubt. Furthermore, the argument does not fit the 1980s and 1990s, when real interest rates were much higher than in the 1970s. As we will show in Chapter 4, there is a large degree of variation in the fiscal performance across countries with relatively similar economic structures and environments, a variety that the conventional arguments cannot explain.

The failure of conventional economics to explain these observations has sparked interest in explanations of a political-economy nature focusing on distributional conflicts. The key questions here are 1) Can we explain large public deficits by political factors? and 2) Can we explain variance in the fiscal performance of different governments by differences in the institutions governing their fiscal policies? Recent literature has developed positive answers to both questions. We review relevant arguments made under both approaches. The main message is that institutions shaping the budget process of a country are an important factor in determining that country's level of public deficits and debts. The implication is that institutional reform of the budget process provides important protection against large deficits and debts.

---

[2] With the two oil shocks, potential output in each country fell. The slowdown in growth had implications for the tax system and for social spending. A Barro-type argument could work initially, as policymakers may have treated the first shock as an aberration. After the second shock, it should be clear something had to be done. Moreover, by 1986, oil prices had returned to their previous levels, so the deficits should have disappeared. They did not.

Deficits and "Raw" Politics

The first strand of literature attempts to explain large government deficits as the result of "raw" politics – political incentives of the parties in government define political processes with no consideration of the institutional environment. Large deficits are a symptom of a government's inability to decide who should pay the cost of its activities. Governments that are politically weak or unstable use the option of deficits to postpone that decision.

This view identifies a number of political fundamentals leading to large deficits. Some authors argue that a high degree of political polarization among the electorate leads to weaker fiscal discipline. Governments expecting to lose power in the near future to an opposition with very different spending priorities may choose to run large deficits. The idea is that an increase in debt service today constrains the spending choices of the opposing party when it gains office (Tabellini and Alesina 1990). The implication of the argument is that the more partisan the political atmosphere, the greater the incentive to run up debt. A related argument focuses on the turnover of government without the partisan edge. Members of the government who expect to lose their positions do not anticipate having to deal with the consequences of their actions today. They therefore saddle future governments with more debt. The expectation in this case is that more frequent government turmoil leads to weaker fiscal discipline (e.g., Persson and Svensson 1989; Roubini and Sachs 1989; Grilli, Masciandaro, and Tabellini 1991; Hahm 1994).

Another body of literature focuses on political competition within governments. Coalition governments have difficulty distributing any painful decisions across coalition partners. During negative fiscal shocks, they cannot agree on which partner's constituency should bear spending cuts and/or tax increases (Roubini and Sachs 1989; Alesina and Perotti 1995). One-party governments, in contrast, do not face this dilemma, and they should be able to react more quickly to negative fiscal shocks. Tsebelis (2002) suggests that partisan differences play an important role – the greater the ideological distance among coalition partners, the harder it is for them to make significant changes.

Because there is a strong link between the electoral system and the number of parties in government, an extension of the argument is to suggest that proportional representation electoral systems lead to larger budget deficits. Under proportional representation, the proportion of seats a party wins in parliament is supposed to correspond to the proportion of votes a party receives in elections. Admittedly, there are differences in how proportional representation is instituted in practice so that there is often not a one-to-one correspondence between vote and seat shares, but in general such systems allow small parties to gain representation in parliament. In contrast, as Duverger (1954) explains, there will generally be only two relevant parties under plurality systems. This means that plurality electoral systems usually produce one-party governments while proportional representation (PR) systems lead to frequent coalition governments. Persson and Tabellini (2000, 2003) suggest that this logic explains why countries with plurality (or, to use their term, majoritarian) electoral systems in their study have lower deficits.

These conjectures have received much attention, but their empirical support has been uneven. Persson and Tabellini (2003), in an empirically sophisticated study of political institutions and economic outcomes, do find that majoritarian electoral systems have smaller deficits. The most recent work on electoral systems and fiscal outcomes, however, has focused only on expenditures and found that overall expenditures are higher in PR systems than under plurality (Bawn and Rosenbluth 2006; Persson, Roland, and Tabellini 2006). Similarly, <u>Roubini and Sachs (1989)</u>, in what has become the landmark article considering the effects of institutional factors on fiscal policy, contend that countries with multiparty coalition governments and with minority governments have the most difficulty maintaining fiscal discipline. In a reconsideration of their dataset, however, Edin and Ohlsson (1991) find that minority governments only are more likely to run large budget deficits. Alesina and Perotti (1995) confirm a link between coalition governments and low success rates in the implementation of fiscal consolidations but discover that minority governments are the most fiscally responsible form of government in their sample. De Haan and Sturm (1994, 1997), in a pooled time-series analysis of European countries, find no statistically significant relationship at all between the form of government and budget deficits. Overall, the empirical evidence produced under this argument is mixed. We will compare these results directly to the third set of arguments concerning fiscal institutions.

A related issue concerns political business cycles. Instead of government instability causing indecision, the possibility of government turnover because of an impending election may lead politicians in office to try to "buy" their reelection through tax cuts and/or more spending in preelectoral years. Such opportunistic political business cycles, which Nordhaus (1975) diagnosed already in the 1970s, may lead to both larger deficits before elections and a ratcheting up of debt levels. Buti and van den Noord (2004b) as well as von Hagen (2006) find such cycles in European countries after Stage III of EMU. Schuknecht (1999), in a study of developing countries, as well as Clark and Hallerberg (2000; see also Clark 2003), who look at the developed world, contend that such fiscal cycles depend upon the underlying mobility of capital and the prevailing exchange rate. They use a Mundell-Fleming model to argue that fiscal policy should be most effective when capital is mobile and exchange rates are fixed. Conversely, monetary policy is most effective when capital is mobile and exchange rates flexible. One should therefore expect fiscal cycles especially under fixed exchange rates. We will examine political business cycles over the entire period in Chapter 4 as well as whether they have become more common under EMU in Chapter 7.

Fiscal Rules

A third approach takes the political context as given and considers explicit fiscal rules. These rules usually set *ex ante* constraints on what the government can do. In practice, the constraints appear as constitutional limits on deficits, debts, and/or spending. A prominent example is a balanced budget law, which requires that a given government propose a balanced budget and/ or finish the fiscal year with the budget in balance. Such rules are most common at the subnational level, and that is also where most of the research has been done. Feld and Kirchgässner (2004), in their study of fiscal performance in Swiss cantons, argue that cantons with explicit fiscal rules that amount to canton-level "debt brakes" have lower deficits. In the American context, some form of balanced budget requirement appears in 49 of 50 states. Poterba and Rueben (2001) argue that markets consider whether American states have fiscal rules in place when pricing bonds during fiscal difficulties. States with balanced-budget rules pay less interest. At the same time, states with tax limits pay more during fiscal difficulties as markets anticipate that they have fewer options to adjust the budget. Alt and Lowery (1994) see an interaction between the political control of government and fiscal rules. They argue that states with balanced-budget laws that restrict the ability of state government to carry over funds to the next year are most effective under unified (rather than divided between Democrats and Republicans) government. They reason that electoral accountability is high under unified government because voters can identify which party is at fault. Eichengreen (1990) shows that the stringency of balanced-budget constraints has a significant and negative effect on a state's debt ratio. However, Eichengreen considers only the level of "full faith and credit" debt, that is, debt that is fully and explicitly guaranteed by the state government. Von Hagen (1991) takes a broader perspective and includes other types of public debt in the empirical analysis, such as debt issued by public authorities. He finds that the stringency of numerical constraints has no effect on the total debt.

The two results are easy to reconcile: they suggest that states subject to stringent numerical deficit constraints tend to substitute debt instruments not covered by the legal rule (resulting from off-budget activities) for full faith and credit debt. Kiewiet and Szakaly (1996) find a similar effect by showing that where more restrictive borrowing constraints are imposed on the state government, municipal governments tend to incur larger debts. Von Hagen and Eichengreen (1996) show in a cross-country comparison that in countries where subnational governments are subject to stringent statutory borrowing constraints, the central government tends to have a higher debt ratio. This indicates a third substitution effect: where subnational governments are not allowed to borrow on their own authority, they tend to pressure the central government to borrow on their behalf. Furthermore, Strauch (1998) shows that constitutional expenditure limits, which are found in many U.S. state constitutions, do not constrain spending effectively. Instead, they induce a shift from the current to the investment budget.

The important insight from these studies is that *ex ante* controls on fiscal choices constrain politicians more effectively in the short run than in the long run. In the long run, policymakers find ways around such controls. Since it is impossible, in practice, to impose rules that cannot be circumvented, and since the individual citizen's incentive to monitor policymakers' behavior and turn to the courts to enforce the rules is weak, the effectiveness of *ex ante* controls seems limited. To the extent that creative practices to circumvent them reduce the transparency of public finances and of the relevant decision-making processes, such controls may actually reduce the voter's ability to monitor the performance of the elected politicians and, therefore, aggravate rather than mitigate the principal-agent problem.

As in other principal-agent relationships, a solution to this problem is to rely on an outside authority that enforces *ex ante* rules effectively. The European Monetary Union (EMU) furnishes a good example of enforcing budgetary rules for its member states through an international organization.[3] In the Maastricht Treaty first, and the Stability and Growth Pact

---

[3] A second possibility could be the International Monetary Fund. Indeed, the Fund seemed to provide this role successfully under the Bretton Woods system, but it does not play an equivalent role today.

later, the EMU states signed agreements committing them to a set of fixed targets. These countries have to submit annual stability programs explaining their governments' strategies to meet these targets. After reviewing these reports and the relevant data, the European Commission issues judgments of the countries' fiscal stance, which become the basis for ECOFIN's assessment and possible recommendations. Before the start of EMU on January 1, 1999, external enforcement power was based on the threat of exclusion from the monetary union. Today, it is based on the threat of public reprimand for fiscal profligacy and the possibility of financial fines.

Chapter 7 will consider the effects of the European level systematically. In the meantime, we note that the success of the European approach has been limited so far. In the run-up to EMU, average debt levels actually increased from 60% of GDP in 1991 to 67% in 1998. They then declined somewhat to 60% in 2004, but there were clear cases of states such as France and Germany flouting the rules.

Political Economy of Government Budgeting

This takes us to the final approach. Once again, the political fundamentals are taken generally as given, but, unlike in the fiscal rules literature, the focus is on the institutional environment in which decisions regarding public finances are made and, in particular, on the budget process itself. Fiscal institutions rather than *ex ante* fiscal rules are most crucial.

In the broadest sense, the budget process is a system of formal and informal rules governing the decision-making process that leads to the formulation of a budget by the executive, its passage through the legislature, and its implementation. These rules divide this process into steps, determine who does what and when, and regulate the flow of information among the participants. The budget process thus distributes strategic influence and creates or destroys opportunities for collusion. The chief constitutional function of the budget process is to serve as the locus of conflict resolution among all competing claims on public finances (Wildavsky 1975). Indeed, a fundamental characteristic of public finances is that they involve spending decisions over other people's money. Above the level of local administrations, governments rarely act like businesses that charge customers fees for particular activities. Instead, those who benefit from a particular program of public policy are generally not the same as those who pay for it. This incongruence makes distributional issues, that is, the question of who pays and who benefits, a central issue in public finance.

Budget processes must deliver two types of decisions simultaneously. They must determine the main fiscal aggregates – spending, revenues, and the deficit – and they must provide a solution to the allocation problem of spending and revenues. That these two types of decisions are intricately related to each other is easily understood by contrasting two alternative forms of budgeting. With bottom-up budgeting, the aggregates follow simply from adding up the appropriations determined individually in the budget process. With top-down budgeting, the aggregates are fixed first, and the individual appropriations determined by dividing up these aggregates.

A budget process can only fulfill its constitutional role effectively if all conflicts among competing claims on public finances are indeed resolved within its framework. Four deviations from this principle undermine the functioning of the budget process. The first is the existence of off-budget funds used to finance government activities. Off-budget funds allow policymakers to circumvent the constraints of the budget process and remove their decisions altogether from being challenged by conflicting distributional interests. Germany's experience in the 1990s is a prime example of the adverse consequences of off-budget funds. In the post-unification period, such funds mushroomed and contributed largely to the federal government's loss of control over public spending (Sturm 1997).

The second deviation is the spreading of nondecisions in the budget process. Nondecisions occur when expenditures included in the budget are determined by developments exogenous to the budget process. Prime examples are the indexation of spending programs to the price level or aggregate nominal income, and open-ended spending appropriations, such as welfare payments that are based on entitlements whose parameters are fixed by simple law or decree, and the government wage bill. Nondecisions conveniently allow policymakers to avoid decisions that would seem "tough" on their constituencies (Weaver 1986) but degrade the budget process to a mere forecast of exogenous developments. Failures to predict these correctly then become a source of excessive spending and deficits.

The third deviation is the existence of mandatory spending, where laws other than the budget make certain government expenditures compulsory. For example, the Italian constitution allows parliament to pass simple laws mandating specific expenditures for which the budget later has to make provision. The budget then becomes a mere summary of the existing spending mandates created by simple legislation. An effective budget process requires a clear distinction between nonfinancial laws (which create the authorization for certain government undertakings) and the budget, which

20

makes specific funds available for a specific period. Legislators should not be able to use items that impact the budget to "sweeten the pot," that is, to widen the policy space when they have difficulty passing a particular bill.

The fourth deviation occurs when the government enters into contingent liabilities, such as guarantees for the liabilities of other public or nonpublic entities. Promises, implicit or explicit, to bail out subnational governments (as in Germany in the mid-1990s), regional development banks (as in Brazil), financial institutions (as in the savings and loans debacle in the United States), or whole groups of companies (as in Korea after the East Asian financial crisis) can suddenly turn into large government expenditures outside the ordinary budget (for the first three examples see Rodden 2006; Rodden, Eskeland, and Litvack 2003; for the Korean example, Lee, Rhee, and Sung 2006). While one must recognize that a proper accounting of contingent liabilities is a difficult task, and that in some sense all government spending is contingent, their existence and importance for the government's financial stance can be called to the attention of decision makers in the budget process by requiring the government to submit a report on the financial guarantees it has entered into as part of the budget documentation.

The core argument of this institutional approach is that greater centralization of the budget process increases fiscal discipline. Off-budget funds, nondecisions on the budget, mandatory spending, and contingent liabilities all occur because there is some decentralization of the budget process. Some scholars in this tradition create indices to measure the degree of budget centralization and have found confirmatory evidence in a variety of settings. On the basis of a survey of Latin American and Caribbean budget directors, Alesina and colleagues (1999) contend that countries with more hierarchical budget systems have smaller deficits than countries with more collegial-based systems. Filc and Scartascini (2006), in an updated and more developed treatment of the coding of fiscal rules, examine the wave of fiscal reforms that swept through Latin America in the past ten years. They find that countries with more centralized fiscal rules have higher budget balances on average. Lao-Araya (1997) reaches a similar conclusion for East Asian countries in the mid-1990s, while Gleich (2003), Yläoutinen (2005), and Fabrizio and Mody (2006) do the same for European Union accession countries.

A literature that focuses in particular on the level of transparency in the budget process also fits this tradition. If populations and markets cannot monitor what governments are doing, it is more likely that politicians will spend more than they should. Milesi-Ferretti (2004) contends that politicians engage in more creative accounting where transparency is low, and he looks specifically at European Union countries (see also Tanzi and Schuknecht 2000, Chapter 8). Alt and Lassen (2006a) correct for possible endogeneity issues and also find that greater transparency in the budget process leads to better fiscal outcomes. Similarly, Alt and Lassen (2006b) find that countries with less transparent fiscal institutions have larger political business cycles, as politicians do more to try to influence the state of the economy where they think that the public cannot observe their actions.

Another set of scholars focus on just one aspect of the budget process or even on just one actor. A common recommendation in this literature is that any reforms strengthen the hand of the finance minister in the budget process. Wildavsky (1975) conceives of the finance minister as the "guardian" of the treasury who keeps the spending of "advocates" (or spending ministers) in check. A strong finance minister can force decision makers to consider the true benefits and costs of increased spending and taxation (von Hagen and Harden 1994, 1995; Hahm, Kamlet, and Mowery 1996). On the basis of this argument, the Inter-American Development Bank (1997) recommended that all Latin American countries that did not already have strong finance ministers adopt reforms that increased the power of this player. Similarly, negotiated spending targets for each ministry can also lead to smaller deficits (von Hagen and Harden 1994, 1995; Hallerberg and von Hagen 1999). This approach examines the structure of other parts of the budget process as well, such as how parliament deals with the government's proposed budget, how the budget is implemented, and whether there are any *ex post* controls. Hallerberg (2004), in detailed case studies, traces the development of fiscal institutions in European Union countries.

With this general approach in mind, policymakers have introduced a range of procedural reforms in the past twenty years with the goal of instilling fiscal discipline. In the United States, much of the political effort to reduce the federal deficit from the Reagan to the Clinton years focused on institutional design: the Gramm-Rudman-Hollings Act imposed deficit targets on the federal budget, for example, while the Budget Enforcement Act protected budget agreements between the president and Congress against subsequent amendments. Such rules did not remain in place under the Bush administration, and members of both political parties have proposed new restrictions to stem mounting federal deficits. In Europe, compliance with the fiscal norms of the Maastricht Treaty became a precondition for entering the Economic and Monetary Union. The Stability and Growth Pact proscribes maximal deficit levels as a percentage of GDP. Following in part the European example, the West African Economic and Monetary Union similarly included fiscal targets (Dore and Masson 2002).

While the statistical evidence in support of the effects of such institutions has generally been stronger, this approach has suffered from three weaknesses. The first is that, despite the work cited previously, we still know little about how budget institutions function in practice in comparative fashion and over time. Even when more information for a given country's procedures is available, all of the studies cited earlier provide cross-sectional data only: that is, they provide information on the budget processes of countries for only one point in time. While cross-sectional studies are certainly suggestive, they do not allow researchers to separate institutional factors from other country-specific effects. Ideally, one would like to observe changes in budget institutions to check whether there are corresponding changes in fiscal performance, but such an analysis is not possible with cross-sectional data. In the one exception to this problem, Hallerberg (2004) does have a longitudinal element, but he does not document in detail the budget institutions in his set of countries.[4]

The second weakness is that these studies generally assume that budget institutions have the same effect in all political settings. A strong finance minister should be able to rein in spending with the same effectiveness in Brazil, Britain, and Botswana. The political context, however, may mean that a fiscal institution that functions well in one setting is ineffective, or even counterproductive, in another. To take a concrete example, a requirement that a budget vote constitutes a vote of no confidence strengthens the prime minister's hand under majority governments, where any defections by parliamentarians whose parties are in government would potentially bring down their own government. This rule represents a strengthening of the budget process. Under a minority government, however, the same rule can weaken budget discipline. A requirement that a majority vote against the budget will bring down the government can leave the minority government hostage to one or more opposition parties, who can then demand that their spending priorities receive full funding. Denmark is a country with frequent minority governments that abolished the link between budget and confidence votes in

---

[4] We do treat this question quantitatively in an article-length piece in Hallerberg, Strauch, and von Hagen (2007).

the 1990s and that then experienced improved centralization of the budget process. Without a sense of how budget institutions function in different political settings, it is difficult to prescribe the appropriate set of institutions for a given country.

The third weakness is that most of the literature does not explain why some states choose a given budgetary institution and others do not. There may be sound reasons why a country does not have a strong finance minister, be they cultural (a reluctance to centralize power in countries with dictatorial legacies; see Hallerberg and Marier 2004's discussion of Latin America) or political (actors in multiparty coalition governments do not want to centralize the process around one actor). An understanding of how governments choose institutions leads to a better understanding of which reforms are, and are not, possible in different settings. Indeed, as we will explain later in this chapter, there is an important causal relationship between the types of political variables discussed earlier in this chapter, such as the electoral system and the number of parties in government, and the types of fiscal institutions that are possible.

The Budget Process within Cabinet Governments

In this section, we review a model of budgeting decisions in a cabinet government.[5] The intuition is straightforward: the structure of the bargaining process within the cabinet affects the size of the budget. If spending ministers are left to determine their own budgets, they will not consider the full tax burden and they will select spending levels that are larger than what is collectively optimal for the government in power. This is the classic common pool resource problem discussed previously. Moreover, it is at the same time a prisoner's dilemma game. All players are better off if they collectively consider the full tax burden. Without an institutional mechanism to get them to the cooperative solution, however, the equilibrium is one where all players "defect." In a multiperiod game, both spending and deficits are higher than the amount the cabinet members themselves want. We then explain two possible institutional mechanisms to remedy the resulting spending and deficit bias, delegation and contracts.

---

[5] See also Krogstrup and Wyplosz (2006) for an intriguing model. They make some additional assumptions, such as considering spending categories such as "productive public spending" and adding an international dimension.

The Model

Consider a government consisting of $i = 1, \ldots, n$ spending ministers. An individual minister has the utility function

$$U_i = -\frac{1}{2} \sum_{t=1}^{2} \delta^{t-1} [x_{t,i} - x_{t,i}^*]^2 - m_i \delta \Gamma(T), \tag{1}$$

where δ is the time discount factor, $0 < \delta < 1$, $x_{t,i}$ is the level of spending allocated to minister i, and $x_{t,i}^*$ is the ideal level of spending from the perspective of this minister. We assume that $x_{1,i}^* = x_{2,i}^* = x_i^*$. The government receives an amount of tax revenue τ_1 in period $t = 1$ which is fixed by past decisions and determines the level of tax revenues in period $t = 2$, T, together with the spending levels in both periods. For simplicity, we set $\tau_1 = 0$. The cost of taxation is

$$\Gamma(T) = \frac{1}{2} \theta T^2. \tag{2}$$

In equation (1), m_i denotes the share of that cost falling on minister i's constituency. Thus, $m_i < 1$. For simplicity, we assume that $m_i = 1/n$.

In the second period, the government receives an exogenous nontax revenue τ_2. The intertemporal budget constraint for the government dictates that

$$T = rB_1 + B_2 - \tau_2, \tag{3}$$

where B_t denotes total expenditures in period t, and r is the gross real interest factor for the government.

Decentralized Budgeting: Fiefdom

We first consider a completely decentralized budget process, in which all spending ministers submit and obtain bids maximizing their individual utility functions (1) taking the other ministers' bids as given. The first-order conditions for spending in periods $t = 1$ and $t = 2$ are

$$\frac{\partial U_i}{\partial x_{1,i}} = -(x_{1,i} - x_i^*) - m_i \gamma \theta T = 0, \tag{4}$$

where $\lambda = \delta r$ and

$$\frac{\partial U_i}{\partial x_{2,i}} = -(x_{1,i} - x_i^*) - m_i \theta T = 0. \tag{5}$$

Summing (4) and (5) over i yields the spending level in period $t = 1$

$$\widehat{B}_1 = \frac{(1 + \theta(1 - \gamma))B^* + \gamma\theta\tau_2}{1 + \theta(1 + \gamma r)} \tag{6}$$

where $B^* = \sum_i x^* i$. Since tax revenues are zero in period 1, this is equal to the deficit in the first period. According to (6), the government deficit increases as λ becomes smaller. This happens because the government discounts the future at a rate larger than the real interest rate: that is, the government is myopic, for example, because of electoral uncertainty. The level of spending in period 2 is

$$\widehat{B}_2 = \widehat{B}_1 - \frac{\theta(1 - \gamma)}{1 + \theta(1 + \gamma r)}[(1 + r)B^* - A]. \tag{7}$$

Using (6) and (7), we obtain the level of taxes in period $t = 2$ as

$$\widehat{T} = \frac{(1 + r)B^* - \tau_2}{(1 + \theta(1 + \gamma r))}. \tag{8}$$

We assume that $(1 + r)B^* > \tau_2$ as the government would not tax in period 2 otherwise. The more the ministers discount the future, the larger the level of taxation in the second period. Equations (4), (5) and (8) imply the following optimal levels for the individual spending ministers:

$$\widehat{x}_{1,i} = x_i^* - m_i\gamma\theta\widehat{T}_2,$$
$$\widehat{x}_{2,i} = x_i - m_i\theta\widehat{T}_2. \tag{9}$$

With these allocations, minister i obtains a utility level

$$\widehat{U}_i = \frac{\delta\theta m_i}{2}\frac{((1 + r)B^* - \tau_2)^2}{(1 + \theta(1 + \gamma r))^2}(1 + m_i\theta(1 + \gamma r)). \tag{10}$$

Fiefdom with Numerical Constraints   Suppose now that this government is subject to a numerical constraint on total spending in the first period, or a fiscal rule demanding that $B_1 \leq M$. Since tax revenues in the first period are exogenous, this is equivalent to a numerical constraint on the deficit in the first period. Assume that if the government violates the constraint, it may suffer a penalty, which could be a financial fine or a loss of political reputation and voter support, and that this penalty occurs with probability $\pi \geq 0$. Obviously, the numerical constraint has no effects if it is not binding, that is, if M is larger than the level of spending the government chooses

The Model

without the constraint. If the constraint is binding, minister i has the following expected utility function:

$$U_i = \frac{1}{2} \sum_{t=1}^{2} \delta^{t-1} [x_{t,i} - x_{t,i}^*]^2 - m_i \delta \theta T^2 - m_i \delta \pi \Lambda, \tag{11}$$

where $m_i \Lambda$ is the utility loss minister i faces, if total spending exceeds the limit. If the government stays within the numerical constraint, it sets $B_1 \leq M$ and the optimal level of spending in period 2 is

$$\breve{B}_2 = \frac{1}{1+\theta}(B^* - r\theta M + \theta \tau_2). \tag{12}$$

The level of taxation in period 2 then is

$$\breve{T} = \frac{1}{1+\theta}(B^* + rM - \tau_2). \tag{13}$$

This is smaller than the level of taxation in the absence of a fiscal rule, if the rule is binding. Assuming that total spending in period 1 is allocated evenly among the spending ministers, $x_{1,i} = m_i M$, and that $x_i^* = x^*$ for all i for analytical convenience, minister i obtains a utility level of

$$\breve{U}_{i,R} = -\frac{m_i}{2}[m_i(M - B^*)^2 + \delta\theta(1 + m_i\theta)\breve{T}^2]. \tag{14}$$

Whether or not the government will stay within the constraint depends on whether or not this level of utility is larger than that resulting from unconstrained maximization of the utility function (1) and suffering the penalty. This is true, if

$$\widehat{U}_i - \breve{U}_{i,R} = \frac{m_i}{2}[m_i(M - B^*)^2 - (\widehat{B}_1 - B^*)^2]$$
$$+ \delta\theta(1 + m_i\theta)(\breve{T}_2^2 - \widehat{T}_2^2)] - \pi m_i \Lambda < 0. \tag{15}$$

Condition (14) illustrates the logic of a rule. Since the spending constraint in period 1 distorts total spending away from what is optimal for the government, the first term inside the squared brackets is positive and the larger; the smaller is the spending limit M compared to the most preferred spending level B^*. The second term is negative, since the level of taxation is smaller given the fiscal rule. Thus, a fiscal rule creates a trade-off between a less preferred level of spending in period 1 and a more preferred level of taxation (and, therefore, spending) in period 2. The greater the distortion in period 1, the greater is the government's incentive to violate the rule. This suggests that, in practice, numerical constraints are unlikely to be kept in times when cutting spending is perceived to be particularly harmful for the government, such as in recessions or close to elections.

The second term in the squared brackets shows that the government's incentive to stay within the constraint depends positively on its discount factor. The more the government discounts the future (the smaller δ), the smaller is its incentive to keep spending consistent with the constraint. Finally, the penalty function indicates that governments will keep the constraint only if the penalty and the likelihood of its being imposed are sufficiently large.[6]

The Delegation Form of Fiscal Governance: A Strong Finance Minister

With delegation, governments lend authority to "fiscal entrepreneurs," whose function is to assure that all actors cooperate. To be effective, entrepreneurs must have the ability to monitor the others, possess selective incentives that they can use to punish defectors and/or reward those who cooperate, and have some motivation to bear the costs of monitoring themselves (Olson 1965; Frohlich and Oppenheimer 1978). Among the relevant cabinet members, finance ministers often play the role of entrepreneurs. Their interests generally coincide with the general interests. Ministers have the responsibility to coordinate the formation of the budget, and, fair or not, the size of the budget deficit is often the principal indicator that others use to judge their effectiveness. Finance ministers often also have only a trivial budget compared with that of other ministers, and they cannot "defect" in the prisoner's dilemma game being played in the cabinet. Finally, finance ministers' staffs provide the means to monitor the actions of the other ministries, and, since ministerial prestige and hence personal benefits depend on the effectiveness of the ministry, they have a private incentive to guarantee that the monitoring occurs. The only question is whether the finance minister has the power to offer selective incentives and/or punishments to the spending ministers.

More formally, consider a centralized budget process in which the minister of finance has agenda setting power over the spending ministers. We

---

[6] It is straightforward to extend this case to a penalty function that increases in the level of spending. If the penalty is quadratic in spending, the total level of spending will be lower than in the unconstrained case even if the government does not stay within the constraint.

assume that the minister of finance internalizes the common pool externality of the budget. Formally, this is reflected in the assumption that the minister of finance maximizes the sum of the individual utility functions,

$$U_{mf} = \sum_{i=1}^{n} U_i = -\frac{1}{2} \sum_{i=1}^{n} \sum_{t=1}^{2} \delta^{t-1}(x_{t,i} - x_i^*)^2 - \frac{\theta\delta}{2} T^2. \tag{16}$$

Comparing (1) and (15) reveals the nature of the common pool problem: the individual spending ministers take into account only the portion m_i of the cost of taxation when making their budget bids, while the minister of finance takes the entire cost of taxation into account.

As an agenda setter, finance ministers choose a budget that maximizes their utility subject to the condition that the proposal must be accepted by the spending ministers. If finance ministers' agenda setting power is unrestricted, they will maximize their own utility function (15) without regard to the utility of the individual ministers. If the agenda setting power is limited, however, finance ministers must make acceptable proposals. Formally, we model this by assuming that finance ministers propose budget bids to each spending minister that maximize the utility function $V = \beta U_{mf} + (1 - \beta)U_i$, where β is a measure of the finance minister's agenda setting power, and $0 < \beta \leq 1$. This yields a total budget

$$\tilde{B}_1 = \frac{(1 + nm\theta(1 - \gamma))B^* + mn\gamma\theta\tau_2}{1 + mn\theta(1 + \gamma r)} < \hat{B}_1, \tag{17}$$

in the first period, with $m = \beta + (1 - \beta)m_i$. The greater the finance minister's agenda setting power, the smaller is the total size of the budget, and, hence, the deficit in the first period. Note, however, that finance ministers who have a low discount factor ($\lambda < 1$) run a larger deficit than finance ministers who have a discount factor corresponding to the real interest rate. The total tax burden in the second period is

$$\tilde{T} = \frac{(1 + r)B^* - \tau_2}{1 + nm\theta(1 + \gamma r)} < \hat{T}. \tag{18}$$

Each spending minister receives allocations

$$\tilde{x}_{1,i} = x_i^* - m\theta\gamma\tilde{T},$$
$$\tilde{x}_{2,i} = x_i^* - m\theta\tilde{T}, \tag{19}$$

in the first and second periods, respectively. Note that this is smaller than the corresponding allocations under the decentralized budget process.

29

The centralized budget process yields a utility level to each spending minister

$$\tilde{U}_i = -\frac{\delta\theta}{2}(m^2(1+\gamma r)\theta + m_i)\frac{((1+r)B^* - \tau_2)^2}{(1 + mn\theta(1 + \gamma r))^2}. \tag{20}$$

Comparing (10) and (19) yields that

$$\tilde{U}_i > \bar{U}_i \Leftrightarrow n > 1. \tag{21}$$

Thus, each spending minister benefits from centralizing the budget process. Given the spending levels of all other ministers, individual ministers can raise their utility by increasing the allocation of their ministry, since they carry only a part of the resulting cost of taxation. But if all ministers act according to this incentive, the total tax burden becomes excessively large and this pulls the individual allocations further away from the ideal points than under the centralized budget process. At the same time, however, the marginal utility of spending on x_i, given that all other allocations correspond to the budget decided by the finance minister, is

$$\frac{\partial U_i}{\partial x_i}\Big|_{x_i = \tilde{x}_1} = (m - m_i)\theta\tilde{T} > 0. \tag{22}$$

Condition (17) says that each spending minister individually would like to deviate from the centralized solution given that all others do not deviate. This reveals the collective decision-making problem arising from the common pool property of the budget. The centralized solution yields higher utility for each spending minister, but it is not a Nash equilibrium. This implies that finance ministers need sufficiently strong enforcement powers to implement their budget. The implementation phase of the budget process must, therefore, vest finance ministers with enough power to prevent the spending ministers from defecting. Similarly, the government's budget proposal as set by the finance minister must be protected against amendments by the legislature.

While we discuss all European Union countries later in the book, a concrete example from the United Kingdom nicely illustrates the delegation approach in practice. The chancellor of the Exchequer, whose position is equivalent to the finance minister in our model, has strong agenda setting power during the making of the budget. He or she chairs a committee of ministers either without portfolios or with ministries with minimal spending needs that sets spending levels for three-year periods. Ministers testify before this committee about their budget needs. After several hours of questioning, the chancellor alone sums up the discussion in the form of a "consensus" that represents the spending requirements of the given ministry.[7] Budget issues therefore are almost never raised before the full cabinet. During the budget's execution, the chancellor has treasury people in every ministry who monitor the spending as it happens. The chancellor also has the right to cut any ministry's budget, and thus to change the spending levels agreed to before his or her committee, if the chancellor indicates that such cuts are needed.

Delegation in Coalition Settings Consider now another budget process in which the finance minister is vested with agenda setting powers. We now assume that the government is composed of different political parties and that the finance minister belongs to a party that particularly favors transfers to constituency $i = 1$. That is, the finance minister's utility function, instead of (15), is

$$U_{mf1} = -\frac{\alpha}{2\beta}[(x_{1,1} - x_1^*)^2 + \delta(x_{2,i} - x_1^*)^2] + \sum_{i=1}^{n} U_i. \tag{23}$$

Thus, with $\alpha > 0$, the finance minister cares more about spending on x_1 than about spending on other items. The finance minister now sets the following budget bids:

$$x_{1,1} = x_1^* - \frac{m\gamma\theta}{1+\alpha}T; \ x_{2,1} = x_1^* - \frac{m\theta}{1+\alpha}T;$$
$$x_{1,j} = x_j^* - m\gamma\theta T; \ x_{2,j} = x_j^* - m\theta T; j > 1. \tag{24}$$

Obviously, for $\alpha > 0$, the finance minister uses agenda setting power to favor his or her own constituency. Defining $\mu = n - 1 + 1/(1 + \alpha)$, this budget process results in the following spending size and tax burden:

$$\ddot{B}_1 = \frac{(1 + m\theta\mu(1 - \gamma))B^* + m\theta\mu\tau_2}{1 + m\theta\mu(1 + \gamma r)} > \tilde{B}_1,$$
$$\ddot{T} = \frac{(1 + r)B^* - \tau_2}{1 + m\theta\mu(1 + \gamma r)} > \tilde{T}. \tag{25}$$

Equations (19) and (20) reveal the principal-agent problem created by delegating fiscal agenda setting powers to a finance minister, when the latter does not share the political preferences of the spending ministers.

[7] The committee was known as the "EDX Committee" under John Major's Conservative government and the "PSX Committee" under the Blair Labour government. For more details on the British version of delegation in practice, see Hallerberg (2004, 68–82).

This new principal-agent problem results in more spending and larger deficits than in cases where finance ministers take the preferences of the spending ministers as their own.

If β and, therefore, m, is a measure of the agenda setting power of finance ministers, we can think of α as the leeway finance ministers have to distort spending in the direction of their most favored constituency. We can then conceive of the design of the budget process as a two-stage process, in which the government chooses the finance minister's agenda setting power, m, first, and the finance minister subsequently chooses the largest α such that his or her agenda setting power is not taken away. In order to secure that, the finance minister must give the spending ministers a level of utility at least equal to what they would obtain under a decentralized process. Setting the utility of a minister $i > 1$ from the process in which the finance minister abuses the agenda setting power equal to his or her utility from (10) yields a relationship between the distortion, α, and the finance minister's agenda setting power, β. Specifically, it is easy to show that

$$\frac{d\mu}{dm}\Big|_{\bar{U}_j = \widehat{U}_{j,j>1}} > 0. \tag{26}$$

Since μ increases with increasing α, condition (21) says that the finance minister will choose a larger distortion in favor of a preferred constituency, if his or her agenda setting power increases. Delegating agenda setting power to the finance minister now has two effects: the common pool externality is internalized and the budget size smaller, but the other spending ministers obtain smaller shares of the budget. Thus, the total utility gain from centralizing the budget process accrues primarily to the finance minister's preferred constituency.

The spending ministers will obviously realize this distortion at the first stage of the design process. As a result, they will give the finance minister less agenda setting power, since this keeps the distortion smaller. This, however, results in a larger budget size. There is, thus, a trade-off between the size of the budget and the deficit on the one hand and the distortion due to the new principal-agent problem on the other. This trade-off makes delegation to a strong finance minister an inadequate solution of the common pool problem in coalition settings where the political preferences differ strongly among the parties forming the government. This point is important, and we will return to it later in this chapter and in the chapter where we focus on institutional choice (Chapter 5).

Negotiating Fiscal Contracts

In contrast to delegation, this form of governance focuses on concrete fiscal targets. With contracts, the government commits itself to a set of fiscal targets collectively negotiated at the start of the budgeting process. The emphasis here is on the multilateral nature of the negotiations, which implicitly forces all participants to consider the full tax burden created by additional spending. In practice, political parties often integrate these contracts into the broader coalition agreement. Detailed targets at the subministry level appear for the life of the coalition.

To illustrate this insight formally, consider a centralized budget process which starts with negotiations over the individual spending allocations x_i among all spending ministers. The outcome of these negotiations is to fix an allocation for each minister. We can use a Nash bargaining solution to derive the result of this process. Assuming that all ministers have equal bargaining power, the Nash bargaining solution maximizes the product of the individual utility functions:

$$V = \max_{x_i} \prod_{i=1}^{n} U_i. \tag{27}$$

Assuming a symmetric equilibrium, in which all spending ministers obtain the same level of utility, yields the equilibrium first-period level of spending and deficit:

$$\hat{B}_1 = \frac{(1 + n\theta(1 - \gamma))B^* + n\theta A}{1 + n\theta(1 + \gamma r)} \le \tilde{B}_1. \tag{28}$$

Again, if $n > 1$, this is smaller than the first-period budget resulting from a decentralized budget process. In this case, it is the bargaining process that reveals the externality of the common tax pool to the agents in the process and leads to its internalization.

The bargaining solution corresponds to the solution achieved by a finance minister with complete agenda setting power ($\beta = m = 1$ in (16)). It follows immediately that each spending minister obtains a higher level of utility under this budgeting process compared to the completely decentralized one. Again, however, it also follows that (23) is not a Nash equilibrium, since each spending minister would like to deviate from it if all others stick to the agreement. As with the budget set by a finance minister with agenda setting power, the bargaining outcome must be protected against defections by sufficient enforcement powers in the implementation phase and against amendments by the legislature.[8]

The ideal case of contracts in the European Union appears in the Netherlands. Coalition partners agree to spending targets for the life of the coalition at the subministerial level, and this agreement precedes any agreement on which party's politician will receive which ministry. The fiscal contract includes detailed rules that indicate what the government will do under a variety of unforeseen circumstances. In the 2003 coalition agreement, the parties (VVD, CDA, and D66) decided that any revenue windfalls would count against the budget deficit and not be spent. Revenue shortfalls would simply be allowed to count against the deficit unless the cyclically adjusted balance was worse than –0.5% of GDP or the actual balance worse than –2.5%, in which case additional measures would be taken. In spring 2004, the actual balance was indeed below –2.5%, and there were 11 billion euros in additional expenditure cuts that the coalition instated.[9] In contrast to the British Chancellor of the Exchequer, the Dutch finance minister has few rights during the making of the annual budget. Parliamentary committees, however, are designed to monitor whether parties are sticking to their contracts. The chair of a given committee usually is from a different party than the minister's party, each committee monitors only one ministry, and committees can compel ministry officials to testify. These powers allow committees to monitor what ministries are doing and whether they are sticking to the fiscal contract.

---

[8] Von Hagen and Harden (1995) consider a budget process in which the spending ministers derive personal benefits from being in office in addition to the benefits from making transfers to their constituencies, and where the personal benefits increase with the size of each minister's allocation. The preference for personal benefits also results in excess spending and deficits. Von Hagen and Harden show that delegating complete agenda setting powers to the finance minister in that context eliminates both the sources of excess spending, while negotiating spending targets among the spending ministers eliminates only the common pool problem as a source of excess spending and deficits.

[9] Author interviews, Dutch Finance Ministry, Central Planning Bureau, The Hague, July 2004.

Comparison of the Two Ideal Approaches

This discussion suggests the availability of two institutional approaches, a delegation and a contractual approach, to overcome the deficit bias in public budgeting.[10] The natural question then is, What determines the choice of governments between these two mechanisms? The formal model presented in the previous section provides a clear answer – the choice depends on the type of government. Specifically, we distinguish two ideal cases: single-party governments where all ministers share the same underlying spending preferences and multiparty governments where party preferences are relatively far apart. Delegation is the proper approach for single-party governments, but difficult for such coalition governments. Contracts is the proper approach for coalition governments where parties have large ideological differences, but more difficult to achieve for single-party governments.

Members of the same political party likely hold similar political views. In terms of our model, members of the same party have the same utility weights apply to the different groups of transfer recipients. The players therefore share the same views regarding the distribution of funds over the various departments, and conflicts of interest arise only from the common pool problem. In a coalition government that would include parties with differing ideologies, in contrast, cabinet members are likely to have different views regarding the distribution of transfers over the groups of recipients. As we illustrate formally earlier, there is a trade-off between the size of the budget and the deficit and the distortion due to the new principal-agent problem. This trade-off leads to an important prediction. As the ideal preferences of parties diverge, they are less and less likely to support delegation to a strong finance minister in the first place. We will discuss the meaning of "preferences" in the next section.

The remaining distinctions between the delegation and contracts approaches only reinforce this point. The second issue is in the scope and strength of the punishments and rewards a finance minister can use to assure the adoption of a proposal. During the budget negotiations, the finance

[10] This discussion bears a superficial resemblance to the rules versus discretion discussion in central banking (Kydland and Prescott 1977), with the first approach largely discretionary and the second focused on rules. Yet the nature of the underlying problems is different. Kydland and Prescott (1977) want to solve a time inconsistency problem, where the government sets an inflation target in period 1 and is then better off in period 2 if it reneges and increases inflation above the target while the population is left worse off. The actors in our model face a prisoner's dilemma. All are better off with the cooperative solution. All are worse off if each player defects and receives an allocation higher than the centralized solution.

minister's power must be backed up by the prime minister and, therefore, depends heavily on the prime minister's relative power in the cabinet. The prime minister in one-party governments especially is the strongest member of the cabinet. The prime minister is the leader of the governing party, and this position reinforces her or his power within the cabinet. The prime minister also can often select cabinet members and can reshuffle the government. Even in the United Kingdom, where the norm of "first among equals" is historically strong, a prime minister dictates the shape of his or her cabinet. If a given spending minister consistently presents unsatisfactory budgets, the prime minister can then replace him or her with someone who will develop more sympathetic policies. Finally, a prime minister can call a vote of confidence on a given issue which puts the very existence of the government at issue if a given minister does not support her or his position (Huber 1996). If the prime minister prefers that the party's ideal budget be reached, as should usually be the case, she or he will have identical preferences on the budget to the finance minister's. The prime minister can then delegate his or her power to the finance minister, and the finance minister will represent a faithful "agent" of the prime minister.

In coalition governments, the finance minister would lack the ability to insist on his or her proposal, because the prime minister cannot give as much meaningful support as in the one-party case. The distribution of portfolios is, as far as the sitting prime minister is concerned, exogenously given, since agreement over forming the coalition determines which parties get which ministries. The prime minister cannot easily dismiss or otherwise discipline intransigent spending ministers from a different party, since that would be regarded as an intrusion into the internal party affairs of coalition partners.

The third important dimension regards the scope of punishments for defecting from the agreed budget. In the one-party case, the ultimate punishment is dismissal from office. Such punishment is heavy for the individual minister who overspends, but generally light for the government as a whole. It is therefore relatively easy for the prime minister to enforce, and ministers who overspend can expect to be dismissed for the good of their political party. In the case of coalition governments, a defecting minister cannot be dismissed easily by the prime minister for the reasons mentioned earlier. The most important punishment mechanism here is the threat that the coalition breaks up if a spending minister reneges on the budget agreement. Overspending by an individual minister from one party in the coalition implies a redistribution of public spending away from the transfer recipients most favored by, and, therefore, implies a cost of political support for the other parties in the coalition. This makes the threat of breaking up the coalition credible from the other parties' point of view. This suggestion is supported by the observation that fiscal targets are often part of the formal coalition agreement. Thus, punishment leads to the death of the government rather than the dismissal of a single individual. There are two important factors which affect the strength of this threat: the existence of alternative coalition partners and, if a new coalition cannot be formed and new elections are necessary, the anticipation of electoral results.

If another partner exists with whom the aggrieved party can form a coalition, the threat to leave the coalition is clearly more credible. The number of parties in parliament is one obvious limit to the number of alternative coalition partners. Even among the parties which do exist, some may be undesirable for policy reasons or may not be considered *koalitionsfähig*, such as the Italian Communist Party. Other parties may simply not be excludable from the coalition formation process. A party is "strong" according to Laver and Shepsle (1996) if it can veto every potential cabinet, and coalition partners may not be able to punish a party that occupies such a dominant position. Yet, to the extent that there are several possible coalitions, reputations will be important. Parties which are known not to keep coalition agreements will have problems finding partners, and as long as parties anticipate that none of them has a reasonable chance of winning an absolute majority of seats in the future they will value the possibility of cooperation in the future. The threat of new elections may also scare a defecting party into meeting its targets, if this party must fear a defeat if elections are called.

For a single-party government, in contrast, the enforcement mechanism of the contract approach is rather weak. To see this, consider a single-party government with a weak prime minister and finance minister. Assume that this government negotiated an agreement on a set of fiscal targets at the outset of the budget process and that an individual spending minister reneges on the agreement during the implementation phase. In this case, the other cabinet members cannot credibly threaten the defector with dissolution of the government, since they would punish themselves by calling for elections. Absent a credible threat, the entire cabinet would just walk away from the initial agreement.

To summarize, we predict that coalition governments with parties that have differing ideal spending preferences will typically choose contracts and single-party governments will typically choose delegation of powers to a strong finance minister as a device to limit the deficit bias.

Political Competition and Ideological Distance

If there is a one-party majority government, the prediction of the model is clear – delegation is the logical form of fiscal governance for the country. If there are regular one-party majority governments, the model suggests that delegation is still feasible if parties have the same, or very close, preferences. How does one know whether parties share the same preferences? As Müller and Strøm (1999) succinctly describe, the literature that focuses on the motivations of political parties makes three arguments, with two of them directly relevant for the design of fiscal institutions. The first is that parties are office-seekers, and that they run in elections in order to enter government. This suggests that delegation works when parties share a common office-seeking interest – the probability of one party's gaining office increases significantly if the other party gains office as well. Such parties usually run together in future elections. They share the same electoral incentive to solve the CPR problem, and delegation to a strong finance minister can benefit all parties in the coalition.

At the same time, parties may want to do different things when they get into office. This leads to a second common assumption in the literature – parties may have real policy differences. The short-lived conservative-communist coalition in Greece in 1989 shared a common electoral goal of denying the socialists (PASOK) power, but they could agree on almost nothing when it came to governing the country. The more parties disagree about the policies that should be implemented, the less likely they will trust that a strong finance minister is taking actions that are in their interests.[11]

Delegation works best when parties share the same fates in entering office or not and when there is no or very little policy discord. If parties do not think their fates are tied together, they will not trust a single player such as the finance minister with strategic powers that could be used only for his or her party's benefit. If they share the same electoral fate, but

[11] Müller and Strøm (1999) would add that parties try to maximize "votes" in addition to maximizing time in "office" and the setting of "policy." This third goal of parties is closely tied to the other two goals: without votes, one cannot gain office and influence policy. We do not see how a common impulse for votes across parties would influence the way governments design fiscal institutions. This common impulse, however, may lead to political business cycles where fiscal discipline slips prior to elections. We explore this possibility in Chapter 4.

there are also policy differences, the parties may choose delegation, but infighting during the life of the coalition should make those institutions less effective. At some point, policy differences may be large enough that the parties want fiscal contracts to spell out planned spending even if they intend to run together in the next election.

We use these insights to predict the ideal form of fiscal governance. There are both further conceptual and measurement issues that require discussion. We treat political competition and ideological distance in turn.

Office-Seeking Competition

Are parties tied to one another when it comes to the probability they enter office? In some countries, such as Finland, the expectation is that parties simply run alone and the set of coalition partners is hard to predict prior to the election. In others, such as France, there are clear blocs of parties that run against each other. If the RPR does poorly in the election, it is unlikely that the RPR and the UDF will be able to form a government.

Empirically, a good proxy for office-seeking competition among parties are the agreements that the parties make with one another on electoral strategy. Nadenichek-Golder (2005) provides a useful dataset on the frequency with which parties sign preelectoral pacts. If there are regular pacts among parties, office-seeking competition is low between them (although it remains high, of course, with their opponents). In Germany, for example, there were electoral pacts in thirteen of the fourteen elections held in the postwar period through 1998. This meant that a voter generally knew which government would form if the parties making the pact won the election. So long as the parties expect to form a pact for the next election, they have a stake in having the whole government succeed in fiscal matters.[12] It is easier in this case to delegate powers to a strong finance minister. In contrast, in a country such as Finland preelectoral pacts are rare events. The shape of a coalition in this case is first discernible after an election. Parties have every incentive to differentiate themselves from one another to voters. Delegating powers to a strong finance minister is not in the interest of the coalition partners.

---

[12] Whether parties will form a future pact is not something we can directly measure. The overall frequencies for pacts that did form should nevertheless be a rough guide.

Table 2.1. *Frequency of Preelectoral Pacts, 1946–1998*

Country	Frequency of Preelectoral Pacts
Spain	1
Germany	0.93
Portugal	0.78
Austria	0.71
France	0.71
Belgium	0.59
Ireland	0.5
Sweden	0.41
Netherlands	0.38
Denmark	0.33
Luxembourg	0.33
Italy	0.31
Finland	0.14
United Kingdom	0.14
Greece	Missing

Source: Data drawn from Nadenichek-Golder (2006) and downloaded from http://homepages.nyu.edu/%7Esln202/, with frequencies computed only for years in which a given country was a democracy.

Table 2.1 provides figures from Nadenichek-Golder (2006) for the EU-15 that are sorted according to pact frequency. Note that such pacts are generally relevant only if there are multiparty coalition governments that form. One would not expect these pacts to be used frequently in the United Kingdom, for example, where the main struggle is between the Conservatives and Labour and where the winner usually forms the government alone. The two countries where one-party majority governments are the norm are Greece and the United Kingdom.

Table 2.1 indicates that preelectoral coalitions are the norm in Spain, Germany, Portugal, Austria, and France. They are more rare (just above one-third of the time or less) in the Netherlands, Denmark, Luxembourg, Italy, and Finland. Belgium has them slightly more than half the time, but they are most common among parties with the same general name that are from different regions, such as between the Flemish and Walloon Christian Democrats.

The dataset ends in 1998, but the pattern is generally consistent with what one has seen through 2006 with one big exception, namely, Italy. Since the reform of the Italian electoral system in 1994, parties before every election have established preelectoral pacts. In fact, since 1996, not only have the parties run together, they have agreed to joint electoral manifestos. There are two clear blocs, one center-Right and another center-Left, that face each other.

Ideological Differences

The next question to consider is how different the parties are from one another when they gain office. For example, there are coalition governments that may approximate a one-party government in terms of spending preferences. The coalition that joined the RPR and the UDF in France in the mid-1990s included two parties of the center-Right that had closely aligned preferences. The parties ran together in elections, and all voters knew before the election that this electoral alliance would govern if they received a majority of votes. With closely aligned preferences and with their electoral fates tied to one another, delegation to a strong finance minister can work well. The key variable for predicting the appropriate form of fiscal governance then becomes the relative ideological distance among the parties. In one-party governments, the distance is simply zero. In multiparty governments, one needs to be able to measure the differences among coalition partners to make an effective prediction.

To get at the measurement issue, there are several approaches in the political science literature. One is that of Tsebelis (2002), who builds on his veto player concept. He argues that one should focus on actors who can veto changes to the status quo. He contends that in the parliamentary governments that one finds in Europe, the relevant veto players are the parties in government. He creates an aggregate measure from three expert surveys of party positions for the ideological distance on a Left-Right scale for most OECD countries, with the range equal to the distance between the two most different veto players (or parties). Datasets for all countries but Greece are readily available at his Web site.[13]

We follow this methodology for determining veto player distances, but we add another way to measure party positions for robustness. An issue with Tsebelis's original measures is that they are fixed: that is, no one has done a time series of successive expert opinions. The relevant datasets have

---

[13] Those expert surveys are Castles and Mair (1984), Warwick (1994), and Laver and Hunt (1992). Tsebelis also averages these three with a foreign policy score that appears in Laver and Hunt (1992), which creates a two-dimensional variable. The one-dimensional measure is most directly relevant for budget agreements, and we use it here.

one score for a given party for the entire period. A change in the core beliefs of a given political party is therefore missed. Two developments from the 1980s illustrate the problem. The Austrian Freedom Party was largely centrist before 1986. Jörg Haider assumed leadership of the party in 1986 and moved it rightward. Similarly, the French Socialist Party (PS) at the beginning of the 1980s was arguably the most leftist socialist party in Europe. By the end of the 1980s under Bérégovoy's guiding hand, the party may have been the most right-leaning Socialist party, and one that may even have been to the right of neighboring Germany's Christian Democratic Party. Such changes in party identity would not be observed using expert opinions from a single point in time. A second problem concerns reliability. There is no common template to measure the polarity of parties when the opinions are from experts who focus only on one country.

An alternative measure appears in the Election Manifesto Project's data (Budge et al. 2001). The group of scholars who make up the project code party manifestos issued before every election. While they also have a multinational team to do the intensive data work, the coding is based on a common standard. This approach also has its own shortcomings, but it nicely allows the party positions to fluctuate over time and it facilitates more consistent comparisons across cases.[14] We therefore supplement the core Tsebelis coding with this coding in empirical work.

Before presenting the data, we need to discuss the appropriate way to aggregate it within countries. This is not as straightforward as it first would seem. Finland, France, and Portugal are three countries in the EU-15 that have what some scholars call "semipresidential" systems (Duverger 1980). In none of these countries does the president have veto power on budget issues, however, so we exclude the president in our coding. Germany adds another complication. Any bill that affects the individual Länder must pass the upper house, the Bundesrat. In practice, the federal budget does not need Bundesrat approval. Moreover, only the lower chamber, the Bundestag, elects the chancellor and his or her government. For both these reasons, we

---

[14] The main disadvantage of this approach is that one has to accept at face value that what parties promise in manifestos reflects their true preferences. Parties presumably write manifestos to appeal to voters and to accent differences they have with their competitors. In cases where there is general agreement across parties, there may be no mention of the issue in the manifesto. In Belgium, for example, discussion of spending caps fell out of party manifestos because the parties no longer disagreed about them (author interview with Belgian parliamentarian, Brussels, 2001). It is also unlikely that the "pain" that is inevitable for some groups in society if fiscal discipline is to be maintained will appear in a manifesto at all. It therefore makes sense to include two different measures for computing ideological distances.

calculate ideological distance on the basis of the parties in government, ignoring for the moment the relevant party constellations in the Bundesrat.[15]

A final complication arises in minority governments. The discussion so far assumes that relevant decisions take place in cabinets. Parliaments are organized according to party membership, and parties support their governments on the budget. We will examine in Chapter 3 whether rules in parliament facilitate government dominance of the budgetary process when the legislature considers it, but there is a fundamental difference between cases where the government has a parliamentary majority and where the only question is whether there is enough party discipline so that the budget passes, and cases where the government lacks a majority and needs to cut deals with one or more opposition parties to pass any legislation. In the latter case, the party veto players in government are not the same as those in parliament. Centralization of the budget process through delegation cannot suffice to solve the common pool resource problem; one or more opposition parties are also part of the decision-making process because their assent is needed for the budget to pass. At the same time, simply taking the budget before parliament and hoping to "buy" enough votes for passage lead to a budget that resembles the one that appears in the fiefdom case no matter how centralized the government made the process in writing its draft budget. Individual members of parliament will ask for additional spending that benefits their constituencies. They have no incentive to consider the overall tax burden. This process therefore increases fiscal damage from the common pool resource problem.

In terms of fiscal governance, the centralizing outcome resembles the majority case. That is, if the distance among parties needed for budget passage is large, a budget that ensures better fiscal discipline under minority governments requires a fiscal contract between the government and one or more opposition parties. Through this procedure, the relevant parties agree to spending levels in all ministries at the same time and, in the process, consider the full tax burden. The particulars of the contract, however, will probably differ. Because the opposition parties are by definition not in

---

[15] If a two-thirds majority exists in the Bundesrat opposing the Bundestag, *all* legislation must pass both houses by a two-thirds majority. While technically this does not force the government's resignation if such a Bundesrat constellation exists, in practice the sitting government could pass nothing without the opposition's assent. This has not happened in the postwar period, although the opposition needed to win only one more Land after Northrhine-Westphalia's switch to a CDU-FDP coalition in May 2005 to have a two-thirds blocking majority in the Bundesrat. The formation of the Grand Coalition between the SPD and the CDU/CSU in fall 2005 made this issue moot.

government, a threat to bring down the government to ensure compliance with the agreement makes no sense. Instead, the agreement is often enshrined in law, as has been the case in Sweden. This has two effects – it increases the costs of noncompliance (a minister is breaking a law if his or her ministry overspends), and it means that a majority of parliament must agree to any changes to it. Another difference with the majority case is the central role a budget committee may play in coordinating the execution of the fiscal contract, as one sees in Denmark. The committee provides a forum for relevant opposition parties that is not needed when the signatories of the fiscal contract are all in government. At the same time, the finance minister may play a more active role in coordinating the budget within the government than in traditional contract states. In cases where the party distances are small, delegation may be possible. The opposition party can be confident that the budget will closely resemble what it would have written had it been in government. Such cases, however, are likely to be rare – parties with similar preferences should be able to form a government.[16]

For the figures on veto distance in Table 2.2, the counting rule is simple – we calculate the party distance among the parties needed to pass the budget in parliament. To do this, we subtract the most Left party score from the most Right party. Under majority governments, the parties considered are those in government. Under minority governments, we calculate the distances on the basis of the party or parties in government plus the parties needed to pass the budget.[17]

---

[16] These differences with the majority case led us previously to consider minority governments as having "hybrid" or "mixed" forms of fiscal governance (Hallerberg, Strauch, and von Hagen 2001; Hallerberg 2004). Here we introduce a common metric, namely, ideological distance. In countries where the ideal preferences of parties are close, more delegation-type fiscal rules work well. Where ideological preferences diverge, contracts make sense.

[17] There is only one exception to this rule. The Swedish Communist Party from the end of World War II to the end of the Cold War promised never to be responsible for the fall of a working-class government. This meant in practice that successive Social Democratic minority governments could, and did, pass the budget without any concessions to the Communists. Given that the Communist preferences on the budget were irrelevant to the outcome, we do not include them in calculations through 1989. From 1998 through 2004, when they support the Social Democrats (after their renaming as the Left Party) together with the Swedish Greens, they are included. Also, we want to be clear that even though we use Tsebelis's data, our coding of minority governments differs from his. Tsebelis assumes that minority governments occupy a center position on the ideological spectrum and can play off the two ideological sides to get essentially what they want. As this section makes clear, we assume that the ideological distance between the government and supporting parties in the opposition affects the type of fiscal governance that centralizes the budget process.

Ideological Differences

Table 2.2. *Ideological Distance Scores, 1985–2004*

Country		Minimum	Median	Maximum	Standard Deviation
United Kingdom	Tsebelis	0	0	0	0
	Manifesto	0	0	0	0
Spain	Tsebelis	0	0	0.37	0.13
	Manifesto	0	0	0.11	0.04
Greece	Tsebelis				
	Manifesto	0	0	0.25	0.09
Portugal	Tsebelis	0	0.17	0.27	0.12
	Manifesto	0	0	0.06	0.02
Germany	Tsebelis	0.03	0.04	0.06	0.01
	Manifesto	0.01	0.1	0.13	0.04
France	Tsebelis	0	0.12	0.18	0.07
	Manifesto	0	0.03	0.1	0.03
Austria	Tsebelis	0.11	0.29	0.39	0.09
	Manifesto	0.03	0.06	0.18	0.05
Italy	Tsebelis				
	Manifesto	0	0.07	0.21	0.08
Ireland	Tsebelis	0	0.13	0.47	0.15
	Manifesto	0.02	0.07	0.28	0.09
Sweden	Tsebelis	0	0.25	0.36	0.09
	Manifesto	0	0.08	0.24	0.07
Belgium	Tsebelis	0.18	0.35	0.5	0.1
	Manifesto	0.07	0.1	0.18	0.04
Luxembourg	Tsebelis	0.19	0.19	0.28	0.02
	Manifesto	0.01	0.11	0.15	0.05
Netherlands	Tsebelis	0.11	0.13	0.54	0.2
	Manifesto	0.05	0.12	0.16	0.03
Finland	Tsebelis	0.19	0.43	0.56	0.14
	Manifesto	0.05	0.15	0.4	0.11
Denmark	Tsebelis	0.18	0.36	0.37	0.13
	Manifesto	0.08	0.16	0.27	0.07

Note: For the Tsebelis data, the statistics are taken from our calculations based on data available at the Tsebelis Web page. He has no data for Greece, and the Italian data end in 1994. We therefore substitute the manifesto data in the regressions that appear in Chapter 4. Although the scaling is somewhat different, this substitution is not problematic because most data points equal zero, which would be the same in both datasets – Greece is 0 for all but a few months in 1989–1990 and Italy is 0 after the 1996 elections. For the manifesto data, the statistics similarly are our own calculations but based on data from Budge and colleagues (2001), which Thomas Bräuninger updated through 2004 and provided to the authors in August 2005. We thank him for his assistance in providing the additional years of data.

Moreover, we standardize the ideological distances to run from 0 to 1 by country for the twenty-year period for which we have detailed data on fiscal rules and institutions (as explained in Chapter 3), or 1985–2004. For the Tsebelis data, which are based on expert opinions, the average distance in the dataset is 0.20, but values range from 0 (the United Kingdom) to 0.56 (Finland's center–Social Democratic coalition government 1983–1986). For the manifesto data, the metric is somewhat different. The minimum and maximum country years are the same, but the overall mean is just 0.08. The same ideological distance under this metric for Finland's center–Social Democratic government is only 0.4.[18]

The country patterns are the ones that are most important in terms of predicting the relevant form of fiscal governance. Table 2.2 provides summary statistics, with the countries listed according to the median in ascending order. The United Kingdom plus the Mediterranean countries of Greece and Spain have median scores equal to zero (or one-party governments), while a fourth, Germany, has a median close to zero. The largest median distances are in Belgium, Finland, and Denmark. As both the standard deviations and the minimum and maximum figures suggest, however, the median scores mask overall developments in the fifteen countries. Some countries such as Italy and Portugal have periods with both a zero distance as well as fairly high distances.

We therefore also graph the scores by country over the twenty-year period as Figure 2.1, and we use this information to make predictions about the appropriate form of fiscal governance. One observes three sets of cases based on the relative stability of the scores. Following the aggregate results closely, the first category includes states with stable ideological distance. One set of countries have zero distance scores the entire time (United Kingdom), a distance usually at zero with a short interruption (Greece and Spain), or a distance that is consistently low (Germany). France is a tougher call; it has a low median score but more periods where the scores are notably above zero than Greece or Spain. Delegation should be the appropriate form of fiscal governance in these countries given that the political parties always run as

---

[18] On a Left to Right scale, with 0 Left and 1 Right, the most left-wing party that is required to pass the budget according to the Manifesto dataset is the Finnish Social Democrats in 1987 with a score of 0.27 while the most rightward party required to pass the budget is the Italian Republican Party (PRI) in the same year with a score of 0.73. The further extremes include parties that do not enter government in our dataset – the entire Manifesto dataset covers both the entire postwar period as well as parties that run for office in OECD countries, and the most left-wing party is the Luxembourg Communist Party in 1979 at 0.13 while the most right-wing party is the Australian National Party in 1954 at 0.93.

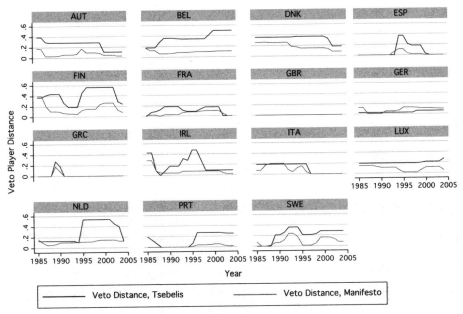

Figure 2.1 Variations of Ideological Distance over Time.

blocs against one another. Similarly, other countries have stable distances that generally score above 0.1 according to both scales that remain above this threshold (Denmark, Finland) or that bounce only once below it (Luxembourg, Netherlands). These scores suggest clear predictions about the most effective form of fiscal governance – delegation is most appropriate for low-score states while contracts are most appropriate for high-score states.

The second group are countries which seem to predict one type of governance in a given, defined period but another type of governance in the remaining period. Italy, for example, has a clear break after 1996, with a distance at zero, while it has a fairly large ideological spread in the first period.[19] Similarly, Portugal begins the period with a score near zero, but the score

---

[19] Readers are reminded that the Manifesto data analyze the manifestos of the parties. The Left and Right blocs ran under common manifestos in Italy in the 1996 and 2001 elections. Our observation of the Italian political scene is that this unity eroded once the parties gained office. Our theory predicts that the effectiveness of delegation fiscal institutions would consequently erode. We have no direct measure of changes in parties once they are in office, and relying on the strict Manifesto codes should understate the institutional effects we are trying to measure.

47

increases in the mid-1990s and remains fairly high. It has again dropped to zero after the 2005 elections (not shown on this particular graph). The final set of countries have scores that bounce around. Ireland moves down and up and down, with some stability at the end. Sweden takes the reader seemingly on a roller-coaster ride, although the only period with the distance at zero is at the very beginning.

To summarize, we can now use these data to label a country with a "small" or "large" ideological distance, which, together with office-seeking competition, can be used to predict the appropriate form of fiscal governance (delegation or contracts). One option would be to code countries by year according to their veto player distance. Yet this does not seem realistic – fiscal institutions take time to reform and, once reformed, to integrate into the budget process.[20] We are also interested in how budgetary institutions perform when veto player distances change. A traditionally small ideological distance country such as France should have difficulty maintaining fiscal discipline as ideological distance increases because it will have a form of fiscal governance that assumes little or no distance. In Chapter 4, in fact, we examine whether ideological distance interacts with a given set of fiscal institutions.

We therefore look for overall trends with relatively clear structural breaks. Greece, France, Germany, Spain, and the United Kingdom are small ideological distance states for the entire period. They either have no deviations from the ideal of no ideological distance or have temporary deviations. They should be appropriate places for delegation fiscal rules. Italy is a delegation state from 1996, when its ideological distance is at zero, and this break occurs shortly after with a change in electoral system in 1994 that encourages two blocs of parties to run against each other. Austria, for its part, broke an almost quarter-century-long pattern of "grand coalition" governments that comprised Christian and Social Democrats with two consecutive governments with the large People's Party and the smaller Freedom Party. From 2000, therefore, the pattern looks "German," and

[20] Political parties themselves decide whether a given government arrangement is temporary and act accordingly. For example, we would expect that parties support contracts where there are regular minority governments where the ideological distance among the different parties required to pass the budget is large. In a country where one party just misses a parliamentary majority and must "buy" one or two votes from the opposition, and where parties anticipate that the winner will gain a majority in the next election, there would be an incentive to maintain delegationlike fiscal institutions. Portugal and Spain are examples of the latter case, while Sweden is an example of the former.

we code it from 2000 as small ideological distance.[21] Similarly, Belgium, Denmark, Finland, Luxembourg, the Netherlands, and Sweden have pretty consistent periods of higher ideological distances. Ireland and Portugal bounce around and are tougher calls. Portugal had a one-party majority government from 1987 to 1995, and for one of the two succeeding minority governments the government lacked only one vote for a majority. We therefore code it as small distance. Ireland, on the other hand, has generally had multiparty coalition governments, but it switches to small ideological distance after 1997.

Predictions about the Ideal Form of Fiscal Governance

This chapter began with a discussion of two separate literatures. The "raw politics" arguments assume that variables such as the electoral system in place affect budgetary outcomes, while the fiscal institutionalists focus on the structure of the budget process. Our introduction of ideological distance scores represents a nuanced way to consider the effects of several political variables. In terms of the effects of electoral systems, plurality electoral systems usually lead to one-party majority governments, and they therefore have ideological distances that equal zero. Proportional representation systems often have many parties that enter parliament, which then lead to governments that have several parties with different ideological views. The qualifier "often," however, depends upon the underlying cleavage structure predominant in a given society. Countries with many social cleavages, such as class, ethnic identity, and religion, will see many parties form under proportional representation systems. In contrast, a country where economic differences are the only relevant cleavage may have a two-party system whether the country uses a plurality or proportional rule in its elections (Cox 1997).

To get a sense for how the predictions of the straight "electoral institutions" (e.g., Persson and Tabellini 2003) and the arguments here may differ when we do the empirical analysis in Chapter 4, Table 2.3 compares the countries with sets of electoral institutions with the measures of office-seeking competition and ideological distance discussed earlier. Following Persson and Tabellini (2003), we also look at the inverse of the district magnitude, with the expectation that the system is more proportional the

---

[21] Germany, of course, looks "Austrian" in terms of the adoption of a "grand coalition" between the Christian and Social Democrats after fall 2005.

Table 2.3. *Comparison of Electoral Systems, Preelectoral Pacts, Ideological Range, and Predicted Forms of Fiscal Governance*

	Electoral System	Inverse District Magnitude	Frequency of Preelectoral Pacts	Ideological Range Small or Large	Predicted Form of Governance
Greece	PR	0.19		S	D
Spain	PR	0.15	1	S	D
Germany	PR	0.52	0.93	S	D
Portugal	PR	0.09	0.78	S	D
Austria	PR	0.05	0.71	L 84–99, S 00–	C 84–99, D 00
France	Plurality	1	0.71	S	D
Belgium	PR	0.14	0.59	L	C
Ireland	STV	0.25	0.5	L 85–97, S 98–	C 85–97, D 98–
Sweden	PR	0.08	0.41	L	C
Netherlands	PR	0.12	0.38	L	C
Denmark	PR	0.11	0.33	L	C
Luxembourg	PR	0.07	0.33	L	C
Italy	PR	0.46	0.31	L 85–96, S 97–	C 85–96, D 97–
Finland	PR	0.09	0.14	L	C
United Kingdom	Plurality	1	0.14	S	D

Source: Data for electoral systems and district magnitude are taken from Persson and Tabellini (2003) and from Guido Tabellini's Web page (http://www.igier.uni-bocconi.it/whos.php?vedi=1168&tbn=albero&id_doc=177 downloaded on August 1, 2006). The data on the frequency of electoral pacts are for the period 1945–1998, and they are taken from Nadenichek Golder (2006). Abbreviations on ideological scores are considered small or large on the basis of the average ideological range and the overall pattern displayed in Figure 2.1.

closer one gets to zero. One can see that plurality systems have governments with low ideological distance and ones that we would therefore
predict should have delegation-like fiscal institutions, but the sample is
quite small – only two of the EU-15 use plurality. The remaining countries
vary more in their attributes than Persson and Tabellini would predict. Five
of twelve countries with proportional representation, or almost exactly half
of the remaining sample, also have small ideological ranges for some time
in the sample and are places where we would predict that delegation fiscal
governance would be most effective.[22]

To get a sense of whether adding the fiscal governance approach to the
more traditional perspective that focuses just on raw politics requires an
understanding of those institutions, Chapter 3 focuses on the budget institutions European Union countries have used in practice. Based on extensive surveys we conducted, it documents the fiscal institutions for the
period 1985–2004. The rules that countries establish do not follow random
patterns. It explains that countries tend to adopt predictable packages of
fiscal rules based upon their form of fiscal governance. Under delegation,
fiscal rules at the different stages of the budget process reinforce the power
of the finance minister. The finance minister, in turn, considers the entire
tax burden when making spending decisions. Under fiscal contracts, rules
that reinforce the negotiation and enforcement of the fiscal contract political parties negotiate among themselves are most important. The finance
minister's role is to monitor the execution of the contract but to remain
largely out of the decision making about the content of the contract. Chapter 4 then investigates empirically the effects of the different forms of fiscal
governance. Chapter 5 returns to some of the themes that first appear here,
and it hammers home the endogeneity question – Why do some countries
adopt expected fiscal institutions while others do not?

---

[22] Readers may notice that the predictions from preelectoral pacts and from veto player
distance are essentially the same. They are clearly related – it is easier for a party to form
an electoral pact with a party that is close to it ideologically. In the regressions presented in
the next chapter, we can comfortably use just the ideological range variable as an explanatory variable. Theoretically, however, we think it important to keep both concepts in
mind. A good example is provided by Poland. In late 2005 two political parties, the PiS and
the PO, finished with 27% and 24% of the vote, respectively, in the parliamentary elections. Together, they had enough parliamentary seats to form a majority coalition. Standard measures of economic ideology would place them as Right parties that would be
ideologically close. The prediction would then be a multiparty government with a strong
finance minister. Yet the parties have enough differences, including a real dislike of each
other among party elites, to keep them apart. The ideological distance measure would not
capture this difference, but office-seeking competition would.

3

An Account of Fiscal Norms and Rules in the European Union from 1985 to 2004

This chapter begins from the premise that budgeting procedures have important consequences for fiscal stability. A budgeting procedure that enables a government to commit itself to fiscal discipline is an essential condition. Commitment mechanisms are important during the three levels of the budget process – preparation of the budget within the government (including planning), passage of the budget law through parliament, and execution of the budget.

We examine this proposition in two versions. Following the fiscal institutional approach discussed in the previous chapter, we begin with a consideration of the "centralization" of the budget process in all countries. Specifically, dominance of the prime minister or finance minister over the spending ministers in setting budget parameters, limitations to modifications of the budget proposal by the legislature, and limitations to budget changes during the execution all centralize the budget process.

The previous chapter also developed the concept of "fiscal governance," which considers whether some set of fiscal institutions is appropriate for one set of countries but not for another. Specifically, some countries benefit from a discretionary system where the finance minister is the most important player at all stages of the budget process. Such countries are known as delegation states because other players in the budget process delegate to the finance minister the power to set, monitor, and correct the budget. Other countries benefit most from setting multi-annual targets that include clear fiscal procedures for what to do under a variety of contingencies. We refer to these countries as contract states because the important players in the budget process (who, in our context, are political parties) agree to what amount to fiscal contracts that set the terms of the budget for several years.

One should note that both ideal forms of fiscal governance centralize the budget process. The underlying theoretical point that centralization of the budget process is needed appears in both approaches. The difference is that the fiscal governance approach claims that one set of rules works best in one political context while another set works best in another.

In order to test the propositions about centralization, one needs to have data on how countries make their budgets. This chapter begins with a description of the budget process and explains the types of data one needs to catalogue the fiscal institutions used in the EU-15 from 1985 to 2004.

The Structure of the Budget Process: Elements of Centralization

In the overview in Chapter 2 we argued that the public budgeting school considers the budget process, in essence, as a device for political conflict resolution. In this section, we explain how the CPR problem, which is a primary force behind these distributional conflicts, may come to the fore in budgetary procedures and which institutions structure the decision-making process so as to contain it.

The budgeting process typically entails three stages. In the first stage, government prepares a budget draft to be presented before parliament. The government comprises spending ministers, a finance or treasury minister presiding over financial resources, and a prime minister. Conflicts of interest among the ministers must be resolved in the drafting process. Preparation also includes planning for future years, which is usually done in a finance ministry on a yearly basis but which can also appear in coalition agreements for the life of a given coalition. In the second stage, the budget is submitted to parliament, which can amend the proposal and either pass or reject it. We think of this primarily as a bargaining process between government, which now represents a unified position expressed in its proposal, and the parties represented in parliament, which either support or oppose the government. In the third stage, the budget law is executed and further modifications of the law may be possible.

To characterize the first stage process, we assume that spending ministers are interested in expanding the resources of their own ministries, but indifferent about the resources of other ministries. In contrast, the prime minister and the finance minister are not bound by particular interests – or not to the same extent – and, therefore, are more constrained by considerations of general public welfare than the spending ministers.

Consequently, one characteristic of the process within government concerns who participates in decisions. The exact details will vary, but there are some general patterns one would expect according to a given form of fiscal governance. In delegation states, there may be bilateral discussions between the finance minister and each of the spending ministers. In France, for example, the finance minister provides each spending minister with a so-called framework letter, which establishes the spending level each ministry should expect to receive in the next budget. There may then be bilateral discussions between the relevant minister and the finance minister, but there is generally not a full cabinet vote on the amount. In Germany, the finance minister derives power from the ability to veto specific spending amounts rather than proposal power. In contract states, in contrast, the cabinet may not be a relevant arena at all because the political parties make the important decisions and incorporate them in the fiscal contract. We can moreover distinguish budget processes by the extent to which they connect the current budget to past and future budgets through multiperiod budget plans. If multiperiod budget plans exist at all, they may be regarded primarily as a general orientation or as a binding constraint.

The government's budget proposal is submitted to parliament, where it becomes subject to another bargaining process. Members of parliament represent local or other constituencies and are, therefore, characterized by a spending bias that is similar to – if not stronger than – that of spending ministers. On the other hand, members of parliament are bound by party discipline. European parties, which are collections of groups of constituencies, are likely to give larger weight to the general interest – as opposed to particular constituencies – in party decisions than individual members of parliament would in the absence of party discipline. Furthermore, for the members of the party or the parties backing the government in office, party discipline entails voting to support the government, even if the outcome does not fully match the preferences of the individual member of parliament.

Parliament's role is to amend the budget proposal, and to pass or to reject it. While government sets the agenda for the parliamentary debate, its proposal will anticipate parliament's reaction to it. The relationship between government and parliament is characterized, first, by the scope of amendments parliament can consider. In the simplest case, there may be no restrictions on amendments at all. Otherwise, amendments may only be permitted for certain parts of the budget, or parliament may be restricted to amendments proposing increases in expenditures only if they identify the necessary sources of additional finance, or only such amendments as do not (or only negatively) affect the overall size of the budget.

The second dimension of the relationship between parliament and government concerns the political implications of rejecting the budget favored by the government. The strategic effect of the potential to reject the budget proposal is twofold. On the one hand, the more likely that a rejection will lead to the demise of the government, the more it is in government's interest to propose a budget that can be expected to find a solid majority in parliament. This tends to weaken the position of government in the process. On the other hand, members of the parties supporting government in parliament will refrain from proposing changes to the budget proposal if doing so may entail the fall of the government, unless the changes are regarded as of outmost importance. This second effect tends to strengthen government's position in the process. While the combined effect is ambiguous, we assume that the latter effect prevails.

Voting procedures within parliament can be characterized by the order and scope of the votes. As within government, they determine the extent to which reciprocity and universalism can prevail. Parliament may debate and then vote on the entire budget in one step. Alternatively, it may discuss and vote on the budget item by item, possibly followed by a general vote on the budget as a whole. Finally, parliament may first vote on the overall budget size and then debate and vote over the individual items. We conjecture that the latter approach is most conducive to fiscal discipline, while the first approach is most likely to result in large budgets and large deficits.

The third stage of the budget procedure contains the execution of the budget law under the control of government. During the execution, new demands for spending or reduced taxation occur in response to unforeseen economic events, as well as discrepancies between planned and actual revenues and expenditures. As in the drafting process, we assume that, for their political interests, spending ministers are more likely to give in to demands for increased spending and more prone to overrunning the limits set by the budget law than the prime minister or the finance minister. Two conflicting forces become important: the degree to which the budget law binds government's actions during the fiscal year and the degree of flexibility to respond to unforeseen events. How binding the budget law is for government depends on the possibility of proposing supplementary budgets during the fiscal year; on the relative importance of open-ended appropriations in the budget, such as social security or unemployment compensation commitments; and on the power of the finance minister to impose spending limits on ministries which exceed their budget norms. The degree of flexibility in the execution of the budget depends on the possibility of transferring expenditures between budget titles, the existence of a budget reserve, and the possibility of carrying unused funds forward.

While budgetary institutions that do not tie the implementation closely to the decision-making process may lead to shirking and overspending, that is, to an aggravation of the CPR problem, one should keep in mind that there may be a trade-off between rigidity and flexibility. Rules that dictate that all money must be spent in a given budgetary year, for example, may encourage spending splurges at the end of the budgetary year. Rather than erode fiscal discipline, the ability to carry over such funds to the next year may encourage it. The policy advice that some international organizations such as the OECD have been giving recently is to increase the flexibility of implementation. One example has been Sweden, which has a provision that departments can both carry over 3% of appropriations and borrow between 3% and 10% from a future year, but the department must then pay back the borrowed amount. Another example is the United Kingdom, where a series of initiatives under Gordon Brown have increased flexibility (Balls and O'Donnell 2002). In practice it may be difficult to determine whether the possible efficiency gains and savings from such flexibility may be overturned by the opportunities of particularistic interests to undermine the fiscal discipline that the government is trying to enforce.

Transparency is another important prerequisite of centralization. Throughout the budget process, greater transparency promotes better fiscal outcomes. It makes it easier for policymakers to understand the consequences of their actions, and it increases the accountability of politicians to voters. It requires that the budget documents are comprehensive and that expenditures are clearly attributed to the relevant spending units within the government. Lack of transparency creates opportunities for collusion among self-interested policymakers and prevents decision makers from developing a comprehensive view of the consequences of their decisions.

Budget Processes in European Countries, 1985 to 2004

Following on this stylized model of the budget process, we present detailed data on the fiscal institutions in place. Our study is primarily based on three surveys that one or more of the authors conducted in 1990–1991,

2000–2001, and 2004 among finance ministries, central banks, and staff members of the budget committee in parliament.[1] In addition, we supplement the surveys with extensive in-person interviews, including in-person visits to all capital cities; primary source material, such as constitutions and laws; and relevant secondary sources that describe the budget process in a given country. The results for the first two surveys appeared in working papers. Von Hagen (1992) used data collected by the European Commission in 1991, the year twelve member states signed the Maastricht Treaty. He and Ian Harden then updated the survey in 1993 to include Austria, Finland, and Sweden, who were to join the European Union in 1995, and presented an analysis in von Hagen and Harden (1994b, 1995).[2] Hallerberg, Strauch, and von Hagen (2001) reported results from a similar survey for the fifteen member states in 2000. Finally, we carried out a third battery of surveys in the summer of 2004 through e-mail and postal correspondence. For all three waves, we made telephone calls where needed if there was confusion about a given item in the survey or we asked follow-up questions in person. While the tables in this section list the dates of the surveys for ease of exposition, we have information for when the major reforms took place for these countries and use the date of change in the empirical analysis in the next chapter.

This section documents and discusses the results from our surveys. In aggregate, we find that there was great variation in budgetary procedures in 1991. By 2000, some parts of the budget process had been strengthened in all countries. Some of this improvement is undoubtedly due to the Economic and Monetary Union. The framework that supports the Stability and Growth Pact requires member states to submit either stability programs (if they are members of EMU) or convergence programs (if they are outside EMU), and these plans now mean that there are medium-term budget plans in every country. However, EMU can explain directly only the improvement of the medium-term plans and not other items. In fact, the amount of change was not the same in all countries: while some, such as Belgium, initiated significant reforms, others, such as Germany and Portugal, did

---

[1] While each institution had a particularly detailed view of one or more stages of the process (budget committee staff person knew the procedures in parliament, etc.), it was important that we received confirmation from other players in the budget process about the rules. When there was a conflict in answers, we asked for specific examples that would indicate what the rule was in practice.

[2] They asked a series of questions in personal correspondence to assure that the information they received about these countries was valid for the same year as the information they had for the original twelve, that is, for 1991.

not make similar improvements. Moreover, the composition of change is consistent with the fiscal governance approach – states where fiscal contracts are most appropriate, for example, have better developed medium-term plans on average. In contrast to shifts in budgetary institutions in the 1990s, we find that there was little change between 2000 and 2004, or in the period after twelve of the states had adopted the euro as their currency. The changes that did occur sometimes strengthened centralization (the Netherlands) and sometimes weakened it (France, Italy). We then consider indices that measure directly the type of fiscal rules we expect to function well under different forms of fiscal governance. Strengthening the role of the finance minister should be most important in delegation states. In contrast, detailed fiscal rules should be most prominent in contract states.

Our discussion of formation, parliamentary passage, and implementation proceeds as follows. Our approach follows von Hagen (1992), who investigates different institutional aspects of the budgetary process: the structure of negotiations within the cabinet, the structure of the parliamentary process, the flexibility of budget execution, and the long-term planning constraint. For the sake of comparability and empirical usefulness, we operationalize and code all institutional items according to their capacity to reduce the CPR problem. In presenting the institutional development, we follow the same approach. The figures for each battery are discussed in detail in the following. At the end of the chapter, we also present comparative data for each period on the type of restrictions national governments place on subnational governments, although we operationalize this in a somewhat different manner in the following empirical chapter through the use of dichotomous variables. The Maastricht definitions for deficits and debts cover general government realizations, not simply central government, and the increased scrutiny of subnational government finance may have led to a change in the relationship among the different levels of government.

Formation of the Budget in Government: Fiscal Targets and the Structure of Negotiations

This aspect concerns the extent to which a country uses multiannual budget plans. The fiscal targets index has four components. The first item indicates whether there is a multiannual target, and, if so, what form that target takes. Countries with no targets receive the lowest, those that focus on either total expenditures or total taxes receive a medium, and those that have total budget size as their target receive the highest score. The second item concerns the time horizon of the plan, with a five-year plan receiving the highest score. The third item concerns the nature of budget forecasts. We distinguish whether forecasts are ad hoc or regularly updated and based on a consistent macroeconomic model. Finally, and crucially, one wants to know the government's commitment to multiannual targets. Targets for internal orientation only receive a low score, while strong political commitment (such as plans written into coalition agreements) receive the highest score.

Before looking at the figures, one should anticipate a large improvement in this index over the 1990s because of the Stability and Growth Pact.[3] All states must submit yearly stability or convergence programs that provide estimates for the budget balance and for macroeconomic developments for a span of five years ($t-1$ to $t+3$), and, after submitting the initial program, states must submit yearly updates. The nature of the target, therefore, improves to the highest score in all cases, and the length of the plan is a minimum of three years ahead. States also connect their plans to macroeconomic models as a rule, with the Netherlands an exception through 2000 that moves to the norm by 2004.

Table 3.1 displays the rules in place concerning long-term constraints, and indeed the change from 1991 to 2000 was fairly dramatic for this index. With a possible maximal score of 16, the average has increased from 7.6 to 13.5. The changes are most notable for Belgium and for Luxembourg, which moved from the minimal possible score (0) to the maximal possible score (16). Except for the one improvement in the use of a macroeconomic model in the Netherlands, there were no changes in the use of long-term constraints from 2000 to 2004.

While the European framework strengthened the planning requirements of governments, it did not require states to link their programs to their annual budget process. In the survey, different degrees of connectedness between these programs and existing national budget planning were reported (see Hallerberg, Strauch, and von Hagen 2001). The role of the programs has increased over time because inconsistencies between programs and other national budget plans became obvious and were hard to maintain. Nevertheless, differences in the commitment governments

---

[3] Council Decision 1466/97 establishes which specific information must be included in each program.

Table 3.1. *Fiscal Targets*

Country	Multiannual Target		Planning Horizon		Nature of Plan		Degree of Commitment		Sum Long-Term	
	1991	2000/04	1991	2000/04	1991	2000/04	1991	2000/04	1991	2000/04
Austria	2	4	2	2	1	4	2	3	7	13
Belgium	0	4	0	4	0	4	0	4	0	16
Denmark	2	4	2	3	2	4	2	2	8	13
Finland	4	4	3	3	4	4	3	3	14	14
France	0	4	1	2	1	4	1	3	3	13
Germany	4	4	3	3	4	4	3	3	14	14
Greece	0	4	2	2	1	4	2	2	5	12
Ireland	4	4	4	2	1	4	3	2	12	12
Italy	4	4	3	3	1	4	3	2	11	13
Luxembourg	0	4	0	4	0	4	0	4	0	16
Netherlands	4	4	4	3	2	2/4	4	4	14	13/15
Portugal	0	4	3	2	1	4	2	4	6	14
Spain	0	4	4	3	1	4	1	2	6	13
Sweden	0	4	0	2	1	4	0	4	1	14
UK	2	4	4	2	4	4	3	3	13	13
Average	1.7	4.0	2.3	2.7	1.6	3.9/4	1.9	3.0	7.6	13.5/13.7

Note: Multiannual target: 4 = total budget size, 2 = spending or taxation, 0 = none; planning horizon: 4 = five years, 3 = four years, 2 = three years, 1 = two years, 0 = none; nature of plan: updated and based on consistent macroeconomic framework = 3, updated but not based on consistent framework = 2, fixed forecast = 1, ad hoc forecast no forecast = 0; degree of commitment: 4 = legal, 3 = political, 2 = indicative, 1 = internal only; 0 = none.

attach to their multiannual fiscal targets at the domestic level remain substantial. This is indicated by the continued variability of figures in Table 3.1.

How the government's annual budget fits into multiannual fiscal targets (if any) depends on how the cabinet formulates its proposal. In line with the previous general characterization of the budget process, we consider four institutional items. The first question concerns whether there is a general constraint on the budget before the cabinet considers it. The tighter this constraint, the higher the score for a given country. The constraints range from no constraint at all, which we assign a score of 0, to preestablished levels of both total spending and the budget balance as a percentage of GDP, which we score as 4.

Table 3.2 indicates that there has been a clear change in the use of such constraints at the governmental decision-making stage. In 1991, roughly half of the states had no or weak constraints, and only three

Table 3.2. *Negotiations in Cabinet*

Country	General Constraint		Agenda Setting		Budget Norms		Structure of Negot		Sum Negot	
	1991	2000/04	1991	2000/04	1991	2000/04	1991	2000/04	1991	2000/04
Austria	0	4	2	4	0	4	2	2	4	14
Belgium	0	4	1	2	0	4	0	2	1	12
Denmark	4	4	3	4	1.33	4	4	2	12.3	14
Finland	1	4	2	2	0	4	2	2	5	12
France	4	4	4	4	4	4	4	4/2	16	16/14
Germany	3	3	1	2	4	4	4	2	12	11
Greece	0	2	1	4	0	4	0	4	1	14
Ireland	2	4	1	4	0	4	0	2	3	14
Italy	2	4/2	1	4	2.66	4	2	4	7.66	16/14
Luxembourg	3	3	4	4	4	4	0	0	11	11
Netherlands	1	3	3	2	2.66	4	4	2	10.7	11
Portugal	1	4	2	2	2.66	4	4	2	9.66	12
Spain	0	3	2	4	4	4	0	4	6	15
Sweden	0	4	0	3	1.33	4	4	4	5.33	15
UK	4	4	3	2	4	4	4	4	15	14
Average	1.7	3.6/3.5	2.0	3.1	2.0	4.0	2.3	2.6	8.0	3.4/13.1

Note: General Constraint: 4 = G/Y, D/Y, 3 = G/Y or golden rule, 2 = B/Y and D/Y, 1 = B/Y, 0 = none; Agenda Setting: 4 = Minister of Finance (MF) proposes, no individual vote on budget bid; 2 = spending minister can ask for individual vote on bid, cabinet can override MF; 0 = MF collects budget bids; Budget Norms: 4 = "broad," 2.66 = "broad" and "specific," 1.33 = "specific," 0 = expenditure/deficit only; Structure of Negotiations 4 = MF bilateral only, 2 = multilateral, 0 = all cabinet ministers involved.

countries received the highest mark. By 2000, however, ten of the fifteen had imposed more specific constraints, with over half now receiving the highest mark. The Maastricht process, which requires states to have budget deficits no larger than 3% of GDP, as well as the Stability and Growth Pact, which establishes that states should have budget balances "close to balance or in surplus," may have led to more consideration of such constraints at the government stage of the budget process. At the same time, these European-level requirements did not prevent some minor backsliding – as Table 3.2 shows, there was a weakening of this constraint in Italy (only) on the 2004 survey, which occurred after the change in government in 2001.

Second, the agenda setting power of the finance minister in government is considered. If the minister simply collects bids from spending ministers, the score on agenda setting equals 0, while the highest score is given to countries where the finance minister (or prime minister) simply determines the budget parameters for the spending ministers. In 1991, the average score was 2.1, and only France and Luxembourg received the highest scores. By 2000, eight had increased the power of the finance minister relative to other ministers while two countries (the Netherlands and the United Kingdom) experienced a slight weakening.

The third item captures the scope of budget norms in the setting of the agenda. If the only norm concerned either expenditures or the deficit only, the country received a 0. A 4 was given where the scope was broad. Once again, there is a clear improvement from 1991 to 2000. On the basis of the answers from the 2000 survey, all countries receive a 4 in 2000. This is (probably) due to the broadness of budget norms that are now required for reporting at the European Union level.

The final item is the structure of budget negotiations, and this again relates to the involvement of the finance minister. If all ministers are involved in budget negotiations, then the country earns the lowest score, while if the negotiations take place bilaterally between a spending minister and the minister of finance, the country receives a 4. In this case, there is not an overall trend to observe, with the average score improving from 2.0 to 2.4. Yet the aggregate number obscures change within a majority of member states – five centralize the structure of negotiations while four decentralize it.

Overall, the structure of the government stage of the budget process has improved 5 points on average, from 8 to 13. Some of the improvements are fairly dramatic – Austria, Greece, Ireland, and Spain all increase their indices at least 9 points.

Structure of the Parliamentary Process

The underlying assumption for the identification of items and their conceptualization in von Hagen (1992) is that the easier it is for parliament to amend the government's budget, the more likely the CPR problem is to creep into the budget process. Parliamentarians then have the possibility to insert their pet projects into the government's proposal, which will increase spending.

The first three items capturing this aspect concern amendments. If parliamentary amendments to the government's budget are limited, the country receives a score of 4, while if amendments are not limited the score is 0. If amendments must be offsetting, that is, if any increase in spending requires a concomitant increase in revenues or decrease in spending in another field, then the country is assigned a 4, while if the amendments are not required to be offsetting the score is 0. If an amendment can cause the fall of the government, then the country receives a 4, while if an amendment cannot lead to a fall in government the score is 0. The rationale on this last item is that the government can threaten to dissolve itself if an amendment is not withdrawn. This threat may increase party discipline within the parties that compose the government. The final question asks whether or not parliament first votes on the total size of the budget before it considers individual items in the budget. We suggest that by forcing a vote on the total budget first the parties in parliament are compelled to negotiate the level of total spending. This in turn will lead them to internalize the common pool problem.[4]

Table 3.3 indicates that, in aggregate, there has been some strengthening of the government vis-à-vis parliament. In terms of specifics, whether or not amendments to the government's budget are limited changed little, with only Greece introducing limitations while Italy, the Netherlands, and Spain loosened limitations. A more notable change concerned offsetting amendments – a majority of states introduced this requirement, and, combined with two states that already had such a requirement in place, ten of fifteen now require offsetting amendments. The change is equally apparent when examining the global vote on the total budget – once again, eight states introduced this requirement that did not have it in 1991. When taken together, the largest aggregate improvements in the index were in Greece, Germany, Italy, and Sweden. While three countries slipped somewhat, the general trend was for stronger governments.

This is one of the most surprising, and potentially one of the most interesting, findings of this exercise. There is no *direct* reason why the Maastricht process should change how parliaments consider government budgets. Nowhere in the treaties are there articles that dictate how national parliaments should do anything on budgetary matters. Yet there does seem to be an indirect effect of the Maastricht process. The larger states of Germany, Italy, and Spain in particular made revisions, and they changed

---

[4] Ferejohn and Krehbiel (1987) provide empirical evidence suggesting that the sequence of decisions is not systemically correlated with the size of the budget in a setting without a common pool resource problem.

Table 3.3. *Parliamentary Stage*

Country	Amendments Limited 1991	Amendments Limited 2000/04	Amendments Offsetting 1991	Amendments Offsetting 2000/04	Amendments Cause Fall 1991	Amendments Cause Fall 2000/04	Expenditures Pass in One Vote 1991	Expenditures Pass in One Vote 2000/04	Global Vote on Total Budget 1991	Global Vote on Total Budget 2000/04	Sum Parliament 1991	Sum Parliament 2000/04
Austria	0	0	0	0	0	0	4	4	0	0	4	4
Belgium	0	0/4	0	0	4	4	0	0	0	4	4	8/12
Denmark	0	0	4	0	4	0	4	4	0	4	12	8
Finland	0	0	0	0	4	4	2	2	0	0	6	6
France	4	4	4	4	4	4	2	0	4	4	18	16
Germany	0	0	0	4	4	4	0	2	0	4	4	14
Greece	0	4	0	4	0	4	0	0	0	4	0	16
Ireland	4	4	0	4	4	4	0	4	0	0	8	16
Italy	4	0	0	4	0	4	2	2	0	4	6	14
Luxembourg	4	4	0	0	4	4	0	0	0	0	8	8
Netherlands	4	0	0	0	4	4	4	4	4	4	16	12
Portugal	0	0	0	0	4	4	0	0	1	4	5	8
Spain	4	0	0	4	0	0	0	0	0	4	4	8
Sweden	0	0	0	4	4	4	4	4	0	4	8	16
UK	4	4	0	4	4	4	4	4	4	4	16	20
Average	1.9	1.3/1.6	0.5	2.1	2.9	3.2	1.7	2.0	0.9	2.9	7.9	11.9

Note: Amendments Limited: 4 = yes, 0 = no; Amendments Offsetting: 4 = any expenditure increases require expenditure cuts elsewhere, 2 = expenditure increases require corresponding expenditure cuts and/or revenue increases, 0 = no; Amendments Can Cause Fall of Government: 4 = yes, 0 = no; Expenditures Pass in One Vote: 4 = chapter by chapter, 0 = not chapter by chapter; Global Vote on Total Budget: 4 = yes, 0 = no.

their indices to the levels already existing in the remaining large countries of France and the United Kingdom.

Budget Execution

This section considers the institutions forging the execution of the budget. A budget may, as proposed and as passed by parliament, be designed to maintain fiscal discipline in a country, but this budget is not enough to ensure fiscal discipline. One possibility is that the easier it is to change the budget during its execution, the easier it is to undermine the discipline in the budget. As discussed earlier, however, this concern must also be weighed with the possible benefits of having a more flexible system to respond to unexpected developments. Our coding of this part of the budget process assumes that more rigid rules "lock in" a level of fiscal discipline agreed to during the budget's formation and approval.

We focus on six items at the execution stage. The first item captures whether or not the finance minister has the power to block expenditures, with affirmative answers receiving a score of 4 and negative answers a score of 0. The second item considers whether spending ministers are subject to cash limits. If they are, it is more difficult for ministers to overrun their budget allocations and the country is scored a 4, while if they are not the country is scored a 0. The third item asks how easily funds can be transferred between chapters. Countries with unrestricted transfers receive a 0, while countries where the transfers can only be within departments, and even then are subject to the finance minister's consent, receive a top mark.[5] The fourth shows how easily the government can change the existing budget law. If it can make changes at its discretion, then it is easy for governments to make constant revisions. The country then receives a 0. If changes to the budget law fall under the same regulations as the ordinary budget, then the country receives a 4. The final item records carryover provisions to the following year. If the unused funds have no restrictions on their carryover, then the country receives the lowest score. If carryovers are not possible, the country receives the highest score.

As Table 3.4 shows, in aggregate there has been less change at this stage of the budget process than at other stages. Moreover, in 1991, the average

---

[5] The original scale reported in von Hagen (1991) ran from 0 to 5. We rescale these numbers to run 0 to 4 so that they are consistent with the other components of the index, which all run 0 to 4.

Table 3.4. *Execution*

Country	MF Block 1991	MF Block 2000/04	Cash Limits 1991	Cash Limits 2000/04	Disbursement Approval 1991	Disbursement Approval 2000/04	Transfers 1991	Transfers 2000/04	Budget Changes 1991	Budget Changes 2000/04	Carryover Provisions 1991	Carryover Provisions 2000/04	Sum Execution 1991	Sum Execution 2000/04
Austria	4	4	4	4	4	4	1.92	4.00	0	0	2.66	2.66	16.6	18.7
Belgium	0	4	0	0	4	0	1.92	0.00	4	0	0	0	9.9	4
Denmark	0	4	4	4	0	0	1.92	0.00	4	3	0		9.9	11
Finland	0	0	0	0	4	4	4.00	4.00	0	0	4	4.00	12.0	12
France	4	4	4	4	4	4	1.92	1.92	4	0	1.33	1.33	19.3	15.3
Germany	4	4	4	4	4	0	1.28	0.64	3	0	2.66	2.66	16.9	11.3
Greece	4	4	4	4	0	4	1.28	1.92	2	0	4	0	15.3	13.9
Ireland	0	4	0	0	0	4	3.20	1.92	4	4	4	1.33	11.2	15.3
Italy	0	4	0	4	0	4	0.00	0.00	1	0	0	0	1	12
Luxembourg	4	4	0	4	0	0	0.00	4.00	4	4	4	4.00	12	20
Netherlands	0	0	0	0	4	0	0.00	3.20	0	0	1.33	1.33	5	1
Portugal	0	4	4	4	4	0/4	0.00	0.00	4	2	2.66	1.33	15	11.3/15.3
Spain	0	0	0	4	0	0	0.64	1.92	4	0	1.33	4.00	6.0	9.9
Sweden	0	0	0	0	0	0	0.00	4.00	4	4	1.33	2.66	5.3	10.7
UK	0	4	4	4	0	4	1.92	1.28	4	4	1.33	0	11.3	17.3
Average	1.3	2.9	1.9	2.7	1.9	1.9/2.1	1.3	1.8	2.8	1.4	2.0	1.7	11.2	12.4/12.8

Note: Finance Minister Block: 4 = yes, 0 = no; Minister of Finance Cash Limits: 4 = yes, 0 = no; Finance Minister Disbursement Approval: 4 = yes, 0 = no; Transfers: 4 = only within departments, require finance minister consent, or not allowed, 3.2 = only within Departments, 1.92 = only within chapters, 1.28 = limited, require finance minister approval, 0.64 = limited, 0 = unlimited; Budget Changes: 4 = no changes allowed, 0 = changes allowed; Carryover Provisions: 4 = carryovers not possible, 2.66 = limited, require finance minister approval, 1.33 = limited, 0 = unlimited.

controls on the execution of the budget were not so high, 11.2 out of a possible 24. By 2000, the average had increased only to 12.4. Yet the aggregate figures again hide important changes in individual countries as well as in values for the individual indices. Three countries (Italy, Luxembourg, and Sweden) improved at least 5 points in the index. On the other hand, another two countries (Belgium and Germany) fell at least 7 points. Concerning the individual indices, the changes in the power of the finance minister went only one way – six states added the power to block spending during the execution of the budget; that leaves only four finance ministers without this ability.

Similarly, three countries added cash limits on ministers, leaving only five countries without such limits. There was also some strengthening of the rules on transfers between chapters, with the most dramatic change in Sweden. The same trend was not evident for the remaining indices. For disbursement approval, budget changes, and carryover provisions there were fewer changes, and those that were made were more likely to lower the index than to increase it. The drop was especially clear for budget changes, with seven of fifteen now allowing changes midyear that did not allow them before. In 2000, only four countries required changes to the budget to go through the same procedure as the passage of the ordinary budget. As is the case for the parliamentary index, none of the changes that occurred is mandated by the Excessive Deficit Procedure or by the Maastricht Treaty. The only changes in execution we found in the 2004 survey were for disbursement in Portugal and transfers in the Netherlands. In both cases, there was some strengthening of the procedures.

Informativeness of the Budget Draft

The working hypothesis is that less transparent budgets make it easier for politicians to hide funds or to obfuscate the true costs of given spending programs. We consider four variables in our survey to measure this concept. The first captures whether or not special funds are included in the budget draft. If so, the country receives the highest score, a 4. If special funds are completely off-budget, which in practice was the case only in Portugal in 1991, then the country receives a 0. Intermediate values indicate cases where some, but not all, funds are included. The second item relates to whether or not the budget is included in one document. If the budget appears over multiple documents, it is more difficult to follow what the government is proposing. Countries that have the budget in one document receive a 4 and those that do not a 0. The third item evaluates whether or not the person interviewed thinks that the budget process in her or his country is transparent. While certainly a subjective judgment, the question allows us to consider the level of transparency in a way that may not be picked up examining the drafting of the budget only. The fourth item shows whether the budget draft is linked to national accounts. Cases where the draft is linked receive higher scores than cases where the draft is not linked. The final item captures whether government loans appear in the budget draft.[6] "Transparency" can be measured other ways, and we include as a comparison the measure that Alt and Lassen (2006a, 2006b) compute for 1999, which is based on ten indicators that do not overlap the indicators we use. They report that their index correlates well with the subjective assessment of transparency provided in von Hagen (1992), which is the basis of the "transparency assessment" variable reported later.

Table 3.5 indicates that there has been a general increase in the level of transparency, from an average score of 13 out of 20 in 1991 to 16.1 in 2000, and that this level of transparency remained constant through 2004. Countries with scores of 10 or below in 1991 all made improvements. The most frequent change was the requirement that the budget draft appear as one document; four of five countries that did not include the budget in one draft in 1991 did so by 2000. Similarly, it is now generally the norm that government loans appear in the draft as well – only in Portugal is this definitively not the case. Four countries increased the linkage of their budget drafts with the national accounts. In aggregate, the most transparent countries are the small northern European ones, with the Netherlands and Sweden having perfect scores and Finland almost perfect at 19. The clear outlier in the other direction is Portugal, which is the only country to have an aggregate score below 10 in 2000. The remaining southern European countries are closer to the mean. In comparison to Alt and Lassen (2006a and b), our overall index is only weakly correlated in 2002/04, at .29, but the subjective assessment variable is correlated at the 0.81, confirming the same result they reported but with more current data.

Relationship between National and Subnational Governments

There is a final category of data that deserves comment, namely, the relationship between national and subnational governments. As the previous

---

[6] The information for this set of items (only) was not included in the 2000 survey. We followed up with relevant contacts in summer 2002 to get the information both as it stood in 2000 and in 2002. None of these items changed in the 2004 update.

Table 3.5. *Informativeness of the Budget Draft*

Country	Special Funds Included		Budget in One Document		Transparency Assessment		Link to National Accounts		Government Loans Included		Sum		Alt-Lassen
	1991	2002/04	1991	2002/04	1991	2002/04	1991	2002/04	1991	2002/04	1991	2002/04	1999
Austria	1	1	4	4	2	2	4	4	4	4	15	15	4
Belgium	2	1	2	4	2	2	0	4	4	4	10	15	3
Denmark	2	2	4	4	2	2	1.33	2.66	4	4	13.33	14.66	3
Finland	3	3	4	4	2	4	4	4	4	4	17	19	4
France	4	4	4	4	4	4	2.66	2.66	4	4	14.66	18.66	4
Germany	3	3	4	4	4	4	4	4	2	2	17	17	2
Greece	3	2	0	4	4	2	1.33	1.33	2	4	10.33	13.33	
Ireland	1	4	0	4	2	2	0	4	2	2	5	16	3
Italy	1	1	0	4	0	2	0	1.33	2	4	5	12.33	3
Luxembourg	4	3	4	4	4	4	4	4	4	4	20	19	
Netherlands	4	4	4	4	2	4	4	4	4	4	18	20	5
Portugal	0	2	4	4	2	2	1.33	1.33	0	0	7.33	9.33	
Spain	3	2	4	4	2	2	4	4	4	4	17	16	
Sweden	1	4	0	4	4	4	4	4	0	4	9	20	4
UK	4	4	0	0	4	4	4	4	4	4	16	16	7
Average	2.4	2.7	2.5	3.7	2.7	2.9	2.6	3.3	2.8	3.5	13.0	16.1	3.8

Note: Special Funds: 4 = yes, 3 = yes but annexed to budget, 2 = most, 1 = some, 0 = none; Budget in One Document: 4 = yes, 2 = recent yes, 0 = no; Transparency Assessment: 4 = fully transparent, 2 = not fully transparent, 0 = hardly transparent; National Account Link: direct link provided = 2.66, provided in separate document = 1.33, possible = 0 not provided; Government Loans Included: 4 = yes, 0 = no.

69

chapter indicated, rules that structure the fiscal relationship between the national and subnational levels can have important effects on budgetary outcomes. Moreover, the Maastricht process defines debt as general government debt, not just central government debt, and states may have taken measures to control the running of deficits and debts at the subnational level. Table 3.6 indicates whether there were balanced budget requirements at the subnational level, whether the national government can restrict borrowing at the subnational level, and whether the various levels of government negotiate internal stability pacts that specify the level of debts each level of government is allowed to run in a given year. Budget restrictions for lower levels of government, in particular municipalities and local districts, have a long tradition in European countries similar to that in other regions (see Eichengreen and von Hagen 1995). From our survey data, one can see that the relationship nevertheless tightened from 1991 to 2000. Sweden introduced a balanced budget requirement for local government. Three countries added the ability of the central government

Table 3.6. *Subnational Restrictions*

Country	Balanced Budget Required, Regional Governments		Central Government Can Limit		Internal Stability Pact	
	1991	2000/04	1991	2000/04	1991	2000/04
Austria	No	No	No	No	No	Yes
Belgium	Yes	Yes	Yes	Yes	No	Yes
Denmark	Yes	Yes	Yes	Yes	Yes	Yes
Finland	No	No	No	No	No	No
France	Yes	Golden rule	Yes	Yes	No	No
Germany	Golden rule	No	No	No	No	No
Greece	Yes	Yes	Yes	Yes	No	No
Ireland	No	No	No	Yes	No	No
Italy	No	No	Yes	Yes	No	Yes
Luxembourg	Yes	No	No	Yes	No	No
Netherlands	Golden rule	Golden rule	No	Yes	No	No
Portugal	No	No	No	Yes	No	No
Spain	No	No	No	Yes	No	Yes
Sweden	No	Yes	No	No	No	No
UK	Golden rule	Golden rule	No	Yes	No	No

Note: "Golden rule" under "Balanced Budget Required" indicates that the government must balance current revenues and expenditures. This means in practice that borrowing is allowed for investment projects. The remaining categories are self-explanatory.

to restrict borrowing, while another three added negotiated internal stability pacts. However, it should be noted that the operation and stringency of these pacts varied considerably, with Austria pursuing a more formal approach including a sanctioning mechanism and Italy having a rather weak arrangement. The only two countries that do not have one of these three restrictions on subnational borrowing in place are Finland and Germany.[7] In these countries, there were efforts to introduce restrictions on lower-level governments. In Finland, a change in local government regulations first introduced in 2000 requires them to present a three-year deficit reduction plan if there is a deficit in earlier years and the government is projected to be in deficit again. There are no sanctions if local governments ignore their plan, however, and as a result in practice "this amendment has turned out to [be] a dead letter."[8] Similarly, in Germany a new regulatory arrangement requires the Financial Planning Council to take into consideration economic and fiscal factors and then make recommendations regarding budgetary discipline for the different levels of government. In particular, it recommends a common expenditure course designed to ensure implementation of European requirements. As was true in 2000, there are no sanctions if Land or local governments ignore these recommendations.

Aggregating the Indices into Measures of Delegation and Contracts

Having described how the structure of the budget process may shape the distributional conflicts pertaining to the CPR problem and having described the respective institutions in the EU-15, we now have to link these institutions to the two forms of fiscal governance identified as coordination mechanisms. Forms of fiscal governance should dictate which elements of a budget process are most important for centralizing the process. That is, some fiscal institutions, such as strengthening the position of the finance minister, may be necessary to ensure fiscal discipline in one country but not in another. Under delegation, a finance minister plays the key role in the making of the budget, including in setting any budgetary targets for the government. He or she maintains a strong position in all budget

---

[7] Local governments in Germany are generally obliged to comply with the golden rule according to Länder financial laws. Similarly to other federal systems, Länder rather than the central government have the supervisory power over local public finances.

[8] Comment from anonymous Finnish official, Finance Ministry, summer 2004.

negotiations. The parliamentary stage could be an opportunity for ministers who "lost" the internal battle on spending priorities with the finance minister to reintroduce the spending items with the help of sympathetic parliamentarians, so restrictive rules at the parliamentary stage reinforce the finance minister's power. This suggests the cabinet and parliamentary stages are most important at the formation stage in delegation states. Similarly, the implementation stage is important to enforce the finance minister's budget. Because of the emphasis on discretion given to the finance minister both in the setting of the annual budget and in its execution, multiannual planning is not expected to be equally developed, or equally important, in delegation states.

In contrast, multiannual targets lie at the very heart of the contracts approach. An index that measures fiscal rules for contract states should include all four items discussed under multiannual planning earlier. Negotiations in cabinet, however, should not have a major impact so long as the parties (and their ministers) are respecting the multiannual plans in the drafting of their budgets at this stage; for example, whether the finance minister formally presents the preagreed budget is not pivotal. Similarly, the rules at the parliamentary stage could in theory be important so that parliamentarians do not undermine the terms of the contract, but one reason to create the contract is to make the parliamentary vote largely pro forma. This is especially true in countries with minority governments, such as those found in Denmark and in Sweden, where the fact that the opposition *could* upset the government's budget in parliament spurs both government and one or more parties in opposition to bargain a comprehensive package of measures. Such countries traditionally have institutionally strong parliaments (Strøm 1990), but robust fiscal contracts mean that these institutional powers are rarely, if at all, used in practice.[9]

However, parts of the delegation index that reinforce the implementation of the fiscal contract could be important. The finance minister is not expected to play an important role in the formation of the budget – the parameters should be set already in the fiscal contract – but this minister

---

[9] Underlying this discussion is the question about where the most important decisions on the budget are made. Under contracts, parties generally set the fiscal targets together outside both cabinet and parliament. The Danish example is illuminating here. There are debates about the budget in parliament in the fall, but the main decisions are taken when party leaders meet in secret at the Finance Ministry's office to hammer out the terms of the fiscal contract. Once it is agreed, both government and a selection of opposition parties that sign it stick to it, and parliament usually passes this contract substantively unchanged. See Hallerberg (2004, Chapter 6) for details about the Danish process.

can play a role in enforcing the preexisting contract. Similarly, restrictions on the transfer of funds should reinforce the contract. If money can be easily shifted, it is hard for coalition partners to know whether the players are violating the contract. At the same time, some flexibility may be acceptable as long as changes, such as carryovers from year to year, abide by the overall, multiannual targets. Because provisions in multiannual contracts could also allow some shifting of funds across years and accounts, there is not an "ideal" set of implementation rules in contract states that we can identify. We explore this question more thoroughly in Chapter 4.

In sum, the fiscal governance approach would expect that different budget rules have different effects depending upon whether a country is expected to be most appropriate for "delegation" or "contracts." Table 3.7 presents the states according to their standardized scores for an aggregate "delegation" index, which aggregates the cabinet, parliamentary, and implementation scores. Since the implementation stage is also deemed to be important for contract states, a reduced delegation index combining the first two stages and the implementation index are shown separately. Columns A–C should therefore be most relevant in delegation states. Column D provides a "targets" index which aggregates the long-term constraints, while Column E provides a "contracts" index that adds two parts of the implementation index – the ability of the finance minister to block changes to spending during implementation and the ability to transfer funds – to create a "contracts" index. Both of these columns should be most relevant in contracts states.

When comparing these aggregate figures, the most obvious pattern is that fiscal institutions centralize the process more in almost all countries from 1991 to 2000/04 according to the aggregate delegation index. There was real variation in 1991, with France having the strongest institutions and Belgium the weakest. By 2004, the overall average had increased 0.15 point, with the weakest country again being Belgium followed closely by the Netherlands. The differences are more distinct under the combined cabinet and parliament index. Greece had a score close to 0 in 1991 while France was at the opposite end. By 2004, France had slipped somewhat, while the United Kingdom had a perfect score. The lowest scores in the latest period were for Austria, Finland, and Luxembourg. The greatest change over the period, however, was for the use of fiscal targets, with the average jumping by 0.36 point. The swings were also the greatest: the two countries that had no fiscal targets in place at all in 1991 – Belgium and Luxembourg – had the most extensive targets by 2001/04. Changes in

Table 3.7. *Comparison of Indices*

Country	Delegation Index (Cab + Parl + Imple)		Reduced Delegation (Cab + Parl)		Implementation		Fiscal Targets (Long-term)		Contracts (Long-term + Two Implementation)	
	1991	2000/04	1991	2000/04	1991	2000/04	1991	2000/04	1991	2000/04
Austria	0.38	0.62	0.23	0.54	0.69	0.78	0.44	0.81	0.59	0.91
Belgium	0.23	0.44/.51	0.13	0.58	0.41	0.17	0	1	0.12	0.75
Denmark	0.59	0.58	0.69	0.64	0.41	0.46	0.5	0.81	0.37	0.66
Finland	0.37	0.52	0.31	0.53	0.5	0.5	0.88	0.88	0.59	0.69
France	0.9	0.81/.77	0.95	0.9	0.8	0.64	0.19	0.81	0.46	0.78
Germany	0.58	0.62	0.48	0.69	0.79	0.47	0.88	0.88	0.77	0.73
Greece	0.23	0.75	0.03	0.84	0.64	0.58	0.31	0.75	0.49	0.75
Ireland	0.35	0.77	0.29	0.84	0.47	0.63	0.75	0.75	0.58	0.75
Italy	0.27	0.73/.69	0.39	0.85	0.04	0.5	0.69	0.81	0.34	0.66
Luxembourg	0.53	0.64	0.54	0.54	0.5	0.83	0	1	0.25	1
Netherlands	0.56	0.47	0.73	0.64	0.22	0.11	0.88	0.81/.94	0.44	0.49/.67
Portugal	0.49	0.54/.60	0.43	0.58	0.61	0.47/.64	0.38	0.88	0.19	0.69
Spain	0.27	0.58	0.29	0.67	0.25	0.41	0.38	0.81	0.23	0.53
Sweden	0.32	0.71	0.37	0.84	0.22	0.44	0.06	0.88	0.03	0.69
UK	0.74	0.87	0.87	0.94	0.47	0.72	0.81	0.81	0.52	0.74
Average	0.45	0.64/.65	0.45	0.71	0.47	0.52	0.48	0.85/.86	0.40	0.73/.74

Note: Values range from 0, where a country would have none of the attributes that would centralize the budget process according to a given approach, to 1, where a country has all of the attributes attributed to a given approach.

implementation were, at least on average, the least impressive, with the aggregate increasing only about 0.05 point. Yet the average covers some interesting changes within the group. Implementation jumps at least 0.20 point in the United Kingdom, Sweden, and Luxembourg. At the same time, it *decreases* by around the same amount or more in Belgium, France, and Germany, while the Netherlands has a score near 0 even in 2004.

The next chapter considers whether these differences in fiscal rules in countries had an effect on fiscal outcomes. The straight centralization argument would expect that the first index would be important in all countries. The fiscal governance argument, in contrast, would argue that the delegation and reduced delegation indices should be most relevant in delegation states, the fiscal targets and contracts index in contract states, and, when implementation is considered separately, that it should be significant in both types of states.

4

How Forms of Fiscal Governance Affect Fiscal Performance

We evaluate here the effects of fiscal institutions on fiscal performance. The previous chapter catalogued the norms and rules found at different stages of the budget process for European Union countries from 1985 through 2004. It created indices to match the theoretical expectations detailed in Chapter 2. The delegation index tests the proposition that the same sort of centralization of the budget process is appropriate in all states. According to the fiscal governance approach, the delegation index should matter most in countries with low ideological distances and low office-seeking competition. In countries with high ideological distances and high office-seeking competition, the fiscal target and contract indices should be most significant.

The most common way to measure fiscal discipline is to look at some sort of measure of the gross debt burden or the budget balance. Consistently with these studies, we expect the various indices to matter most for changes in the gross debt burden over time as well as in the overall budget balance.

While the results confirm that the delegation indices matter most for expected delegation states and the contracts indices the most for expected contract states, there is an important finding about the effectiveness of those institutions that emerges. The very effectiveness of a given set of fiscal institutions can be undermined if the underlying ideological distance changes. That is, institutions that seem to guarantee a strong role for the finance minister work when there is a one-party government but become increasingly ineffective as policy differences among coalition partners increase. Similarly, fiscal targets by themselves are most useful as policy differences become greater but have little impact if they are in place and a one-party government replaces a preexisting multiparty coalition government.

We also expand our study of the effects of institutions to a broader set of concerns. First, there is a debate about whether there are biases in the macroeconomic forecasting errors that governments make. We find that there are systematic differences in the errors that states make according to whether they are appropriate for delegation or fiscal contracts, with expected contract states more conservative in their forecasts than expected delegation states. We hypothesize that more conservative forecasts make it less likely that the relevant players will have to renegotiate the "fiscal contract."

Second, we address the debate about the effectiveness of different consolidation strategies. Earlier literature has pointed out that the quality of fiscal consolidations has implications for their success in terms of debt reduction, persistence, and macroeconomic impact. In this context, "quality" refers to the kind of consolidation effort. "Good quality" consolidations put most of the effort on the spending side of the budget, while "bad quality" consolidations rely mainly on increasing taxes. We investigate the role of our measures of centralization in that context and find that budgetary procedures strongly centralizing decision-making power in expected delegation states support good quality consolidation efforts.

Fiscal Discipline and Fiscal Institutions: Debts and Deficits

The first question that we address is whether centralization of the budget process leads to greater fiscal discipline. To measure "discipline," we look first at the gross debt burden as a percentage of GDP. An advantage of using the gross debt figures is that essentially everything the government does appears on these accounts, and that means that they are much less subject to direct accounting tricks. Dafflon and Rossi (1999) contend that several European Union states used accounting tricks to get their deficits below 3% in the run-up to Economic and Monetary Union, while von Hagen and Wolff (2006) find evidence of such tricks continuing once the euro is introduced in 1999. The gross debt ratio over time is generally not stationary, however, so we first examine differences and consider changes instead of levels of the debt ratio. We also look at general government budget balance figures, which receive the lion's share of attention. In contrast to the debt ratio, budget balances have been stationary over the period for which we have institutional data, or 1985–2004, and we look at the level version of this variable.[1]

In terms of independent variables, we include a set of economic and political variables that we anticipate may both be associated with fiscal discipline and correlated with the variables we care most about, namely, the institutional measures. To deal with autocorrelation and because past budgets likely affect current ones, we include a lagged dependent variable. We also include a lag of the level of the debt ratio. The assumption is that countries will have a more difficult time raising funds when debt levels are high, and this will put pressure on governments to reduce debts/deficits. Changes in gross domestic product and in the unemployment rate measure the effects of the business cycle. Countries with weak or negative growth or with an increasing number of citizens receiving unemployment benefits should experience a deterioration of their budget balances as automatic stabilizers do their work. Similarly, interest rates that governments pay on their debt are not directly under the government's control, and we include a variable for debt servicing costs. High debt payments may also increase the public pressure on governments to consolidate and reduce the amount of tax revenues which has to be accrued to this budget item. Countries with more open economies may have an easier time borrowing abroad than countries with more closed economies. We follow the literature to measure openness as exports plus imports divided by GDP. Countries with larger populations may be able to enjoy economies of scale in the provision of public services. They may also face fewer international constraints on their budget behavior. Finally, the period under consideration includes the years prior to qualification for Economic and Monetary Union. Countries with deficits above 3% of GDP may have taken additional measures to adjust their budgets, and their sensitivity may have increased the higher their deficit was above the Maastricht deficit criterion. We include a variable that measures the amount the deficit was above 3% prior to 1998.

---

[1] For the entire period, the coefficient on a lagged dependent variable of debt levels is 0.992, which strongly suggests a unit root. A simple look at the increase in debt in some countries, such as in Greece and Italy, indicates as well that there is a time trend. Finally, the Im-Pesaran-Shin panel unit root test with the assumption of a lag of 1 indicates that one cannot reject the hypothesis that at the 0.1 level that the debt level has a unit root. In contrast, the same test rejects the hypothesis at the 0.026 level that there is a unit root in the budget balance data (because of a two-year gap in Luxembourg's budget balance data in the late 1980s, the test had to exclude Luxembourg from the dataset in order to run).

The remaining independent variables follow from the discussions in Chapters 2 and 3. To summarize the predictions from the fiscal governance approach, delegation institutions should be effective when veto player distance as well as office-seeking competition are small/low (expected delegation states), while contracts should be most effective when veto player distance and office-seeking competition are large/high (expected contract states). This prediction has two implications for the empirical model. First, we divide the sample in two according to whether states are predicted to be appropriate for delegation or contracts. Second, in some specifications we include an interaction term between the relevant institutional index and veto player distance. Our expectation is that the effectiveness of the institution declines as the actual veto player distance diverges from the ideal (either small under delegation or large under contracts).[2] To keep the analysis tractable, we report results with the Tsebelis coding for veto player distance.[3] Finally, we include additional political and institutional variables that may matter. Governments may intentionally let fiscal discipline slip before elections in an effort to buy votes. Such opportunistic political business cycles should lead to increases in the debt burden prior to elections. We use Franzese's (2002) method of coding elections, which considers the proportion of a given year. Given that all figures are in terms of general government, we include a dummy variable for whether there is a ban on subnational borrowing in a given country.[4]

[2] An alternative, and equivalent, specification would be to employ triple interaction effects, that is, to add a dummy variable for delegation/contracts, then interact that with the veto player times institutional variable.

[3] We replicated the results with the Manifesto Project data. Although the correlation between the Tsebelis and Manifesto is not high, the results are nevertheless quite close. They are available upon request.

[4] See Rodden (2006) for more details about the use of such bans. We also include in regressions not reported here additional variables. Following the literature on transparency, we consider the transparency index as presented in Chapter 3 as well as a measure for economic volatility, with the rationale for the latter that economies with greater swings may have more difficulty keeping fiscal discipline under control (Hallerberg, Strauch, and von Hagen 2006). We also include just the "subjective evaluation" of overall transparency, which the previous chapter indicated was closely correlated with the Alt and Lassen (2006b) measure. The variation among European countries in the Alt and Lassen measure is much smaller than their overall sample, which includes a country such as New Zealand with perfect transparency according to their measure and a country such as Japan with no transparency at all, so the fact that we do not get interesting results with this measure is not surprising. None of these variables is significant in any regression, so there is no reason to have them take away degrees of freedom and we do not include them in the reported results.

The most interesting variables for our purposes are the ones that measure directly the strength of fiscal institutions. Each column in Table 4.1 considers a different hypothesis. In column 1, the question is whether a centralization of the cabinet, parliament, and implementation stages (the delegation index) is equally effective in all countries, as the centralization hypothesis elaborated in Chapter 2 would suggest. The straight centralization hypothesis from Chapter 2 would assume that this index would be statistically significant for all countries in the sample. Column 1 in Table 4.1 presents the regression evidence for the EU-15 for the period 1985–2004. It indicates that the delegation index is statistically significant in the expected negative direction, but only at the 0.1 level.

The remaining variables have coefficients that we would expect – real growth reduces the change in debt, increases in unemployment increase the debt, and preelectoral years also lead to increasing debt burdens. Note that more extensive fiscal targets have no statistically significant effect.

The fiscal governance approach, in contrast, assumes that the delegation index should be most effective in places that should be delegation states and fiscal targets in expected contract states. Columns 2 and 3 break down the EU-15 into expected forms of governance and rerun the same regression equation. In expected delegation states, the delegation index is now significant at the 0.01 level, with a coefficient almost a third higher than in the regression that included all of the states. There is a more practical interpretation of this variable. The constant term is 5.61 and statistically significant. If countries score a 1 on the delegation index and have average growth for the period (2.8% in the EU-15), the linear combination of the constant term, growth, and the delegation index is indistinguishable from zero.[5] Expected delegation countries with centralizing budgetary institutions and higher than average growth in a given year experience a decline in their debt burdens, while those that have a bad growth year have an increase in the debt burden. "Fit" institutions allow the automatic stabilizers to do their job. It should be noted that the targets index has the expected negative sign but is not significant.

We observe a similar pattern for expected contract states for the targets index. While fiscal targets were completely ineffectual in the full sample and only marginally significant in the delegation states, in expected contract states they have the expected negative effect. In this case, the constant is not different from zero and the sign on economic growth remains

---

[5] In particular, the term then has a coefficient of 1.42 with a standard error of 0.99.

Table 4.1. *Regression Results for Change in the Gross Debt Ratio*

	All Countries	Expected Delegation	Expected Contracts	Expected Delegation	Expected Contracts	Expected Delegation	Expected Contracts	Expected Delegation	Expected Contracts
Fiscal Institutions									
Delegation Index	-1.82 (1.15)	-3.04 (1.40)*	2.05 (2.72)	-3.6 (1.48)*	0.77 (2.83)	-4.00 (1.47)**	2.26 (2.80)	-2.97 (1.34)*	4.11 (3.53)
Delegation Index (Multiplicative)									
Delegation*Veto				18.58 (14.66)		31.26 (12.80)*		23.37 (13.68)†	
Delegation (Multi)*Veto									
Targets Index	-0.71 (0.47)	-1.69 (0.92)†	-1.40 (0.65)*	-0.98 (1.01)	1.44 (1.70)				
Targets*Veto					-10.85 (6.19)†				
Contracts Index						1.82 (0.85)*	0.55 (2.36)		
Contracts*Veto							-11.91 (8.74)		
Contracts Index (Multiplicative)								0.62 (0.79)	-1.74 (2.57)
Contracts (Multi)*Veto									-.20 (10.85)

(continued)

Table 4.1 (*continued*)

	All Countries	Expected Delegation	Expected Contracts	Expected Delegation	Expected Contracts	Expected Delegation	Expected Contracts	Expected Delegation	Expected Contracts
Remaining Variables									
Lag Dependent Variable	0.29 (0.07)**	0.16 (0.07)**	0.29 (0.08)**	0.16 (0.07)*	0.27 (0.08)**	0.15 (0.07)**	0.26 (0.08)**	0.16 (0.06)*	0.30 (0.08)**
Lag Debt	-0.02 (0.01)**	-0.03 (0.01)**	-0.03 (0.01)**	-0.03 (0.01)**	-0.03 (0.01)**	-0.03 (0.01)**	-0.02 (0.01)*	-0.04 (0.01)**	-0.03 (0.01)**
Real GDP Growth	-0.34 (0.12)**	-0.41 (0.17)*	-0.24 (0.13)†	-0.42 (0.17)*	-0.26 (0.13)*	-0.38 (0.16)*	-0.24 (0.13)†	-0.36 (0.16)*	-0.24 (0.13)†
Change Unemployment	1.10 (0.27)**	0.79 (0.33)*	0.28 (0.32)**	0.79 (0.33)*	1.22 (0.32)**	0.79 (0.32)**	1.29 (0.33)**	0.78 (0.31)*	1.25 (0.32)**
Debt Servicing Costs	0.30 (0.16)†	0.16 (0.19)	0.77 (0.22)**	0.14 (0.19)	0.72 (0.21)**	0.13 (0.19)	0.73 (0.22)**	0.18 (0.19)	0.82 (0.22)**
Openness of Economy [(exports + imports)/GDP]	0.00 (0.00)	-0.02 (0.01)	0.01 (0.00)*	-0.02 (0.01)†	0.01 (0.00)*	-0.03 (0.01)*	0.01 (0.01)*	-0.02 (0.01)**	0.01 (0.01)†

Population	-0.01	-0.01	0.08	-0.01	0.07	-0.02	0.07	-0.02	0.07
	(0.01)	(0.01)	(0.02)**	(0.01)	(0.02)**	(0.01)†	(0.02)**	(0.01)†	(0.02)**
Election Year	1.11	2.09	0.28	2.15	0.25	2.19	0.28	2.21	0.27
	(0.47)*	(0.60)**	(0.61)	(0.61)**	(0.60)	(0.61)**	(0.61)	(0.62)**	(0.62)
Veto Player Distance (Tsebelis)	-1.39	1.53	0.96	-9.97	8.39	-18.5	6.44	-7.78	20.53
	(1.10)	(2.18)	(2.00)	(9.28)	(4.54)	(8.39)*	(4.42)	(5.52)	(2.95)
Convergence	-0.15	-0.28	0.19	-0.29	0.16	-.36	0.16	-0.31	0.21
	(0.18)	(0.15)*	(0.22)	(0.15)*	(0.21)	(0.15)	(0.21)	(0.15)*	(0.22)
Pre-EMU	-0.32	1.1		0.96		0.49		0.72	
	(0.42)	(0.71)		(0.72)		(0.67)		(0.65)	
Federal Borrowing Constraint			-2.08		-1.98		-2.85		-2.14
			(0.68)**		(0.66)**		(0.87)**		(0.75)**
Constant	3.8	5.61	0.6	5.79	-0.43	6.00	-0.20	5.08	0.62
	(1.09)**	(1.33)**	(1.68)	(1.32)**	(1.73)	(1.36)**	(1.75)	(1.22)**	(1.3)
Observations	296	136	160	136	160	136	160	136	160
Number of Countries	15	9	9	9	9	9	9	9	9

Note: Standard errors in parentheses. † significant at 10%; * significant at 5%; ** significant at 1%

negative, so a country with fully centralized targets would be whittling down its debt burden rather than keeping it the same if economic growth were positive.

This difference in the operation of an appropriate set of institutions bears some explanation. Our suspicion is that strong finance ministers found in true delegation states want to maintain an even keel through the economic waters they encounter, both good and bad. True contract states, in contrast, face a possible breakdown of the contract itself when the seas turn rough. They may want to build a safety margin into the contract to minimize the impact of worse-than-expected economic performance. We consider this possibility in more detail in the next section, when we investigate the forecasting records of expected delegation and contract states.

The remaining columns consider first an interaction term between veto player distance and a given institutional index and veto player distance as well as different ways of coding the appropriate index for expected delegation and contract states. Our theory predicts that countries that traditionally have been one type of state or the other will have institutional breakdowns when the veto player distance moves away from what has traditionally been found in a country. For example, a web of institutions supports and reinforces the powers of the chancellor of the Exchequer in the United Kingdom, and they have generally performed well in fiscal terms under both Conservative and Labour one-party governments. However, if the Liberal Democrats became a more powerful third party in the next election and no party won a majority, a coalition government would be the likely result. Our argument is that the preexisting institutional structure would no longer be appropriate. Unless fiscal contracts were introduced, the system would not function well.[6] Similarly, a state that usually has multiparty coalitions would suffer difficulties if a one-party majority government formed after an election. In terms of conditional coefficients, our expectation is that the delegation index is most negative when the veto player distance is zero (i.e., a one-party majority government), and that the effect of delegation institutions erodes as veto player distance increases. The opposite is expected in contract states for the effect of fiscal targets – targets under governments with veto player distances of zero should have

[6] A case that is not hypothetical is the switch from a Red-Green coalition under Gerhard Schröder in Germany, where the ideological distance between the parties was low, to a Grand Coalition of Christian and Social Democrats under Angela Merkel, where the distance is higher. See Hallerberg and von Hagen (2005) for a brief discussion of the German situation.

no effect, while they should become increasingly, and (statistically) significantly, important as veto player distance increases.

On the basis of these expectations, we calculate the conditional coefficients for the delegation and contract indices, respectively, *given* a certain veto player distance. Given that the conditional standard errors cannot be calculated directly from Table 4.1 and that (Tsebelian) veto player distance ranges in practice from 0 to 0.5, in Figure 4.1 we present the conditional coefficients based on columns 4 and 5.

Filled areas represent the part of the line where statistical significance in a two-tailed test is $p < 0.05$ or below.

The first conditional coefficient is for the delegation index in expected delegation states. The coefficient under one-party majority governments, that is, when veto player distance is zero, is about -3.5. The curve increases, however, as veto player distance increases and quickly becomes statistically insignificant at a veto player distance of about 0.05 (Germany 1998–2005). The reverse is the case for the conditional coefficient of the targets index. It is positive and statistically insignificant under one-party governments, but it has a negative slope and becomes statistically significant at about 0.25 (Netherlands 1994–2003). These results provide strong empirical evidence for the proposition that the effectiveness of a given set of fiscal institutions depends upon the underlying political climate.

The remaining regressions consider different ways to measure the role of institutions in expected delegation and contract states. Column 6 and 7 use a "contracts" index, which is simply the targets index plus two items from the implementation stage, whether the finance minister can block spending and how easily spending can be transferred within departments. This index is again standardized to run from 0 to 1. The coefficients for the institutional variables then become somewhat larger in the expected directions, with the delegation index now almost -4. The interaction term for the contracts regression also becomes more negative; a more negative slope for the conditional coefficients line results. When calculating conditional coefficients, the fiscal contracts index becomes significant at the 0.05 level at a veto player distance of 0.25. Columns 8 and 9 use multiplicative instead of additive versions of the institutional indices. The idea behind a multiplicative index is that failure to centralize the budget at any one stage of the process would lead to lax discipline. The results are broadly similar to the additive regressions – the multiplicative version of the delegation index is around -3 and statistically significant when veto player distance is zero or very low, while the multiplicative contracts index

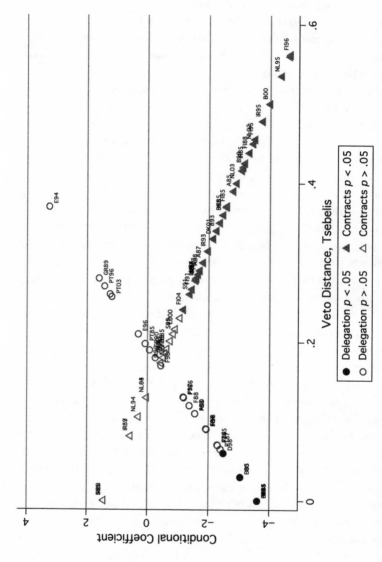

Figure 4.1 Conditional Coefficients of Delegation and Targets Indices in Expected Delegation and Contract States, Change in Debt Levels. Filled areas represent the part of the line where statistical significance in a two-tailed test is $p < 0.05$ or below.

is statistically significant and increasing in value when veto player distance is high.[7]

One question to address is whether there are issues of endogeneity, which would affect our results. The first issue involves the potential endogeneity of contemporaneous macrovariables. Economic growth, the unemployment rate, and the interest rate (relevant for debt servicing costs) may be affected by contemporaneous fiscal shocks. A second potential issue concerns the validity of our institutional measures. Changes in budgeting institutions may be endogenous components of the fiscal adjustment strategies countries used to comply with the Maastricht criteria.[8] If they are, the OLS estimates would be biased. To tackle this issue, we conduct a Hausman specification test for endogeneity of the macroeconomic and institutional variables (see Wooldridge 2002). For the macroeconomic variables, we also check for the impact of lagged variables in levels and first differences in the first-stage regression.[9] Since our sample includes annual data, we use a maximum of two lags. Then we add further variables to the model, that is, the output gap, long-term interest rates, and the contemporaneous U.S. real GDP growth rate, the change in the U.S. unemployment rate, and the U.S. real long-term interest rate.[10] These variables are kept in the model when they increase the overall explanatory power of the first-stage regression model.

To control for the endogeneity of budgetary institutions, we instrumentalize the change in the delegation and targets indices using the institutional setting and the debt level in 1991 and use the specifications for Models 2 and 3. The debt level in 1991 captures the need for fiscal restraint over the coming years in order to maintain or achieve fiscal sustainability. It should therefore be correlated with the institutional reform efforts made later on, but since it precedes the convergence process starting in 1992, it is uncorrelated with the structural error term.

The results of the tests are presented in Table 4.2 and suggest that endogeneity is a problem in only one case – expected delegation states when

---

[7] In particular, the multiplicative delegation index is no longer significant at the $p < 0.05$ level when veto player distance is greater than .05, while the multiplicative index for contracts is significant when veto player distance is equal to or greater than .16.

[8] An important question to consider is why countries change their budget institutions. We seek to answer this question in the next two chapters.

[9] This is to reflect the different approaches to instrumentalizing variables in dynamic panel models using GMM estimators (see Baltagi 2005).

[10] See, e.g., Gali and Perotti (2003), who also use U.S. GDP data for this purpose. The role of the U.S. long-term bond yields for financial conditions in Europe is well documented (see Favero et al. 1997; Cordogno, Missale, and Favero 2004).

Table 4.2. *Hausman Tests for Endogeneity of Macroeconomic and Institutional Variables*

Variables		
Endogeneity of Macrovariables	10.07	22.57*
Endogeneity of Macro- and Institutional Variables	3.05	20.00
Nobs	160	136
Country	Expected Contract States	Expected Delegation States

Note: The dependent variable is the change in gross general government debt as share of GDP. Asterisks indicate statistical significance at the 10% (*), 5% (**), and 1% (***) levels. The H0-hypothesis of the Hausman test is that the difference in coefficients is not significant. The three macroeconomic variables GDP growth, change in unemployment, and debt servicing costs were instrumentalized using all exogenous variables of the model described in Model 1 plus lags of the output gap and real GDP growth, lagged changes in unemployment, lagged long-term interest rates, and U.S. GDP and long-term interest rates. The delegation index and fiscal targets index were instrumentalized using the debt level and institutional setting in 1991.

macrovariables only are included. The institutional coefficient we care about, namely, the delegation index, weakens only somewhat, from –3.0 to –2.58, and remains statistically significant, albeit only weakly for a two-tailed test. If the full set of instruments are included, the Hausman test suggests that there is no reason to include the instruments in the first place.

The next set of results reported in Table 4.3 considers budget balances as the dependent variable. The figures are levels instead of changes, and the expected sign of the variables we care most about reverses. The delegation index, for example, should have a positive rather than a negative sign if the centralization thesis is correct. We keep the remaining independent variables.

The results for the budget balance regressions are quite close to the change in debt level results. The aggregate measure for centralization, the delegation index, is only statistically significant at the $p < 0.1$ level for the entire sample but, as before, has a higher coefficient and is statistically significant at the $p < 0.05$ level in expected delegation states. The interaction effects parallel the debt results as well, with the conditional coefficient for expected delegation states significant only when veto player distance is zero or very low and significant when veto player distance is high. Figure 4.2 presents the conditional coefficients for the regressions in columns 4 and 5.

Table 4.3. *Regression Results for Budget Balance as Percentage of GDP*

	All Countries	Expected Delegation	Expected Contracts	Expected Delegation	Expected Contracts	Expected Delegation	Expected Contracts	Expected Delegation	Expected Contracts
Fiscal Institutions									
Delegation Index	0.89 (0.61)	1.62 (0.80)*	−0.94 (1.42)	1.51 (0.77)*	0.42 (1.50)	1.49 (0.81)†	−0.61 (1.52)		
Delegation Index (Multiplicative)								1.42 (0.81)†	−2.59 (1.61)
Delegation*Veto				4.34 (9.75)		−7.78 (8.31)			
Delegation (Multi)*Veto								−7.68 (7.02)	
Targets Index	0.54 (0.35)	1.30 (0.67)†	0.94 (0.49)†	1.48 (0.82)†	−1.94 (1.23)				
Targets*Veto					11.04 (4.18)**				
Contracts Index						1.21 (0.85)	−1.63 (1.66)		
Contracts*Veto							12.1 (5.62)*		
Contracts Index (Multiplicative)								0.64 (0.64)	−0.38 (1.51)
Contracts (Multi)*Veto									8.03 (5.07)

(continued)

Table 4.3 (*continued*)

	All Countries	Expected Delegation	Expected Contracts	Expected Delegation	Expected Contracts	Expected Delegation	Expected Contracts	Expected Delegation	Expected Contracts
Remaining Variables									
Lag Dependent Variable	0.86 (0.04)**	0.67 (0.09)**	0.82 (0.06)**	0.67 (0.09)**	0.78 (0.06)**	0.69 (0.09)**	0.79 (0.06)**	0.70 (0.09)**	0.80 (0.06)**
Lag Debt	-0.00 (0.00)	0.00 (0.01)	-0.01 (0.01)	0.00 (0.01)	-0.01 (0.01)	0.00 (0.01)	-0.01 (0.01)	0.01 (0.01)	-0.01 (0.01)
Real GDP Growth	0.20 (0.07)**	0.31 (0.09)**	0.10 (0.10)	0.31 (0.09)**	0.12 (0.10)	0.30 (0.09)**	0.11 (0.10)	0.29 (0.09)**	0.12 (0.11)
Change Unemployment	-0.56 (0.13)**	-0.23 (0.17)	-0.82 (0.20)**	-0.23 (0.17)	-0.71 (0.19)**	-0.26 (0.18)	-0.75 (0.20)**	-0.28 (0.18)	-0.81 (0.20)**
Debt Servicing Costs	0.11 (0.07)†	0.26 (0.12)*	-0.12 (0.09)	0.26 (0.12)*	-0.06 (0.10)	0.23 (0.12)†	-0.07 (0.10)	0.22 (0.12)†	-0.10 (0.10)

	(1)	(2)	(3)	(4)	(5)	(6)	(7)	(8)	(9)
Openness of Economy [(exports + imports)*GDP]	0.00	0.01	0.00	0.01	-0.01	0.01	-0.01	0.01	-0.01
	(0.00)	(0.01)	(0.00)	(0.01)	(0.00)	(0.01)	(0.00)†	(0.01)	(0.00)†
Population	-0.01	0.00	-0.05	0.00	-0.05	0.01	-0.05	0.01	-0.05
	(0.01)	(0.01)	(0.01)**	(0.01)	(0.01)**	(0.01)	(0.01)**	(0.01)	(0.01)**
Election Year	-0.63	-0.98	-0.33	-0.96	-0.30	-0.99	-0.32	-1.00	-0.31
	(0.24)**	(0.38)*	(0.36)	(0.39)*	(0.33)	(0.41)*	(0.35)	(0.41)*	(0.36)
Veto Player Distance (Tsebelis)	0.35	0.22	-1.12	-2.47	-8.61	5.15	-6.72	3.45	-2.82
	(0.62)	(1.54)	(1.26)	(6.40)	(3.30)**	(5.62)	(3.15)*	(3.05)	(1.83)
Convergence Pre-EMU	-0.09	0.16	-0.32	0.16	-0.28	0.12	-0.29	0.12	-0.31
	(0.08)	(0.12)	(0.10)**	(0.12)	(0.09)**	(0.12)	(0.10)**	(0.12)	(0.10)**
Federal Borrowing Constraint	0.04	-0.15	0.50	-0.18	0.40	-0.27	0.94	-0.09	0.99
	(0.27)	(0.40)	(0.41)	(0.41)	(0.38)	(0.50)	(0.51)†	(0.48)	(0.50)*
Constant	-1.33	-4.15	0.84	-4.14	1.98	-3.98	1.72	-3.46	1.48
	(0.56)*	(1.14)**	(1.00)	(1.14)**	(1.13)†	(1.18)**	(1.19)	(1.12)**	(0.90)
Observations	293	136	157	136	157	136	157	136	157
Number of Countries	15	9	9	9	9	9	9	9	9

Note: Standard errors in parentheses. † significant at 10%; * significant at 5%; ** significant at 1%

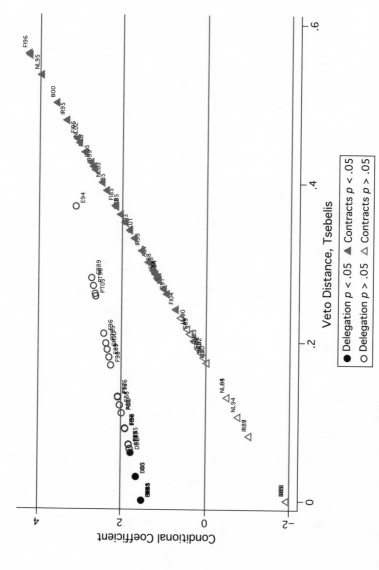

Figure 4.2 Conditional Coefficients of Delegation and Targets Indices in Expected Delegation and Contract States, Budget Balance. Filled areas represent the part of the line where statistical significance in a two-tailed test is $p < 0.05$ or below.

One peculiarity is that the slope of the delegation conditional coefficient is positive instead of negative, but it becomes statistically insignificant at almost the exact same level of veto player distance.

The institutional variables in the last four regressions are, however, somewhat less effective than in the debt change regressions. Why are there differences between the two? A likely explanation is that Economic and Monetary Union changed the way that states reported their budget balances. Under EMU, the European Commission evaluates whether countries have "excessive deficits" and makes a recommendation to the Council of Ministers based on its decision. The figures used in practice to decide whether or not there is an excessive deficit are the budget balances. Countries with deficits close to or above 3% of GDP are subject to most scrutiny. As a result, governments have an incentive to use accounting devices to move funds off the budget, especially when they approach the 3% limit. This explains why some unfunded expenditures raise public debt but do not appear in the budget deficit. Von Hagen and Wolff (2006) find that the correlation between budget balances and debt declines precipitously after 1999, the beginning of Stage III of EMU, and does so when countries approach the deficit limit. Table 4.4 displays the regression coefficients just for the institutional variables for the nine regressions if the sample is restricted to the period before 1999.

The effects of the Delegation index in particular become larger, and more statistically significant, when the period is restricted to before 1999. Not coincidentally, expected delegation states like France, Germany, Italy, and Portugal all had problems keeping their deficits below 3% of GDP.

The Quality of Budgetary Forecasts in Europe – The Track Record of Stability and Convergence Programs

Introduction

This section considers how forms of fiscal governance affect the performance of multiannual budget projections of governments. From the perspective of macroeconomic policymaking, there are few forecasts that have similar importance. Multiannual budget plans are a crucial element of the budgeting decision, since they put the current budget in a medium-term perspective. They also provide outside observers with key information

Table 4.4. *Coefficients for the Institutional Variables, 1985–1998 Only*

	All Countries	Expected Delegation	Expected Contracts	Expected Delegation	Expected Contracts	Expected Delegation	Expected Contracts	Expected Delegation	Expected Contracts
Delegation Index	1.27 (0.69)†	1.76 (0.71)*	-0.34 (1.45)	1.77 (0.68)**	0.90 (1.56)	2.29 (0.64)**	-0.48 (1.55)		
Delegation Index (Multiplicative)								2.70 (0.64)**	-2.01 (1.80)
Delegation*Veto				-0.55 (9.42)		2.36 (9.84)			
Delegation (Multi)*Veto								-3.61 (6.49)	
Targets Index	0.44 (0.39)	-0.05 (0.74)	0.86 (0.49)†	-0.08 (0.74)	-1.94 (1.42)				
Targets*Veto					10.36 (4.80)*				
Contracts Index						1.73 (1.17)	-0.91 (2.07)		
Contracts*Veto							10.15 (6.88)		
Contracts Index (Multiplicative)								1.33 (0.64)*	1.08 (2.07)
Contracts (Multi)*Veto									4.98 (6.74)

Note: Standard errors in parentheses. † significant at 10%; * significant at 5%; ** significant at 1%

about the government's views and intentions, which in turn shape economic and political behavior. Getting these forecasts wrong can have fiscal implications, such as a need for unforeseen spending cuts. They can similarly have political consequences if a government fails to carry out an anticipated consolidation of public finances. For this reason, the assumption that governments strive to maximize forecast accuracy may be rather heroic. However, so far little cross-country analysis of forecast behavior has been done for industrialized countries, and for European countries in particular, to explore whether there are any significant deviations and differences across countries.

One problem that has traditionally prevented comparative analysis in this respect is the scarcity of comparable data. The set of stability and convergence programs published by European governments provides such data. The submission of multiannual budget programs is a key element of the surveillance process installed at the European level through the Maastricht Treaty and the Stability and Growth Pact. Within this framework EU member states have the obligation to submit either convergence or stability programs by the end of the year. The programs are then scrutinized and assessed by the European Commission and the ECOFIN Council to detect budgetary imbalances that could imply risks for fiscal sustainability. Several governments only started to proclaim multiannual budgetary targets in the course of the Maastricht convergence process, or they adjusted their time horizon to the one requested for the programs. As such, the budgetary projections and underlying growth forecasts provide the first fairly homogeneous dataset of government forecasts for European countries. Analyzing these data thus not only provides a unique opportunity with a view to the multiannual budgetary projections in general, but also bears implications for the operation of the European fiscal framework. Given the newness of the dataset, we provide more detail than we did in the previous section.

Descriptive Statistics and Simple Tests of Efficiency

We look at standard descriptive statistics evaluating forecast performance such as the mean error (ME), the mean absolute error (MAE), and the root mean squared error (RMSE) of the program forecasts of budget balances and economic growth. The forecast error e is defined as the actual value minus the forecasted value. Thus a negative sign indicates that one has overestimated the budgetary balance or growth and experienced a negative

Table 4.5. *Convergence and Stability Programs, 1991–2004*

Country	Program (Date of Release or Submission)
Austria	05/95, 05/96, 10/97, 11/98, 03/00, 12/00, 11/01, 03/03, 12/04
Belgium	06/92, 04/93, 03/94, 12/96, 12/98, 12/99, 12/00, 11/01, 11/02, 11/03, 12/04
Denmark	02/94, 11/94, 03/96, 05/97, 10/98, 12/99, 12/00, 02/02, 12/02, 11/03, 11/04
Finland	09/95, 09/96, 09/97, 09/98, 09/99, 09/00, 11/01, 11/02, 11/03, 11/04
France	10/93, 02/97, 12/98, 01/00, 12/00, 12/01, 12/02, 12/03, 12/04
Germany	10/91, 10/93, 02/97, 01/99, 12/99, 10/00, 12/01, 12/02, 12/03, 12/04
Greece	02/93, 06/94, 07/97, 06/98, 12/99, 12/00, 12/01, 12/02, 12/03
Ireland	08/94, 05/97, 12/97, 12/98, 12/99, 12/00, 12/01, 12/02, 12/03, 12/04
Italy	10/91, 09/92, 06/97, 12/98, 12/99, 12/00, 11/01, 11/02, 12/03, 12/04
Luxembourg	02/99, 03/00, 12/00, 12/01, 01/03, 11/03, 11/04
Netherlands	04/92, 10/94, 12/96, 10/98, 11/99, 09/00, 10/01, 06/03, 10/03, 11/04
Portugal	11/91, 11/93, 03/97, 12/98, 02/00, 01/01, 12/01, 01/03, 12/03, 12/04
Spain	04/92, 07/94, 04/97, 12/98, 01/00, 01/01, 12/01, 12/02, 01/04, 12/04
Sweden	06/95, 11/95, 04/96, 09/96, 04/97, 09/97, 12/98, 11/99, 11/00, 11/01, 11/02, 11/03, 11/04
United Kingdom	05/93, 02/94, 03/95, 04/96, 03/97, 09/97, 12/98, 12/99, 12/00, 12/01, 12/02, 12/03, 12/04

"surprise," and a positive sign implies the opposite. The ME, MAE, and RMSE are computed as follows:

$$ME = \frac{1}{N}\sum_{i=1}^{N} e_{i,t+h}, \quad MAE = \frac{1}{N}\sum_{i=1}^{N} |e_{i,t+h}|, \quad RMSE = \sqrt{\frac{1}{N}\sum_{i=1}^{N} e_{i,t+h}^2}$$

We use two specifications. First, N is the number of observations for each forecast horizon $t + h$ across programs i. Later on, we compute these measures for all programs i of a country over all forecast horizons up to $t + h$, such that $N = i \cdot h$. Table 4.5 displays the programs used in the sample.

Table 4.6. *Forecast Errors by Forecasting Horizon, 1991–2004*

Program Year	Obs	ME	MAE	RMSE
Balance				
Current	154	0.10	0.84	1.29
1	140	−0.04	1.14	1.56
2	122	−0.36	1.43	2.01
3	102	−0.77	1.70	2.33
Balance (programs from 1998 onward)				
Current	105	−0.11	0.78	1.25
1	91	−0.32	1.15	1.62
2	73	−0.85	1.57	2.11
3	60	−1.49	1.95	2.50
Growth				
Current	151	0.27	0.73	1.11
1	139	−0.05	1.07	1.60
2	120	−0.34	1.15	1.79
3	100	−0.59	1.00	1.46

We code all data on forecasting errors on the basis of our analysis of these programs.

We start by looking at these measures for different program years since the difficulty of precisely forecasting economic growth and public finances increases with the forecasting horizon. The ME figures in Table 4.6 indicate that governments on average predicted the budget surplus fairly well and that forecast errors were distributed equally around the actual value. This outcome is obviously the result of symmetrically distributed forecast errors as the MAEs indicate. The MAE increases from 0.84 for the current year to 1.70 for the three-year-ahead forecasts. These figures reflect the increasing uncertainty of future budgetary outcomes. Since the RMSE is always larger than the MAE, a considerable proportion of forecast errors are large errors above 1 percentage point. A short look at growth projections indicates that the ME for economic growth is less downward biased and more accurate than projections of budgetary balances.

The bias, though not the overall accuracy, of budgetary forecasts changes considerably when we look at the shorter sample period after 1997. This year is the last one when projections should not be affected by the unexpected downturn starting in 2001. At the same time it presents an institutional shift since the Stability and Growth Pact took force. For

Table 4.7. *Forecasting Errors for Budgetary Balances (by Country)*

Country	Obs	ME	MAE	RMSE
1991–2004				
Austria	33	0.11	0.65	0.82
Belgium	37	−0.02	0.43	0.61
Denmark	38	0.43	0.79	1.02
Finland	34	0.44	1.12	1.64
France	30	−0.83	0.91	1.42
Germany	34	−0.63	1.06	1.52
Greece	32	−2.65	2.99	3.83
Ireland	31	0.48	1.70	2.20
Italy	34	−1.10	1.33	1.71
Luxembourg	22	0.06	1.67	2.23
Netherlands	29	−0.39	1.26	1.63
Portugal	34	−1.08	1.13	1.78
Spain	34	−0.03	1.02	1.52
Sweden	50	0.55	1.45	1.69
United Kingdom	46	0.56	1.22	1.49
1998–2004				
Austria	21	−0.13	0.66	0.87
Belgium	22	0.10	0.27	0.33
Denmark	22	−0.03	0.55	0.72
Finland	22	0.37	0.99	1.46
France	22	−1.02	1.09	1.68
Germany	22	−1.18	1.33	1.75
Greece	21	−3.31	3.38	4.11
Ireland	22	−0.17	1.17	2.15
Italy	22	−1.21	1.35	1.67
Luxembourg	22	0.59	1.67	2.23
Netherlands	19	−0.74	1.52	1.91
Portugal	22	−1.47	1.47	1.85
Spain	22	0.29	0.69	0.85
Sweden	26	−0.36	1.36	1.67
United Kingdom	22	−0.11	1.09	1.30

this period, the ME shows the same trend, but starting from a small negative value for the current year it falls to −1.5, roughly double the size of the ME for the entire sample.

Until now we have analyzed how forecast errors performed over the course of the program. A more important aspect is whether forecast errors vary by country. Table 4.7 lists the ME, MAE, and RMSE for each EU member state pooled over all forecast horizons for each country. One has to assume that forecast errors are stationary to ensure the validity of this approach. The number of observations in the table are correspondingly all forecast errors from $t + 1$ to $t + 3$ available for that country. Looking at country performance for each projection horizon would have drastically reduced the number of observations and might therefore not lead to reasonable results. Since the projection horizon is standardized to three years ahead according to the stipulations of the Stability and Growth Pact and censoring of data at the end of the sample period affects all countries similarly, we should not incur any systematic mistakes when pooling observations over projection horizons.[11]

From this perspective Greece has the largest negative ME, followed by Italy, Portugal, France and Germany, and the Netherlands. Then there is the group of countries with very small ME, including Spain, Belgium, Luxembourg, and Austria. Finally, there is the third group with positive ME all between 0.4% and 0.6% of GDP, including Denmark, Finland, Sweden, Ireland, and the United Kingdom. For the subsample from 1998 to 2004, this ordering changes somewhat for the last two groups with the United Kingdom, Sweden, and Ireland moving downward relative to others. The results for the group of countries with large negative ME are rather stable, but showing somewhat larger ME in absolute terms. There is only a partial correspondence of these biases with the overall accuracy of budgetary forecasts. Taking the RMSE as a benchmark, results show that Greece followed by Luxembourg and Ireland perform worst for the entire sample as well as for the post-1997 period. Countries with a smaller bias, in particular Belgium and Denmark, perform best.

An obvious question is to what extent the larger forecast errors for the budget balances during the 1998 to 2004 period can be explained by deviations of actual from predicted economic growth or whether one has to look for different factors to explain differences in forecast performance over the cycle. One can answer this question by empirically estimating the elasticity of the budget balance with respect to GDP forecast errors based on the dataset of stability and convergence programes. Simply regressing budgetary forecast

---

[11] One should keep in mind that accounting concepts were not fully harmonized before 1998. This could distort cross-country comparisons for the initial years. Moreover, we do not correct actual budgetary outcomes for ex post revisions, but take the data vintage of autumn 2005 as point of comparison. Given the different size of ex post revisions, this may also affect cross-country comparison.

errors on deviations of actual growth from projections yields the following result for the entire sample and the 1998 to 2004 subperiod:

$$e_{balance} = -0.17 + 0.54 \cdot e_{growth} + v$$
$$\phantom{e_{balance} = }(-1.77) \quad (9.71)$$

$$e_{balance} = -0.43 + 0.46 \cdot e_{growth} + v$$
$$\phantom{e_{balance} = }(-4.60) \quad (6.81)$$

Numbers in parentheses are t-statistics.[12] The estimate indicates that generally for each percentage point by which actual output growth exceeds forecasts, budgetary balances deviate 0.5% from budgetary plans. This is a sizable effect which lies close to the normally assumed budget elasticity to output fluctuations. The unexplained bias captured by the constant is small and borderline significant at the 10% level. Looking at the sample of programs starting after 1997, the budgetary elasticity with respect to growth decreases somewhat and the estimate of the overall bias becomes larger in absolute terms and statistically more significant. From these results, one can conclude that errors in growth projections cannot fully explain why mean errors worsened during the downturn from 2001 onward.

Finally, governments may nevertheless have used all information efficiently when projecting budgetary balances and simply had "bad luck" and could not have done better. A way to analyze whether governments have used all information efficiently when producing their forecasts is to examine whether they improve on either simple models or competing forecasts. In this context, comparison with forecasts from the European Commission are particularly interesting from an institutional perspective, since the commission is the "guardian of the Treaty" and has a prevailing role in the surveillance process.[13]

---

[12] The regressions were conducted using simply country-year observations over all countries and forecast horizons. The number of observations is 503 for the regression including the entire sample and 323 for the 1998–2004 sample period. The t-statistics are based on Newey-West standard errors allowing for a MA(3) process.

[13] We are assuming for the sake of argument here that the commission conducts forecasts independently of national governments. The commission does conduct forecast meetings with national delegations, where these delegations make their case for their respective projections. However, there is no legal obligation for the commission to follow member state dictates even though in practice commission forecasts may match national government forecasts for some countries. This is also an empirically interesting question in any event – if these forecasts had to be approved by the respective governments, one should not see differences because governments would obviously impose their own numbers. And even if there is some influence, this does not invalidate the argument – to the contrary, the commission would be doing better than governments *despite* their influence.

Table 4.8. *Test for Efficiency of Surplus and Growth Forecasts (by Forecast Horizon)*

Horizon	Program	EC
	Growth	
Current	0.46 ($\beta = 1$: 5.27**, $\beta = 0$: 4.14**)	0.64 ($\beta = 1$: 2.49, $\beta = 0$: 7.75***)
1	−0.19 ($\beta = 1$: 14.78***, $\beta = 0$: 1.41)	1.19 ($\beta = 1$: 0.32, $\beta = 0$: 12.15***)
2	−0.46 ($\beta = 1$: 26.68***, $\beta = 0$: 2.64*)	1.27 ($\beta = 1$: 1.02, $\beta = 0$: 22.51***)
	Balance	
Current	0.15 ($\beta = 1$: 34.21***, $\beta = 0$: 1.17)	0.85 ($\beta = 1$: 1.06, $\beta = 0$: 33.58***)
1	0.32 ($\beta = 1$: 7.39***, $\beta = 0$: 1.60)	0.66 ($\beta = 1$: 2.03, $\beta = 0$: 7.46***)
2	0.12 ($\beta = 1$: 8.36***, $\beta = 0$: 0.15)	0.74 ($\beta = 1$: 1.32, $\beta = 0$: 10.57***)

Note: Asterisks indicate significance at the 1% (***), 5% (**), and 10% (*) level. Numbers in parenthesis are F-statistics.

Therefore we apply a standard forecast encompassing test for the different forecast horizons to see whether program forecasts encompass commission projections or vice versa. Following Diebold (2000: 295), we estimate the following equation:

$$y_{it+h} = \beta_1 f^p_{it+h} + \beta_2 f^{ec}_{it+h} + \varepsilon_{it}.$$

Y is the actual outcome, f are the h year-ahead forecasts released in a program (p) or by the European Commission (ec) for country i. If (β_1, β_2) = (1, 0) it is said that the program forecast encompasses the commission forecast. For (β_1, β_2) = (0, 1), the opposite holds. For this exercise program projections were matched with the European Commission forecast data being released closest to the date when the program was published. Since commission forecasts are not generally available for the horizon $t + 3$, the comparison is only possible up to the two-year horizon.[14]

Table 4.8 depicts the coefficient estimates and the F-statistic for the respective restriction on the coefficients. For economic growth, one can reject for all forecast horizons that the coefficients are 1, while it cannot be rejected with one exception that they are 0. The opposite holds for the commission forecasts, where the hypothesis that β is 1 can never and that it is 0 can always be rejected, thus indicating that the information content of commission forecasts actually encompasses program projections. Budgetary

---

[14] In case the release of a program fell just in the middle of the time span between two forecast publications (usually April and November), the commission forecast with the longer horizon is used.

forecasts provide an even clearer picture, since for no program horizon the restriction that β is 0 can be rejected. This would suggest that little additional information can be learned by looking at program projections when assessing future fiscal developments in EU member states. This result is somewhat counterintuitive if the objective of governments were to minimize forecast errors. Generally one would assume that the information set available to the European Commission is a subset of the information accessible to the government. The government may have special confidential databases and models and inside information on policy measures, whereas the European Commission possibly has to rely on information made available by the government or on news available to the public. Under this assumption, our finding indeed indicates that governments could more efficiently make use of the available information in order to improve forecasts or did not use it effectively to maximize forecast accuracy.

Toward a Political Economy of Forms of Fiscal Governance and Budgetary Projections

To understand how institutional factors may affect the budget, it is useful to review why such errors may arise. First, there may be unforeseen economic developments. Under this scenario, presumably there is not sufficient time for the government to respond. If this is the only source of the error, there should be no particular bias to the error. Second, the government may choose to ignore spending limits it sets for itself. The forecasts assume that the spending limits are respected, so there is forecasting error. Forecasts in this case should be too optimistic. Third, governments may introduce an intentional bias to their forecasts. They may want to limit the risk of an unexpected deficit. Forecasts are then pessimistic.

The form of fiscal governance affects the relative weight of each source of forecasting error. The fragmented budgetary system found under a fiefdom form of fiscal governance should result in larger absolute forecast errors and an overly optimistic forecast. Since the budget process is decentralized, spending limits are more likely to be ignored. Moreover, the aggregation of spending pressures may lead to an asymmetric reaction to random shocks, that is, large increases in spending under negative economic shocks but no consolidation under positive economic shocks. The main reason for forecast errors in this case is the lack of budgetary control.

The prediction for contract states is the opposite of the one for fragmented states. The contracts approach relies on explicit numerical targets.

Deviations from the targets are presumably costly because they imply re-negotiation of the contract. Under the assumption that renegotiating budgetary shortfalls is more costly for all coalition partners than distributing unexpected budgetary slack, there should be a cautionary bias. As the empirical data in Chapter 3 have already indicated, in fact, expected contract states generally have contingency rules for budgetary windfalls or shortages. This suggests that governments are well aware of renegotiation costs and try to circumvent them.

Finally, states with a delegation form of fiscal governance should not experience any systematic bias in forecasts at all. If an unexpected fiscal shock arises, the finance minister has the power to make an adjustment to the budget so long as there is sufficient time to respond. There is also no need to have overly pessimistic forecasts so long as the finance minister is indeed strong.[15]

The argument for a fiefdom form of fiscal governance in particular suggests that governments when announcing forecasts may have an asymmetric loss function. One well-known functional form of asymmetric loss is the "quad-quad" function (see Elliott et al. 2003),

$$u(e) = \begin{cases} ae_j^2, & e \leq 0 \\ be_i^2, & e > 0 \end{cases}$$

where e again indicates the forecast error. When $b/a < 1$, there is a higher loss from negative forecast errors, that is, underprediction; otherwise over-prediction is less desirable. Given the political economy of contracts, one would assume that governments under contract regimes tend to have a co-efficient close to 1, or, if they have cautionary bias, below 1. There is no particular prediction for delegation states. Following Artis and Marcellino (2001), we can determine the parameter value b/a for our sample assuming that forecasts are optimal given governments' loss function and setting $u(e)' = 0$.[16] Under this assumption the ratio of coefficients can be computed as $b/a = \sum e_i^2 \big/ \sum e_j^2$.

Table 4.9 shows the coefficient for forecasts of budgetary balances and the prevailing type of fiscal governance in each country. Looking at the entire sample of countries, contract forms of governance predominantly

---

[15] Indeed, overly pessimistic forecasts are a clear indication of the weakness of the finance minister. If the finance minister can respond during the execution of the budget, there is no need to introduce an intentional bias.

[16] Elliot et al. (2003) present a GMM approach to estimate parameter values of the loss function directly. Unfortunately, the number of observations per country and forecast horizon is too small in our sample to replicate their analysis.

Table 4.9. *Asymmetry of Loss Function for Budgetary Forecasts and Forms of Fiscal Governance (1991–2004)*

Country	b/a (1991–2004)	b/a (1998–2004)	Expected Form of Fiscal Governance
Austria	0.64	1.07	Delegation
Belgium	2.45	0.45	Contract
Denmark	0.19	1.20	Contract
Finland	0.24	0.24	Contract
France	172.81	248.64	Delegation
Germany	8.30	71.3	Delegation
Greece	41.4	969.48	Fragmented, delegation
Ireland	0.74	1.69	Contract
Italy	35.7	63.61	Fragmented, delegation
Luxembourg	0.96	0.96	Contract
Netherlands	3.99	5.83	Contract
Portugal	14.41	18153	Fragmented
Spain	2.39	0.16	Delegation
Sweden	0.62	3.23	Fragmented, contract
United Kingdom	0.29	1.46	Delegation

Note: The values indicate the parameter values *b/a* as estimated for each country pooling errors over the entire forecast horizon.

show an asymmetry factor below 1. In the cases of the Netherlands and Belgium, values are 2.5 and 4, respectively. This would imply less political concern about budgetary optimism, but the values nonetheless remain small compared to those obtained by most delegation countries. Countries with fragmented and delegation forms of governance have mostly para-meter values substantially above 1, indicating that they put relatively less weight on underprediction. The notable exceptions are Austria and the United Kingdom.[17] When looking at the subperiod from 1998 to 2004, utility values generally increase and the difference between contract and delegation states becomes more pronounced. Values for contract states mostly remain below 1 or, when above, in the vicinity of 1. Values increase to 5.8 for the Netherlands and 3.2 for Sweden. For most delegation states,

---

[17] France has an extreme value of 172.8. This implies that there were few and small forecast errors when France underpredicted its budgetary balance, while this scheme was much more equally weighted, say, in Germany (8.33).

however, the skewedness of the utility function toward underprediction of deficits is reflected in high values above 60 for Italy and Germany and above 100 for France and Greece, which are only topped by those for Portugal, which is characterized by a fragmented form of governance.

Multivariate Analysis

While this nonparametric evidence is indicative of the bias in delegation states particularly during the economic downturn after the year 2001, there are competing explanations for this pattern. A more refined multivariate analysis is required to control for these factors. For this purpose, the following model is estimated:

$$f_{it} = \alpha + \beta_1 X_{it} + \beta_2 P_{it} + \varepsilon_{it}$$

where f presents the fiscal variable under consideration for program i at time t. For the forecast error this is the mean error, for the projected and actual fiscal stance these are annual observations. ε is a random error. X is the vector of economic control variables, $X = \{$gap, volatility, conv$\}$. *Gap* indicates the lagged output gap. This controls for the cyclical situation during the budgetary planning stage. Cyclical fluctuations create uncertainty about future developments and possible turning points. They may also induce a forecasting bias if people are tempted to expect better times in busts and are overly optimistic during booms. *Volatility* is the standard deviation of real GDP growth over the cycle. In line with the literature on European business cycles, we use eight years to compute this measure (see Bouthevillain et al. 2001). Higher output volatility could lead to a cautious forecast bias if policymakers are risk averse. Finally, *conv* indicates the convergence need, that is, the distance between the actual balance and the "benchmark" reference value at the time when the program was released. The European fiscal framework itself sets incentives for strategies of "blame avoidance" (Weaver 1986), which could lead to forecast biases. Conversely, not complying with projections similarly should have caused peer pressure. In case countries run the risk of an excessive deficit, this could have even formal procedural consequences leading from an early warning to the decision to fine a euro area country.

P comprises the vector of political and institutional variables, $P = \{$elect, veto, contract, delegate$\}$. *Elect* captures the preelection year. Upcoming elections may induce governments to paint a more rosy picture of the future and at the same time embark on a spending spree not foreseen in

105

earlier budget plans. The variable is operationalized as a continuous and not as a dummy variable: that is, it captures the time span of the pre-electoral year falling in the calendar year when the election actually takes place in the following calendar year. *Veto* indicates the ideological complexion of government.

Contract and *delegate* capture the respective expected fiscal governance structures. Because our theoretical expectation is about the effects of the general form of fiscal governance on forecasts, we use a dummy variable in our regressions for the actual form of fiscal governance instead of the various indices considered earlier in the chapter. The variable is 1 for a delegation regime if a country has a delegation form of fiscal governance. A contract dummy is coded 1 if the contract mechanism is regularly applied by government coalitions to commit to budget aggregates. In all other cases, representing a fiefdom form of governance, the two variables are coded 0. These dummy variables can be considered fixed effects that capture the performance of these regimes relative to the fragmented structure, which is the default.

Our data constitute a cross-sectional time series dataset, which is relatively small on the time and cross-sectional dimension, and where observations from programs and their updates are clustered for individual countries. Moreover, some key variables such as the form of fiscal governance show little or no time variation for several countries. These features restrict clearly the econometric specification which we can apply. We therefore have to use standard OLS without country effects. Robust standard errors allowing residuals to be correlated within countries are computed to accommodate the potential clustering of observations. The robustness of results is checked extensively by dropping individual countries from the sample to control for the impact of unobserved measurement errors or other factors affecting observations in a country.

Table 4.10 presents the results for forecast errors of budgetary balances. Over the entire decade, all variables turn out to be statistically significant at standard levels. The results indicate that a favorable cyclical position is associated with less positive or more negative forecast errors. In other words, booms induce overly optimistic forecasts. Conversely, cyclical downturns reduce this bias or even lead to an overly cautious forecasting stance. This pattern could be the outcome of a turning point problem. Countries had problems in correctly predicting the recovery after the slowdown in the early 1990s and the downturn following the boom in the late 1990s until 2001. Therefore, they, respectively, under- and overpredicted budgetary balances. Moreover, output volatility significantly affects

Table 4.10. *Forecast Errors – Budget Balance (OLS-Regression)*

	1991–2004	1998–2004	1991–2004	1998–2004
Constant	–0.55	–0.75	–0.70	–0.84
	(0.34)	(0.55)	(0.55)	(0.98)
Output Gap (lag)	–0.30***	–0.23	–0.27***	–0.23**
	(0.07)	(0.13)	(0.07)	(0.11)
Output Volatility	0.29**	0.31*	0.10	–0.0006
	(0.11)	(0.15)	(0.12)	(0.25)
Convergence Need	0.07*	0.08	–0.04	–0.23
	(0.04)	(0.15)	(0.07)	(0.28)
Election			–0.32	–0.27
			(0.35)	(0.29)
Veto-player			–0.76	–0.73
			(1.07)	(1.24)
Delegate			0.04	–0.26
			(0.32)	(0.39)
Contract			1.16***	1.41**
			(0.38)	(0.51)
R^2	0.21	0.06	0.30	0.26
F-test	12.51***	3.14*	9.07***	30.80***
Nobs	153	104	153	104

Note: Asterisks indicate significance at the 1% (***), 5% (**), and 10% (*) level.

forecast errors: that is, governments in more volatile economies tend to have more cautious forecasts leading to positive errors. Finally, a positive coefficient for the convergence need would indicate a similar stance being related to the deviation from the reference values. But the latter two results lose statistical significance when we reduce the sample period and/or control for political variables.

Columns 3 and 4 show the estimates including the political and institutional variables. The positive and significant coefficient on the dummy for contract states indicates that forecasts are more cautious under this regime. Delegation, in contrast, shows no statistically significant difference to the performance of fragmented governance. This supports our hypothesis that contract states may face stronger incentives to avoid unexpected deficits.

These findings of the multivariate analysis support the conjecture that fiscal forms of governance affect forecasting performance. Contract states make more cautious forecasts then delegation states. Importantly, this result holds even if we control for the convergence need under the European fiscal framework at the time when the program was written. The evidence casts doubts on the argument that forecast behavior is actually driven by the European fiscal framework and that there is simply observational equivalence between delegation states and those countries not complying with the European budgetary requirements.

Delegation, Rules, and the Structure of Fiscal Consolidations

Introduction

The result in the last section about the optimistic bias for projected consolidations in delegation states raises the question whether fiscal institutions play any role in the form a consolidation takes, that is, whether the consolidation is mostly on the spending or revenue side of the budget. Some empirical studies find that the type of consolidation affects its persistence. Alesina and Perotti (1997); Perotti, Strauch, and von Hagen (1998); von Hagen et al. (2002); von Hagen and Strauch (2001); and Mulas-Granados (2003) all show that expenditure-based consolidations tend to be more persistent and run less risk of subsequent reversal. These studies also indicate that the start of consolidation efforts and the choice of the consolidation strategy are not random. Von Hagen and Strauch (2001) argue that the cyclical position of the domestic and international economy as well as the initial debt level and the fiscal stance in other countries affect the likelihood of fiscal consolidations as well as the consolidation strategy. Similarly, Mulas-Granados (2003) finds that the degree of fragmentation in decision making, as measured by the size of the cabinet, and the proximity of an election determine the likelihood and duration of consolidations. The ideological orientation of the government is more important for the choice of the consolidation strategy, with leftist governments being more prone to engage in revenue-based consolidations.

In this literature, the role of budgetary institutions in the occurrence and quality of fiscal consolidations has not been included. A priori there is good reason for the lack of previous research on this topic. Conceptually, there is no immediate link between the frequency of consolidation episodes and the functioning of a delegation or contracts form of fiscal governance. On the one hand, one might expect that "better" institutions lead to more timely consolidations. On the other hand, the need for consolidations may be reduced under "better" institutions in the first place. Moreover, the formal model we use for the common pool resource problem does not give us guidance about the type of strategy one should use to increase the chances of successful consolidations. The model in Chapter 3 indicates only that developed delegation and contract forms of government equally reduce the spending bias. This refers essentially to spending levels and does not necessarily imply that a short-term balancing of the budget has to be achieved only through spending reductions.

Nevertheless, since public sector spending tends to be rather high and inertial in European countries, one could speculate that governments operating under delegation and contract forms of governance are indeed more hesitant to increase taxes and maintain high spending levels than those with fiefdom forms of fiscal governance. Centralized budgetary institutions also lower the transaction costs of expenditure reduction. Fiscal institutions that induce more centralized decision making may in turn increase the likelihood that consolidation decisions are implemented. Empirical evidence from the American state context (Poterba 1994, Strauch 1998) suggests that strict fiscal rules and budgetary centralization lead to spending adjustments. The expectation, therefore, would be that delegation and contracting forms of fiscal governance should have more expenditure-led consolidations than fiefdom forms of governance.

Descriptive Statistics on the Role of Forms of Governance

The first issue is the definition of fiscal consolidation episodes. Some studies (e.g., Alesina and Perotti 1995, 1997) focus on one- or two-year periods with strong changes in the fiscal stance. The main drawback of this method is the arbitrariness of the time spell and the benchmark set for the strength of the adjustment effort. Others (e.g., von Hagen et al. 2002, Mulas-Granados 2003) have therefore opted for an endogenous definition of consolidation efforts that considers consolidation spells over the entire period when the fiscal stance improves. In order to prevent a single blip in revenue or spending flows which can be the result of a minor idiosyncratic factor or measurement error from distorting the picture, von Hagen and associates (2002) define consolidation episodes as those periods when the fiscal stance improves by a minimum of 0.5% over the adjustment spell. For our analysis we apply the same definition to define fiscal consolidation episodes for changes in the primary balance.

Table 4.11 shows the distribution of consolidation spells for expected delegation and contract states. The total number of episodes varies for the different definitions but does not reveal large discrepancies. It shows that more than half of the consolidation episodes occurred in expected contract

Table 4.11. *Occurrence of Consolidations According to Different Fiscal Measures*

	Primary Balance	Fiscal Stance (Commission CAPB)	Fiscal Stance
Contract	31	37	36
Delegation	28	25	28
Contract			
Rules (nonstringent)	19	22	23
Rules (stringent)	12	15	13
Delegation			
Index (decentralized)	10	9	10
Index (centralized)	17	16	18

Note: The fiscal stance in the second column is defined as the change in the primary cyclically adjusted budgetary balance as computed by the European Commission. As an alternative measure the fiscal stance (third column) is computed as $f = \Delta s - \varepsilon \Delta y$, where s is the balance, y is the real GDP growth rate, ε the budgetary elasticity with respect to output growth, and Δ the first difference operator. Budgetary elasticities are taken from van den Noord (2000) and Bouthevillain et al. (2001) for Luxembourg.

states. The difference between contract and delegation states is more sizable for the two measures of the fiscal stance adjusting budgetary flows for the impact of the cycle. As a next step, we look at the occurrence of consolidations within each form of fiscal governance and distinguishing between tight and weak fiscal rules, respectively, centralized and fragmented budgetary procedures using the median value as the benchmark to categorize our institutional indices. In expected contract states, fiscal consolidations occurred more often under weak rules according to all measures. In delegation states, however, clearly more episodes of fiscal tightening took place under more centralized budgetary procedures.

Table 4.12 depicts different measures of the quality of fiscal consolidations by distinguishing between revenue- and expenditure-led episodes based on four definitions of expenditures (primary and current primary expenditures as well as two measures of cyclically adjusted primary expenditures). Expenditure-led consolidation episodes are defined as those when spending accounts for more than 50% of the adjustment.

Using this definition, one can cross-tab the quality of consolidations with the expected fiscal form of governance or institutional setting and test whether there are significant differences using a standard Pearson's chi-square test statistic. For the countries with expected delegation and contract fiscal forms of governance, no significant difference exists with

Table 4.12. *Occurrence of Expenditure-Led Consolidations*

Strategy	Primary Expenditures		Current Primary Expenditures		Cyclically Adjusted Primary Expenditures (European Commission)		Cyclically Adjusted Primary Expenditures	
	Rev. led	Exp. led	Rev. led	Exp. led	Rev. led	Exp. led	Rev. led	Exp. led
Contract	11	20	11	20	17	20	19	17
Delegation	13	15	13	15	14	11	16	12
Pearson chi_2	0.73		0.73		0.603		0.12	
Contract								
Rules (nonstringent)	7	12	10	9	11	11	11	12
Rules (stringent)	4	8	7	5	6	9	8	5
Pearson chi_2	0.04		0.10		0.36		0.63	
Delegation								
Index (decentralized)	9	2	11	0	7	2	8	2
Index (centralized)	4	13	8	9	7	9	8	10
Pearson chi_2	9.12***		78.58***		2.71*		13.32*	

Note: Asterisks indicate significance at the 1% (***), 5% (**), and 10% (*) level.

Table 4.13. *Size of Expenditure Reductions during Consolidation Spells According to Different Fiscal Measures (in Percentage Points of GDP)*

	Primary Expenditures	Primary Current Expenditures	Cyclically Adjusted Primary Expenditures (European Commission)	Cyclically Adjusted Primary Expenditures
Contract	−2.74	−1.94	−1.53	−1.96
Delegation	−1.64	−0.80	−1.02	−1.11
Contract				
Rules (nonstringent)	−3.28	−2.27	−1.74	−1.96
Rules (stringent)	−1.88	−1.42	−1.23	−1.97
Delegation				
Index (decentralized)	−0.50	−0.18	−0.81	−0.28
Index (centralized)	−2.38	−1.20	−1.14	−1.57

regard to the quality of the consolidation experiences. For the fiscal measures, which are not cyclically adjusted, there tend to be more expenditure-led consolidations in expected delegation and contract countries, but this does not hold entirely anymore for the cyclically adjusted measures. Within the group of countries where a contract form of fiscal governance would be expected, we distinguish again between those with tight and weak fiscal rules. It shows that for those with weaker fiscal rules there were roughly as many expenditure-led as revenue-led consolidations, while the distribution for those countries with tight fiscal rules depends very much on the expenditure measure under consideration. Clear differences emerge in the group of countries with the expected delegation form of governance. Expenditure-led consolidations occur more often under centralized budgetary procedures according to all spending measures.

On the basis of the previous result, we ask whether these differences are also reflected in the size of the expenditure adjustment during consolidations. Table 4.13 shows the average accumulated expenditure reductions as percentage of GDP during consolidation episodes. The higher frequency of consolidations in expected contracts regimes is reflected in larger expenditure reductions. The same holds for the set of expected contract states with respect to the less stringent fiscal rules. Expenditures are on average reduced more in cases with a lower than median value of the fiscal rules index. For the index on the centralization of the budget process, the result is the opposite. More centralization and a larger share of expenditure-led consolidations are reflected in a more sizable cut in spending levels. The difference between more fragmented and highly centralized procedures is smallest for the cyclically adjusted measures of the European Commission.

Multivariate Analysis

The pattern of institutional settings and the quality of fiscal consolidations has so far been extracted from simple descriptive statistics. For a multivariate analysis, however, the model used in the first section of the chapter needs to be adjusted for two reasons: First, conceptually, several structural variables – such as openness of the economy or population size – are determinants of longer-term spending and revenue levels rather than short-term adjustment dynamics and can therefore be excluded from the econometric model. Second, the small number of observations clearly reduces the degrees of freedom and the possible set of variables that can be included in the model. On the basis of these considerations and the existing evidence on determinants of fiscal consolidations we first estimate a probit model for the occurrence of expenditure-led consolidations using the lagged debt level, real GDP growth, change in the unemployment rate, and veto power of parties in government as covariates. The model is estimated separately for expected delegation and contract states. In the baseline model the unemployment variable affects negatively the probability of expenditure-led consolidations. This result is in line with Mulas-Granados (2003). The other variables are insignificant at standard levels. Coefficient estimates for the institutional indices, when added to the model, are shown in Table 4.14. The coefficients for the delegation index are all positive, but only statistically significant at the 10% level for current primary expenditures. For the contract index there is no indication that it would weaken the tendency to conduct expenditure-led consolidations, as one might have inferred from the descriptive statistics. Since the impact of the delegation index may not be linear with respect to the discretionary dependent variable, the dummy variable for centralized budgetary procedures is used as an alternative specification. For this measure there are indeed more indications that delegation improves the likelihood of expenditure-led consolidations. All measures show such a positive relationship with the exception of the indicator derived from the European Commission measure of cyclically adjusted expenditures.[18]

---

[18] No coefficient is shown for the current primary expenditures since the occurrence of consolidations is perfectly predicted by the high delegation index dummy and this variable is therefore dropped from the estimation.

Table 4.14. *Occurrence of Expenditure-Led Consolidations*

	Primary Expenditures	Primary Current Expenditures	Cyclically Adjusted Primary Expenditures (European Commission)	Cyclically Adjusted Primary Expenditures
Delegation Index	2.92 (2.02)	5.37* (3.13)	0.42 (1.77)	0.40 (1.91)
Contract Index	0.65 (1.01)	0.49 (1.09)	–0.23 (0.75)	–1.33 (1.08)
Delegation Index (centralized – dummy)	3.43** (1.47)	–	1.04 (0.74)	1.76* (0.92)
Contract Index (stringent – dummy)	0.62 (0.62)	0.07 (0.63)	0.40 (0.51)	–1.71 (0.92)

Note: The dependent variable is the probit of an expenditure-based consolidation. ***, **, and * indicate significance at levels below 1%, between 1% and 5%, and above 5% and below 10%, respectively. Figures in brackets are standard errors. Estimates for the delegation index are based on the observations for expected delegation states. Estimates for the contract index are based on the sample of expected contract states.

The dummy variable for the occurrence of expenditure-led consolidations strongly condenses the information content of our indicators for the quality of public finances. As an alternative to check the robustness of results, we estimate a regression model using the expenditure contribution to the consolidation effort as dependent variables. OLS estimates for the sample of expected delegation states are shown in Table 4.15. The dummy variable indicating the degree of delegation carries a positive coefficient for all spending measures, with the exception of the European Commission's cyclically adjusted measure. However, the result is statistically significant for total primary expenditures and the cyclically adjusted measure based on the method proposed by Hughes Hallet, Strauch, and von Hagen (2001). Finally, the model is expanded by using the index values for more centralized delegation regimes with the veto variable. The results show the expected sign in the regression using the primary balance as dependent variable. Strong delegation procedures support a higher expenditure contribution to fiscal consolidations, but the impact is undermined increasingly by the ideological dispersion of the government. A similar positive impact can be found for the cyclically adjusted budgetary measure of Hughes Hallett and colleagues

Table 4.15. *Fiscal Forms of Governance and Expenditure Contributions to Consolidations*

	Primary Expenditures	Primary Current Expenditures	Cyclically Adjusted Primary Expenditures (European Commission)	Cyclically Adjusted Primary Expenditures
Delegation Index (centralized – dummy)	77.95*** (29.32)	31.55 (21.51)	−2.76 (30.69)	114.58*** (26.78)
Contract Index (stringent – dummy)	30.83 (19.69)	13.08 (15.25)	75.00** (29.31)	0.63 (21.05)
Delegation Index (centralized)	83.98** (33.47)	11.31 (24.12)	−5.03 (36.95)	76.03** (31.84)
Delegation * Veto	−148.44 (414.37)	523.34 (320.11)	97.54 (829.06)	658.42* (333.03)

Note: The dependent variable is the contribution of expenditures to the consolidation. ***, **, and * indicate significance at levels below 1%, between 1% and 5%, and above 5% and below 10%, respectively. Figures in brackets are standard errors. Estimates are based on the observations for expected delegation states. Data were cleaned for extreme outliers.

115

(2001). The interaction with the veto variable carries a positive coefficient, which is statistically significant at the 10% level. However, when the regression is replicated using actual expenditure reductions over the consolidation spell as dependent variable, the specification based on this cyclically adjusted measure carries a negative and statistically significant coefficient for the index value (pointing to the expenditure reducing impact) and a coefficient of the opposite sign for the interaction term.[19] Overall, while there is considerable evidence that budgetary procedures entailing a high degree of delegation support the quality of fiscal consolidations, the importance of the interaction with the ideological constellation in government cannot be fully determined for the limited sample under consideration although some results are in line with the overall argument of this chapter.

Conclusion

The chapter evaluated the effect of different measures for the form of fiscal governance on a set of outcomes. The results are consistently strong for changes in the debt ratio and for the level of the budget balance. A particularly important finding is that the effects of a given set of institutions depend upon the underlying political alignment. Institutions consistent with a delegation form of fiscal governance are effective only when there is little or no ideological conflict within government. In contrast, institutions that are consistent with a contracting form of governance are most effective when ideological distance is large.

The findings for government forecasts also suggest that differences in the form of fiscal governance have clear effects. Expected contract states have more cautious forecasts than expected delegation states. Such governments presumably want to avoid renegotiation of the fiscal contract. Finally, we link our work with the literature on the type of budget consolidations. The results here are less persuasive, but they do suggest that expected delegation states with centralized budgetary procedures initiate more expenditure-led fiscal consolidations.

The results beg the question why countries adopt the fiscal institutions that they do. This is the theme of the following two chapters, with the first looking at Western Europe while the second examines institutions in the Central and Eastern European countries that joined the European Union in 2004 and 2007.

---

[19] The values are –2.50 (standard error 1.30) for the index term and 14.15 (standard error 13.64) for the interaction term with the veto variable.

5

Why Do Countries Have Different Fiscal Institutions?

A culture of public spending was pervasive in the political scene. Politicians scored points against their opponents by promising more and more spending for policies benefiting specific groups of voters, and the amount of spending they managed to obtain for their ministries, often despite what had been foreseen in the budget, was a measure of success for individual cabinet members. The government was often in minority and had to secure the support of one or more opposition parties in the parliament. In such situations, governments simply "bought" the support of an opposition party to ensure the passage of the budget through greater levels of spending. When economic growth was robust, none of this provoked much concern in the public debate. But when the crisis hit, the currency crashed, and public debt rose from a seemingly comforting 42% of GDP to over 72% within three years, it became obvious to the population that the country had to change the way fiscal policy was conducted.

A person widely respected for his knowledge and expertise served as finance minister, and he proposed a series of austerity measures to rein in the deficit. Despite his rhetorical ability and the respect he generally commanded, his cabinet colleagues refused to support his proposals, and he soon resigned. The government proposed a more scaled back version, yet parliament balked at even these measures, and soon the government itself resigned. As matters continued to worsen, the budget deficit slipped first to 10% of GDP in one year and to 15% of GDP the next.

Markets became increasingly concerned about whether government would be able to pay their debts, and the central bank was forced to raise overnight interest rates to an astounding 500% in defense of the currency. Pressure from markets did not abate, and two months later the central bank admitted defeat and let the currency float. The currency then depreciated by more than 20%. The fiscal and exchange rate crises had real effects on the economy, with economic growth declining by 1% one year and 2% the next. Just cleaning up the banking sector cost taxpayers an estimated 2% of GDP, with costs not reflected in the deficit but accounting for part of the surge in government debt.

The country is Sweden and the crisis hit in 1991. It provides an example of a success case that managed to get out of its culture of weak fiscal discipline. Eventually, the government responded to the crisis by introducing a fundamental reform of its budget process. The main insight behind the reform was the necessity to force all politicians involved in decisions over public spending to move beyond the narrow perspective of their constituencies' interests and take a comprehensive view of the budget, recognizing the true costs and benefits of all public policies. To achieve this, the budget was transformed from a mere enumeration of annual public spending into a contract among the ruling parties specifying their intended fiscal policies for the next few years (e.g., Molander 2000; Wehner 2007).

One of the main changes was the introduction of overall expenditure targets and clear budget frames that broke the overall target into twenty-seven categories. These targets are negotiated during the Swedish "conclave," a meeting of the members of the cabinet and the leaders of the coalition parties at the beginning of the annual budget process, which ends with an agreement on the spending framework for the following year. Parliament first votes on the overall target, with the vote generally taking place in the spring. In the fall, parliament passes the expenditure frames that must aggregate to the total limit agreed to earlier. This forces an explicit consideration of trade-offs between different types of spending. Today the country also sets an overall target of a budget surplus of 2% of GDP on average over the economic cycle. This is put in place both to make Sweden more responsive to future economic shocks and to prepare the country for future spending challenges due to the aging of the population.

Thanks to the new system, the culture of political debate has changed dramatically in Sweden. Instead of jockeying for who can spend more, politicians must now fit their proposals into the overall framework. The political discourse focuses on where to raise, and where to lower, spending under the same set of general expenditure targets.

Fiscal performance has improved substantially under this revised system. Since 1997, when the reforms were all in place, the country has generally run budgetary surpluses. The exception was during the same economic shock that the rest of the industrialized world experienced from 2001 to 2003, but even then the government experienced a deficit of merely 0.5% of GDP. Meanwhile, Sweden's debt burden has decreased again to below 50% of GDP. Overall economic growth has also been impressive. While real growth in the ten years prior to 1994 averaged about 1.5% of GDP, it doubled in the ten years that followed to an average of almost 3% of GDP.

Yet the Swedish success story leads to a host of new research questions. The finance minister originally tried to consolidate the budget yet failed. In other countries, however, finance ministers have more power in the process, and consequently more success in changing the budget. It is hard to imagine a Gordon Brown as chancellor of the Exchequer having the same difficulties as his Swedish counterpart. Why do finance ministers succeed in some countries but not in others? Are the types of fiscal targets the Swedes put in place substitutes for a strong finance minister, or are they complements?

Building on the previous chapters, which first identified the fiscal institutions in place as well as indicated that fiscal performance is best in countries where the fiscal institutions fit the expected form of fiscal governance, this chapter considers in more detail why countries have the fiscal institutions that they do.

Argument

As we have already indicated in Chapter 2, we expect that the ideological distance among the relevant veto players as well the competitiveness of the political system together determine the form of fiscal governance that is most appropriate to a given country. Countries with small ideological distance are appropriate for a delegation form of fiscal governance, while places with high ideological distance are most appropriate for fiscal contracts. Similarly, if parties expect to run together in elections, they can delegate some strategic power to a finance minister, while if they anticipate running against each other they want fiscal contracts.

We also by now know something about what type of environment of electoral institutions tends to have small or large ideological distance. Countries with plurality electoral systems approximate two-party systems, and they usually have small ideological distances in government. Proportional representation systems are somewhat more complicated.

As Chapter 2 explained, some "proportional" systems are in practice rather disproportional. They may have a minimal electoral threshold for parties to enter parliament as well as rounding rules that favor large parties over small. Small numbers of candidates elected per district (or district magnitude) also make it more difficult for small parties to enter parliament and, if they do get in, to win many seats. In our sample, Greece and Spain both have proportional representation systems that are rather disproportional and in which often one party has enough seats on its own to form a one-party majority government. The Netherlands, which has one electoral district for the whole country, is the most proportional. Ideological distance tends to be high the greater the proportionality.

Concerning the likelihood that parties run together, Chapter 2 examined evidence from Nadenichek-Golder's (2006) study of preelectoral pacts. It found that for the EU-15, ideological distance and preelectoral pacts predicted roughly the same set of countries should have either delegation or fiscal contracts. It is indeed likely that parties that are closer to one another ideologically have an easier time forming preelectoral pacts with one another.

A straight functionalist argument would suggest that countries would, over time, adopt the institutions that are most effective for them. Countries that have regular one-party majority governments should strengthen their finance ministers over time, while countries with regular multiparty coalitions where the parties in government have real ideological differences should develop fiscal contracts.

This logic leads to two testable hypotheses from a functionalist perspective:

Hypothesis 1a. Countries adopt fiscal institutions that are most fiscally effective. Small ideological distances mean delegation to a strong finance minister while large ideological distance means the development of fiscal contracts.

Presumably countries that have the same ideological distance over long periods have the opportunity to consolidate their fiscal institutions according to a given form of fiscal governance. The United Kingdom, for example, has almost always had one-party majority governments in the postwar period. In countries where there are regular shifts in ideological distance, institutions have less time to "gel." This suggests:

Hypothesis 1b. States with more variation in ideological distance over time have weaker fiscal institutions.

While there is certainly something to the functional argument, it tells us only which solution to the common pool resource problem a government may use, not why it would want to solve the problem in the first place. The formal model for the common pool resource problem we develop in Chapter 2 indicates that politicians face incentives to focus only on their constituencies. The basis of the CPR problem is that policymakers consider the net benefits of public spending accruing to their constituencies only. Presumably the constituents reward their representatives for acting this way. Farmers, for instance, care most about agriculture subsidies as well as the taxes that farmers bear. They will reward electorally a politician or party that maximizes the gains for farmers. In the aggregate, all constituencies are worse off if they elect politicians who worry about the narrow benefits and costs and not the costs to the whole population. The key question to ask is why constituents, and the politicians who represent them, should care about the whole and about "fiscal discipline" per se. One possibility is that constituents inherently understand the consequences of the CPR problem and that they dislike budget deficits and debts, so they elect only politicians who worry about the whole tax burden. The population is simply fiscally conservative. While this story may be able to explain variation across countries, it cannot account for variation across time.

A more plausible argument is that populations only realize the benefits of fiscal reforms if they have had a previous fiscal crisis. They push for fiscal reforms that are meant to prevent future crises. The institutions also help to "lock in" this desire to prevent crises – as other problems arise and the deficit returns to normal levels, the attention to the deficit is reduced and the tendency for overspending and excessive deficits rises again. At that point, centralization of the budget process can be an important mechanism to preserve the collective memory of the previous crisis. The Swedish example that began the chapter is illustrative. The deep economic crisis Sweden suffered in the early nineties created the momentum that triggered a political debate on institutional reforms. Politicians then initiated and passed several reforms that increased the level of centralization of budgetary decision making. Similarly, in Kneebone and McKenzie's (2000) study of budgetary reform in the Canadian province of Alberta, they find that the perception of a fiscal crisis in the early nineties induced the newly elected government to introduce immediate measures to reform the budget process (the Deficit Elimination Act and the Balanced Budget and Debt Reduction Act).[1]

---

[1] Additional authors see fiscal difficulties as necessary for reform; see, e.g., Rubin (1990).

There is also an interesting extension of the argument about fiscal and economic crises. The formal model in Chapter 2 indicates that the smaller share of the overall tax burden falling on each of groups, the greater the size of the CPR problem. This suggests that the more constituencies there are in a society, the more likely it is that there has already been some sort of breakdown.

Hypothesis 2a. Fiscal crises raise the public's demand for reforms. Those states have more fiscal centralization consistent with their form of fiscal governance than states that have not had fiscal crises.

The CPR model developed in Chapter 2 suggests that increasing numbers of constituencies should lead to a bigger CPR problem. These countries, in turn, should be more likely to have experienced a fiscal crisis earlier than countries with fewer constituencies. To make this argument more concrete, political scientists have classified the number of politically relevant cleavages in developed countries. One may expect that countries with more cleavages have "fitter" institutions.[2]

Hypothesis 2b. States with more politically relevant cleavages in society are more likely to have had a fiscal crisis in the past. They should have more fiscal centralization than countries with fewer cleavages.

---

[2] There is one more element to the discussion that bears examination. So far we assume a political system with competitive elections. That is, if politicians do not respond to populations who learn about the consequences of CPR problems and insist that they make changes to their institutions to make such fiscal crises less likely, the people will elect another party or group of parties that will make those changes. A history of a fiscal crisis, therefore, may not be sufficient to explain the extent of reforms. Hallerberg (2004), for example, suggests that fiscal problems in Italy in the late 1970s and 1980s did not lead to meaningful reform because there was no plausible alternative to parties already in government. The Cold War and the history of the Italian Communists meant that no non-Communist party would form a coalition with the Communists, and the Communists could not win an absolute majority on their own. Similarly, Molander (2000) emphasizes that the fiscal crisis in Sweden in the 1990s did not automatically cause the institutional reform, but it presented a general climate for reform. This suggests that there have to be electoral consequences to leaving the institutions the same, that is, to making it more likely that there will be fiscal crises again in the future. To state this another way, populations must care about fiscal policy to begin with and be able to reward governments that introduce and maintain institutions that centralize the budget process and punish those that do not. Hallerberg (2004) indicates that the political systems of the EU-15 were generally competitive by the mid-1990s, with Italy one of the last to increase competition. Given that the level of competition does not vary over the period that is the focus of the book, we do not discuss it further here, but work applied to other countries should consider the interaction between a window of opportunity for reform and whether there is political competition to fill that window.

Empirical Evidence

Bivariate Comparisons

We have information on fiscal institutions for the period 1985–2004. We want to stress at the beginning our humility with regard to the amount of data we have and what we can infer from those data. There are just fifteen countries in our sample. Over our period we have one "reform" per country, so it does not make sense to do more sophisticated models such as a pooled probit. We begin with mostly bivariate comparisons, and we finish with ordinary least squares techniques for a cross section of countries. The results are strongly suggestive even if we would prefer to have more cases to analyze for robustness.

Table 5.1 presents information from Table 3.7 in Chapter 3 that compares the various indices. Given that the empirical results reported in Chapter 4 were almost identical to the various indices, we focus here on a subset, namely, the "delegation" and "contracts" indices, respectively. There is also almost no change in fiscal institutions from 2001 to 2004, so we focus on the period 1991–2001.[3] The table adds two columns that indicate the change in fiscal institutions over the period 1991–2001, and it divides the countries according to whether they are expected to use delegation or contracts over the entire period as well as whether they "switched" the expected form of fiscal governance during the period. Chapter 2 indicates that Austria, Ireland, and Italy all began the period as expected contract states but then moved to expected delegation states in the mid-1990s. A purely functionalist argument would assume that these states would begin the period with a relatively low delegation index and would be more likely to make bigger changes on this score than countries that did not experience a similar change.

Several patterns are evident. First, there is a general increase in both indices over time. Yet the pace of change differed depending upon the expected form of fiscal governance. The average increase in the expected delegation states was 0.16 versus a slightly lower 0.13 in contract states. The most interesting finding is for the states that switched to expected delegation – among those three, the average delegation score increased 0.37, or three times the change in score for the expected contract states.

---

[3] Something that jumps out from Table 3.7 is that only five countries make any changes to their fiscal institutions over the period 2001–2004, and only in the Dutch case did the index increase or decrease by more than 0.06. We will discuss the changes in the Netherlands over this period at the end of the chapter.

Table 5.1. *Data for Tests of Functional Arguments*

Country	Delegation Index 1991	2001	Change	Contracts Index 1991	2001	Change	Ideological Distance, Standard Deviation
Expected Delegation, Entire Time							
France	0.9	0.81	−0.09	0.46	0.78	0.3	0.05
Germany	0.58	0.62	0.04	0.77	0.73	−0.04	0.01
Greece	0.23	0.75	0.52	0.49	0.75	0.26	0.08
Portugal	0.49	0.54	0.05	0.19	0.69	0.5	0.12
Spain	0.27	0.58	0.31	0.23	0.53	0.3	0.13
United Kingdom	0.74	0.87	0.13	0.52	0.74	0.22	0
AVERAGE	0.54	0.70	0.16	0.44	0.70	0.26	0.07
Expected Contracts 91, Expected Delegation 01							
Austria	0.38	0.62	0.24	0.59	0.91	0.32	0.07
Ireland	0.35	0.77	0.42	0.58	0.75	0.17	0.16
Italy	0.27	0.73	0.46	0.34	0.66	0.32	0.09
AVERAGE	0.33	0.71	0.37	0.50	0.77	0.27	0.11
Expected Contracts, Entire Time							
Belgium	0.23	0.44	0.21	0.12	0.75	0.63	0.09
Denmark	0.59	0.58	−0.01	0.37	0.66	0.29	0.01
Finland	0.37	0.52	0.15	0.69	0.69	0	0.14
Luxembourg	0.53	0.64	0.11	0.25	1	0.75	0.01
Netherlands	0.56	0.47	−0.09	0.44	0.49	0.05	0.21
Sweden	0.32	0.71	0.39	0.03	0.69	0.66	0.13
AVERAGE	0.43	0.56	0.13	0.32	0.71	0.40	0.10

Note: The ideological distance scores are for the period 1985–2001 rather than through 2004, and they therefore differ slightly from the standard deviations reported in Table 2.2, Chapter 2.
* indicates statistical significance < 0.10, ** < 0.05.

This suggests that there is a functional logic to the choice of fiscal institutions that depends on the underlying political environment (i.e., the ideological distance). Similarly, there are differences in the change in the contracts index; the increase in both expected delegation and in "switchers" was about the same (0.26 and 0.27), while the increase in expected contracts states was higher (0.40).

The gap between the expected contract and remaining states is especially noteworthy given the requirements from the European Union to make changes on items that were components of this index. A brief history is in order here to explain why. The Maastricht Treaty that the heads of government and state agreed to in December 1991 makes clear that "member states shall regard their economic policies as a matter of common concern and coordinate them in the Council" (Article 99(1)). The council was also expected to monitor member state policies, but the treaty did not provide any details on this issue. In December 1993, the council passed a regulation that required member states to send reports twice a year to the European Commission. States were expected to provide information on their budget deficits and their debt levels, investment and interest income, and gross domestic product. They were also expected to report on how they planned to reach their medium-term objectives.

In the mid-1990s, the European Commission was generally dissatisfied with the amount, and the quality, of information contained in the reports. In particular, there was no requirement that there be a justification for any of the numbers that the member states submitted, so it was difficult for the commission to understand the basis for the member state projections. In July 1997, the European Council passed a new regulation that systematized the reporting requirements. Eurozone countries were required to submit "stability programs" while noneurozone countries had to file "convergence programs," but the content of both of the documents was to be the same. Budget forecasts were to be over four years (t to $t + 3$), and states needed to explain how they would reach the medium-term objective of a deficit "close to balance or in surplus" as well as details on how they planned to meet this objective. They also had to explain how changes in underlying macroeconomic assumptions would lead to different outcomes. All programs were to be made public. The regulation also formalized the relationship among the member states, the Economic and Financial Committee, and the Council (specifically ECOFIN). The commission was to issue recommendations on each program. ECOFIN then was to consider the council's recommendations and issue a decision where it recommended what additional steps (if any) member states should take.[4]

---

[4] There was a further revision of the process in March 2005 as part of the more general revision of the Stability and Growth Pact. Member states would be providing country-specific medium-term objectives. States that had met the objectives were expected to take measures conditional on the economic cycle. Moreover, if states were making structural reforms, they were allowed to deviate from their objectives (see Morris et al. 2006). For a more detailed discussion of the evolution of the European Union level rules prior to 2005, see Hallerberg (2004, 48–59). For more discussion of the implications of those rules for the fiscal policies of the member states beyond the institutional changes discussed here, see Chapter 7.

These European Union rules had implications for the domestic fiscal institutions in place in the member states. Beginning in 1994, there was an expectation that member states submit some sort of document to the European Commission about their multiannual plans. By 1997, all member states were required to report to the European Commission the same set of information covering a period at least three years in advance. The European level also provided the accounting rules for the programs that standardized the data that were reported (Savage 2005). These changes increased the values of all four variables for the "contracts" index discussed in Chapter 3 – "multiannual target" and "nature of plan" increased to perfect scores, while the minimal score a country can receive on the remaining two, "planning horizon" and "degree of commitment," is a 2 (or three-year planning horizon). A score of 12 out of 24, or 0.5, is therefore the default for any European Union member beginning in 1997.[5]

The evidence on the "functionalist" argument is therefore strong so far. Consistent with Hypothesis 1a, countries made greater improvements over time to the fiscal institutions that best "fit" them. Hypothesis 1b states that countries that change their ideological distance from election to election will have less time to build their fiscal institutions appropriately. We therefore compute the standard deviations of ideological distance for all countries, and we calculate Spearman rank correlations with both the level and the change of a given index in 2001 that we report in Table 5.2. The correlation scores, however, suggest only a weak link – while they are in the expected direction for the level variables, only the level variable for fiscal contracts is statistically significant at the 0.10 level, and no correlation is significant at the 0.05 level.

The next set of arguments to consider focus on the effects of fiscal crises. Table 5.3 presents preliminary data on fiscal crises data to test Hypothesis 2a as well as data on the political cleavage structures of the EU-15 for Hypothesis 2b. The main issue concerns how to identify a "fiscal crisis" in the first place. One possibility is to designate any increase in the debt burden beyond a certain point as a fiscal crisis. The rationale here is that debt can increase so quickly that the population as well as politicians fear a default. If one looks at the period 1982–2001, the average

---

[5] The Netherlands is the only exception. States were supposed to link their stability/convergence programs to their macroeconomic estimates. Initially the Dutch refused and assumed simply that economic growth would be 2.5% each year. By 2004, the Dutch had dropped the growth assumption and linked the budget directly to macroeconomic forecasts.

Table 5.2. *Spearman Rank Correlations, Standard Deviation of Ideological Distance with Indices for 2001*

	Std Dev, Ideo Dist	Delegation	Contracts	Δ Delegation	Δ Contracts
Std Dev, Ideo Dist	1				
Delegation	−0.39	1			
Contracts	−0.45*	0.42	1		
Δ Delegation	0.26	0.31	0.11	1	
Δ Contracts	−0.13	−0.02	0.32	0.19	1

Note: Δ indicates the change in the institutional index between 1991 and 2001. **indicates significance at levels < 0.10.*

increase in the debt burden was slightly positive at 0.74%. The 95th percentile for the changes in the debt ratio in the period 1982–2001 is an increase of 8.2%. Taking this as a threshold, one identifies eight countries with a fiscal crisis. They are clustered either in the early 1980s or in the early 1990s, times when there were general recessions in Europe. Another option is to look at gross debt ratios themselves in level terms instead of changes in the ratios. The expectation would be that countries with large debt ratios would face the most difficulties in financing them. Yet it is unclear what level of debt burden represents an unsustainable one. Both Belgium and Italy have had gross debt burdens above 100% of GDP for many years while Japan currently has a debt burden above 150% since 2006. All three countries were able to obtain additional financing in the world market despite these high levels. There are some who argue that one should combine both debt and deficit figures to serve as early warnings for possible unsustainable debt in the future (e.g., Balassone, Franco, and Zotteri 2006).

A critique of this type of approach, however, is that *any* cutoff point is necessarily arbitrary. What is theoretically interesting from our standpoint is whether populations *perceive* that there is a fiscal crisis and whether they then put pressure on governments to act. Table 5.3 therefore lists approximate dates when the literature indicates that populations sensed a "fiscal crisis." Some countries had a significant crisis prior to the start of our time frame (or before 1985). In France, for example, there was a consensus that part of the more general crisis of the Fourth Republic involved economic policy, and fiscal policy in particular (Wildavsky 1986). Similarly, the United Kingdom was forced to go to the International Monetary

Table 5.3. *Fiscal Crises and Political Cleavages in the EU-15*

Country	Above 95% Change in Debt, 82–01	Crisis Years	Number of Cleavages	Ethnic, Religious Cleavage High
Expected Delegation, Entire Time				
France	No	1950s	2.5	0.0
Germany	No	1920s	3.0	1.0
Greece	1993	Early 1990s	1.5	0.0
Portugal	No	?	2.5	0.0
Spain	1993	Early 1990s	2.5	1.0
United Kingdom	No	1970s	1.5	0.0
AVERAGE			2.3	0.3
Expected Contracts 91, Expected Delegation 01				
Austria	No	?	1.5	0.0
Ireland	1982, 1986	Mid-1980s	1.5	0.0
Italy	1993	Early 1990s	3.0	1.0
AVERAGE			2.0	0.3
Expected Contracts, Entire Time				
Belgium	1982–2003	Early 1990s	3.0	1.0
Denmark	1982–2003, 1993	Early 1980s	2.5	0.0
Finland	1991–2003	Early 1990s	3.5	1.0
Luxembourg	No	?	2.0	1.0
Netherlands	No	Early 1980s	3.0	1.0
Sweden	1982, 1992	Early 1990s	2.5	0.0
AVERAGE			2.8	0.7

Source: Data on whether a country is above the 95% level in change in debt are from the dataset assembled for Chapter 4. "Crisis years" data are from Hallerberg's (2004) case studies as well as from Wildavsky (1986). Lijphart (1999) provides the number of cleavages and whether there was an ethnic and/or religious cleavage.

Fund in 1976 for a loan to stave off a general default. Other countries, however, did not experience crisis environments until the early 1990s. The EMS crisis in autumn 1992 in particular concentrated popular attention on the fiscal policies of governments in Italy and Spain (Hallerberg 2004).

A comparison of the two crisis measures is revealing. Of the eight cases where the debt level was above the 95% threshold, seven overlap with the more subjective measure for a "fiscal crisis." The one exception is Belgium, which had especially bad budgetary figures in the early 1980s but waited until the sense of crisis built to the point that there was a constitutional revision in 1993. There is also one case where a country had a fiscal crisis according to the literature but did not exceed 95%, namely, the

Netherlands in the early 1980s. It, too, had fairly large increases in its debt level (6% in 1983), but here, too, there was a slight lag with the worst figures posted in 1979 and 1980 (Hallerberg 2004, 120). Despite these discrepancies, the data suggest that the two measures are picking up essentially the same phenomenon.

The second set of measures considers the cleavage structure of a given society, and there is an established literature that examines them. In particular, Lijphart (1984, 1999) maps the level and the number of social divisions in thirty-six democracies, which include all of the European Union countries. He argues that there are seven possible cleavages in any society: socioeconomic, religious, cultural ethnic, urban-rural, regime support, foreign policy, and postmaterialism. In cases where a division is high, the country receives a score of 1, while in cases where the cleavage is medium the country receives a score of 0.5. The scores for the seven divisions are then summed into one number that represents the number of dimensions. Ethnic and/or religious cleavages can be especially contentious, and we separate out whether one of these cleavages exists in a given European Union country.

The data indicate that expected contract states generally have more social cleavages and are more likely to have at least one ethnic and/or religious cleavage. There are some exceptions in each group – Germany and Italy have a large number of cleavages. If Hypothesis 2b is correct, expected contract states should have more centralized budgetary institutions that are appropriate to their form of fiscal governance than expected delegation states.

Table 5.4 presents correlation coefficients for the delegation and contracts indices in 1991 and whether a country had had a fiscal crisis prior to the early 1990s and its cleavage structure. The evidence suggests that prior fiscal crises had a significant, and positive, effect on both the delegation and contract indices, with the effect on the delegation index being especially strong. This provides support for Hypothesis 2a that countries improved their fiscal institutions after such crises. In contrast, there is no support for Hypothesis 2b. More divided societies were not any more likely to have had a prior fiscal crisis, and as a consequence the number of cleavages does not affect the strength of fiscal institutions.

Yet one should not write off the relevance of cleavages – there are some effects on the organization of parliaments that have a direct bearing on the passage of budget legislation. Table 5.5 presents Lijphart's classification of the number of cleavages, and it compares the number of dimensions with

Table 5.4. *Spearman Rank Correlations, Fiscal Crises, and Political Cleavages with Indices for 1991*

	Fiscal Crisis Pre-1991	Number Cleavages	Ethnic and/ or Religious Cleavage	Delegation	Contracts
Fiscal Crisis pre-1991	1				
Number Cleavages	−0.07	1			
Ethnic and/or Religious Cleavage	−0.22	0.71**	1		
Delegation	0.73**	−0.06	−0.23	1	
Contracts	0.44*	−0.11	−0.06	0.35	1

Note: * indicates statistical significance < 0.10, ** < 0.05.

the indices for the strength of parliament in the formation stage and in *ex post* control. For the formation stage, a country receives a score of 1 for each item that strengthens the role of the parliament legally in the formation of the budget.[6] For the *ex post* stage, data come from Mattson and Strøm's (1995) study that documents the ability of parliamentary committees to monitor the government.[7] Once again, the table also divides countries according to whether or not they have a major ethnic cleavage and/or a major religious cleavage. These cleavages tend to be especially difficult to manage. Government accountability in such situations extends to more than simple accountability to a majority in the legislature. Religious or ethnic minorities may demand that the government be accountable to them in parliament even if (or because) they are routinely in the minority.

Table 5.5 indicates that societies that are more divided also involve parliament more in the budget process. The average score on the ability of the legislature to influence the budget is 1.3 points higher in societies where there is a prominent ethnic and/or religious cleavage than in

---

[6] Those items appear in Chapter 3 and are the following: whether parliament can amend the budget (yes scored 1); whether amendments are limited (no scored 1); whether amendments must be offsetting (no scored 1); whether parliament may submit a separate budget from the government (yes scored 1).

[7] The items coded here are as follows: "Ministerial correspondence" refers to cases where a given parliamentary committee matches exactly a given ministry (yes coded 1); whether the committee chairs are awarded proportionately on the basis of a party's representation in parliament (yes coded 1); whether a committee can compel representatives from the government to give testimony before the committee (yes coded 1); and whether a committee can compel the release of government documents to it (yes coded 1).

Table 5.5. *Cleavages in Society and Strength of Parliaments in the Budget Process*

Countries	Ethnic or Religious Cleavage High	Issue Dimensions (Lijphart)	Legal Ability to Influence Budget	*Ex Post* Power
Finland	1	3.5	2	2
Belgium	1	3	4	2
Netherlands	1	3	3	2
Germany	1	3	2	2
Italy	1	3	2	1
Spain	1	2.5	3	4
Luxembourg	1	2	3	3
AVERAGE	1	2.9	2.7	2.3
Portugal	0	2.5	3	3
Sweden	0	2.5	3	3
Denmark	0	2.5	3	3
France	0	2.5	1	2
Greece	0	1.5	0	0
Ireland	0	1.5	0	0
United Kingdom	0	1.5	0	0
AVERAGE	0	2.1	1.4	1.6

countries where this cleavage is absent.[8] Moreover, the *ex post* power of the legislature is 0.7 point higher in the divided societies. Another way to consider the effects of cleavages is to use the broader Lijphart measure of the number of cleavages in society. The correlation between this broader measure and both indices is in the expected positive direction. The ability of the legislature to influence parliament is 0.64, while the correlation with the *ex post* power index is 0.47. These results suggest that societies with more social divisions place a greater premium on legislative participation in the budget process.[9]

[8] It is uncertain what to do with Austria here. Lijphart (1999) indicates that it has only 1.5 relevant dimensions. Yet the Left-Right dimension has been so divisive that its intensity and effect resemble those of an ethnic or religious cleavage for the purposes of this table. *Proporzdemokratie* was established to moderate the severity of the conflict, which approached a civil war. We therefore leave out Austria because it is a clear outlier. When it is included in the table, the averages move somewhat closer to one another if it appears in the bottom group and diverge somewhat if it is included in the top group.

[9] One could probably go one step further with this analysis. Three countries – Denmark, Portugal, and Sweden – that look like exceptions in the noncleavage part of Table 5.4 also have regular minority governments. Because the government by definition does not have enough sure votes on a given bill, it must share some power with one or more opposition parties in parliament. One would therefore expect parliaments to be stronger in such countries. Of the remaining four countries that then remain in the group, all but France grant their parliaments no amendment power and no direct ability to control the government *ex post*, and the French National Assembly itself is weak.

Taken together, this work would seem to present a puzzle. From an efficiency standpoint, one would perhaps expect that greater parliamentary involvement would decentralize the budget process and lead to greater inefficiency. Spending on the budget should be higher when parliament is involved. Budget deficits should be higher. Yet the evidence presented in Chapter 4 suggests that the powers of parliament are not crucial for expected contract states. While there is little direct effect on the budget, stronger parliaments may play important roles in diffusing conflicts in multicleavage countries.

Multivariate Analysis

So far the discussion has looked generally at bivariate correlations and means. What does the analysis tell us if we make it multivariate?

We are interested especially in the change in fiscal institutions over the period 1991–2000, so the changes in the delegation and contract indices, respectively, serve as our dependent variables. States that already have strong institutions in place should not make many changes over the period, so we include the level version of the given variable as an independent variable. The standard deviation of ideological distance is included to examine the argument that greater deviation slows institutionalization. The functionalist argument states as well that expected delegation states should have stronger delegation institutions while expected contract states should have stronger contracting institutions. Finally, countries that experience a fiscal shock after 1991 may feel more pressure to initiate institutional changes. Given that the fiscal crisis discussed previously takes a value of 1 when the crisis was before 1991 and a 0 afterward, we expect the sign of the coefficient to be positive.[10]

Table 5.6 presents the regression results for the EU-15. As expected, countries with higher initial scores of either index made fewer changes over the period. The standard deviation of ideological distance, in contrast, has the correct sign in both regressions but is statistically significant only for changes in the contracts index. This suggests that it is harder to establish regular fiscal contracts when the ideological differences among coalition partners vary a lot. Also consistently with the functionalist argument,

---

[10] With the political cleavages not correlated with fiscal crises and with an *n* already low at 15, we spare the two degrees of freedom and do not include either measure of political cleavages.

Table 5.6. *Regression Analysis of Changes in Indices*

	Change Delegation	Change Contracts
Delegation (1991)	−0.72 (0.19)**	
Contracts (1991)		−0.99 (0.16)**
Std Dev Ideo Dist	−0.49 (0.50)	−1.05 (0.54)*
Expected Delegation (2001)	0.12 (0.055)*	
Expected Contracts (2001)		0.01 (0.07)
Fiscal Crisis	0.11 (0.07)	−0.04 (0.07)
After 1991		
Constant	0.45 (0.13)	0.82 (0.10)
N	15	15
R^2	0.80	0.82

Note: * indicates statistical significance < 0.10, ** < 0.05.

countries that were expected delegation states made bigger changes, all else equal, than countries that were not expected delegation states. The expected contract state dummy, in contrast, was not statistically significant for the contracts index, but there is a ready explanation for this – as explained earlier in the chapter, much of the change for the contract index is due to the new European Union reporting requirements. If everyone has to develop multiannual plans, it does not matter whether one is an expected delegation or contract state.

In comparison to the support for the functionalist arguments, the results for the fiscal crisis variables are weak, with none of the coefficients statistically significant. One reason here may be simply that the "adjustment" to the centralization scores happened already for the countries that had higher initial scores in 1991. As mentioned earlier, the correlation between countries that had fiscal crises before the 1990s and the delegation index in 1991 was positive as expected and statistically significant. The effects of the fiscal crises on the delegation index may be swamping out the effects of crises in the 1990s. It could also be that there was something different about the shocks in the 1990s and the shocks in earlier times. Finland, for example, started with a fairly strong set of contracting institutions, yet the collapse of both the Soviet Union and the country's own banking system at about the same time was something that those institutions could not prevent.

In sum, the results are consistent with the functionalist argument that countries do make reforms consistent with their form of fiscal governance. The results also suggest that fiscal crises prior to the 1990s may have affected the level of centralization consistent with delegation. The next section traces the development of fiscal institutions in a particular contract country, the Netherlands, in the most recent period to provide a more longitudinal study of institutional reform.

The Dutch Example

The Dutch case since 1998 illustrates how a country follows an expected path of reform based upon its form of fiscal governance. It has served as perhaps the prototypical "contracts" state. When it found itself in trouble after 2001, its reaction was to strengthen the elements of fiscal contracts and not to do anything on the "delegation" side.

The Netherlands first introduced elements of fiscal contracts in the early 1980s. The country suffered a serious economic downturn that exacerbated a fiscal situation that had been deteriorating since 1974. The new government in 1982, which drew together the Christian Democrats and the Liberals, agreed upon detailed multiannual fiscal plans meant to last for the life of the coalition. The finance minister, H. Onno Ruding, oversaw the execution of the "contract" and was closely associated with it. It included cuts in unemployment compensation and more generally restraints on spending. The change to fiscal contracts coincided with a broader push to reconcile capital and labor, which put an important brake both on inflation and on public wages. The Agreement of Wassenaar in November 1982 ended automatic wage indexation, and it also ended the tracking of public wages with private ones. When the public judged these contracts a success and reelected the government in 1986, the "contracts" became a permanent feature of the Dutch system.[11]

While the initial model of fiscal governance was generally considered a success, the Dutch continued to tinker with it in subsequent years. In particular, Finance Minister Gerrit Zalm under a Social Democratic–Liberal coalition elected in 1994 introduced a series of reforms that tightened the agreement the coalition parties reached on the budget. The government issued series of rules that specified what to do given unforeseen shocks. It also decided that all planning would assume a future growth rate of a little more than 2% of GDP. The intention was to make it more likely that the country would experience "positive" rather than "negative" fiscal shocks. The system worked well, and the Netherlands qualified for Stage III of

---

[11] See Hallerberg 2004, 116–127, for more details about this earlier period.

Economic and Monetary Union with a general government deficit of just 1.1% of GDP in 1997. By 2000, the government, which had been reelected handily in 1998, was running a surplus at 1.5%.

Yet something happened on the fiscal side that bears explanation. Alone among expected contract states, the Netherlands had a budget deficit above the critical 3% level by 2003.

In purely technical terms, much of the explanation was on the revenue side. Revenues fell by more than the Central Planning Bureau (CBP), the main forecasting organ, expected given the drop in growth. In practice, the CPB had forecast in September 2001 that the government would have a surplus of 1% of GDP in 2002. The actual outcome, however, was −1.6%. As late as October 2003, the government was telling the European Commission in its updated stability program that the 2003 balance would be –2.3%. The actual deficit for 2003 was almost a full percentage point higher. There were several reasons for this: a tax cut in 2001 lowered rates; housing prices increased, thus increasing the level of mortgage interest deductions; pension payments, which were tax-deductible, increased; and because corporations can spread losses over years, corporate tax collections dropped precipitously.

There was also an expenditure side story, but it is more nuanced. Successive governments had successfully defended the overall spending caps. The only overrun was in 2003, and it amounted to just 300 million euros. Yet two points are relevant here: First, the subcaps were not usually kept. The Dutch had targets for central government, health care, and social security. Under the Kok II government (1998–2002), social security spending was lower than expected because of strong economic growth, and education, safety, and health care were allowed to exceed their caps (more on health later).

Second, there was political instability during the period, which upset the fiscal plans. A first government was formed under Jan Peter Balkenende in July 2002 that entered into a coalition with the Pim Fortuyn List that gained both seats and office for the first time, but that government lasted only eighty-seven days. A caretaker government then remained in power through the following May. What is notable for our study is how the successive governments reacted to fiscal problems – after elections, the new coalition agreement that the Christian Democrats, Liberals, and D66 signed did include real expenditure cuts. In fact, the three governments over the period July 2002–April 2004 passed multiannual expenditure cuts either in their coalition agreements or in two austerity packages that added up to a combined 6.5-billion-euro cut in spending in 2003 and 11-billion-euro cut in 2004 (or 2.25% of GDP).

But the new governments also allowed for an update of the expenditure ceilings that, in the health care case in particular, meant that the caps crept up.[12] The government was unable to stay below even the higher revised ceilings. Actual spending appears to have been another 800 million euros above the second cap. On the basis of some figures from the central bank, the EMU budget balance should have been –2.9% (rather than –3.4%) had the health care caps in the first agreement been kept. Respect for the caps, therefore, would have kept the country below the critical 3% level (author interview at the Netherlands Bank, The Hague, July 2004).

There were at least three important reasons for the increases in health care spending. First, there was a landmark court case in 2000 that ended the previous caps. The court ruled that access to health care was a basic right, and that the government could not impose caps on the number of operations, and the like, for cost reasons. Second, there was a sense among the public encapsulated in the phrases "public poverty, private wealth" and "more hands on the [hospital] bed" that more money should go into health care during the Dutch economic boom, and it was hard to turn this off when the economy soured. Finally, health care had been an important source of job creation during a recession – 40% of all new jobs between 2000 and 2002 in the Netherlands were in this sector (author interviews, Central Planning Bureau, Finance Ministry, The Hague, July 2004).

Finally, there was a general government story. The assumption at the central government level was that local governments would have balanced budgets. Information on local governments, however, was given to the central government slowly. Figures for 2002 were not available until 2004. Figures for 2003 were available a few weeks later, but after the budget year of course had ended. Local governments technically must run "balanced budgets." The accounting standards at the local and EMU levels, however, differed. Local governments had their figures in accrual terms, and they cared about capital only for depreciation purposes. They therefore ran balanced budgets in their terms but, importantly, not according to the accounting standard of ESA 95 that was used at the European level. Local governments ultimately accounted for around 0.7% of GDP of the general

---

[12] For example, for 2003 the expenditure increased 1.6 billion euros from the first coalition agreement in July 2002 to the second in May 2003.

government deficit in 2003 (author interviews, Central Planning Bureau, Finance Ministry, The Hague, July 2004).

In summary, the basic attitude in an expected contract state such as the Netherlands remained the same. Different levels of government followed the "rules." The overall spending caps were generally kept at the central government level, while local governments generally kept to their balanced budget rules. These rules were not, however, completely compatible with EMU rules. The government elected in 2003, therefore, approved a new set of rules. Subcaps were to be tightened so that they would be more likely to be honored, and that meant that overruns in health care should not be compensated elsewhere. There was also a "trip wire" in the coalition agreement that said that if the general government balance is forecast to be −2.5% or worse, the government must approve a new set of measures. One of the fiscal rules to deal with unanticipated shocks also changed. All anticipated tax revenue was to count against the deficit instead of some sort of split between deficit reduction and tax cuts as was the case under the previous Kok government (and which led to tax cuts in 2001). There was also a discussion to revise the rules at the local government level, although less progress was made on that front. In the meantime, there were efforts to improve local government reporting during the budget year. This again would make it easier to abide by the fiscal contracts at all levels of government. If the Netherlands had been an expected delegation state, one would have anticipated moves to strengthen the role of the finance minister.

Under these somewhat modified rules, the fiscal situation in the Netherlands improved. By 2006, the country had a general government with essentially a balanced budget (surplus of 0.1% of GDP).

Conclusion

This chapter considered different explanations for why countries have different levels of budget centralization. It built on Chapter 2, which predicted under what political conditions one would expect either delegation or fiscal contracts to be more effective. That chapter concluded that delegation worked best when ideological distance was low while fiscal contracts worked well when ideological distance was high.

A straight functional argument would predict that countries would adopt the fiscal rules and institutions that led to the best policy. The chapter found some support for this argument – states did make reforms that were consistent with their form of fiscal governance. Yet efficiency alone does not explain why countries make changes. We found evidence that countries with previous fiscal crises generally had fitter fiscal institutions. This story fits with the version of the common pool resource model we discuss in both Chapter 2 and the Appendix – if policymakers experience a CPR problem, why would voters necessarily want to solve that problem? We posit that the populations learn through fiscal crises the potentially disastrous consequences of having decentralized fiscal institutions in place. Politicians can then win votes through fiscal reforms.

This story is necessarily somewhat speculative because we are discussing countries with relatively long institutional histories. Getting the causal story straight is not easy. In the next chapter, we examine a set of new democracies that essentially begin their fiscal lives from scratch after the fall of communism, and we consider why they introduced the fiscal reforms that they did.

6

Institutional Choice in New Democracies

FISCAL GOVERNANCE IN CENTRAL
AND EAST EUROPEAN COUNTRIES

The first four chapters concentrated on the design and effect of forms of fiscal governance in the countries that composed the European Union until 2004. The fifth chapter discussed why those countries adopted the fiscal institutions that they did. The focus was on the effects of deep fiscal crises, the competitiveness of the political system, and ideological distances within the government, which affect the choice of one form of fiscal governance or the other. Here we broaden the study to include the Central and Eastern Europe countries that joined the EU in May 2004, the Czech Republic, Estonia, Hungary, Latvia, Lithuania, Poland, Slovakia, and Slovenia, as well as Bulgaria and Romania, which became members in January 2007.

This is a particularly interesting sample for our purposes. Government budgeting in the sense the term is used in modern, market economies did not exist under central planning, and the countries we consider had to create new legal frameworks, organizational modes, and decision-making structures from scratch. This makes the sample uniquely interesting for a study of institutional choice, because, unlike in the countries considered in the previous chapter, the weight of history and tradition in shaping the new institutions is very low. At the same time, we observe a fair degree of variation across the budgeting institutions of the countries. This raises the question of how the variation can be explained.

This chapter begins with a discussion of the evolution of budgeting institutions in the ten sample countries. We use the summary characterizations of budgeting institutions for our sample countries developed in Gleich (2002), and we cite additional material where appropriate from Yläoutinen (2005). Both authors have tested empirically the effects of

139

fiscal institutions in this set of states, with Gleich looking at an earlier period (through 1998) and Yläoutinen both expanding on and extending to 2003 Gleich's work. The most recent article on this topic, Fabrizio and Mody (2006), uses Gleich's coding of fiscal centralization and updates it through 2003 with an impressive, and exhaustive, battery of econometric tests. The three sets of authors all reach the same conclusion – increasing budget centralization in this set of countries increases fiscal discipline.

Rather than replicating this excellent work on the effects of the fiscal institutions, our focus in this chapter is on institutional choice in the new member countries. We begin with a discussion of the budgetary systems of the ten countries, and we compare the countries according to the indices developed in Chapter 3. Effective multiannual fiscal targets require a high level of technical capacity to execute, and we find that none of the new member countries has institutions consistent with a "contracts" country. Yet there is some basic level of centralization of the budget process that benefits all countries, which the Gleich (2003) coding of fiscal institutions measures. We use this coding scheme to consider why countries adopted the institutions that they did. We find that more divided societies – both politically and ethnically – were most likely to centralize their budget processes. Following the structure of the previous chapter, which finished with a discussion of the Dutch case, we conclude with a case study of Poland that we use to illustrate the main themes.

Fiscal Institutions in Central and Eastern Europe

Delegation and Contract Indices

The first step is to compare these countries with their Western European counterparts to create the same sorts of indices that we presented in Chapter 3. Figure 6.1 compares the EU-27 (with the exception of Cyprus and Malta) according to the delegation and contracts indices elaborated in Chapter 3 on the basis of available data in Gleich (2003) and Yläoutinen (2005). We stress that these figures are not complete; we do not have the same panel of data for the new member countries that we have for the EU-15, and even then the survey used in Gleich (2003) did not include two of the twelve items in the delegation index. The comparisons are also for the latest year for which we have data,

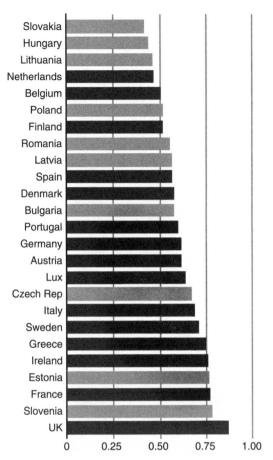

Figure 6.1 "Delegation" and "Contracts" Indices, 2003 Accession and 2004 EU-15.

or 2002/03 for new member countries and 2004 for the EU-15; that means that we are comparing a set of countries shortly before they join the European Union with a set that were already members.

Nevertheless, the initial comparisons are informative. Each graph in Figure 6.1 shades darkly a member of the EU-15 and lightly a new member country. There is a difference especially between the two groups for fiscal contracts, with new member countries generally having the lowest scores. Perhaps the most important component of the "contracts" index is the commitment countries make to their fiscal plans; elaborate multiannual projections have less effect on policymakers when they are mostly statistical exercises than when political parties make political commitments to abide by them. Looking at this measure, no new member country has a commitment to a multiannual plan at anything greater than the indicative level. Given that this is the most important attribute of the contracts approach, it suggests that no new member country should be considered strictly a "contracts" state.

The previous two chapters indicate that weak targets are not an issue if a country is an expected delegation state, yet it is clear that all of them but Hungary should be considered expected contract states. As Yläoutinen (2005, 63) illustrates well, these countries have electoral systems that encourage multiple-party representation in parliament. They all have some version of proportional representation. They also include a minimal threshold of the percentage of votes for a party to gain seats, which in most cases is 5% for parties running alone and sometimes higher for parties running together as one coalition. The thresholds make the systems less proportional than a straight PR system would be, but they still encourage the development of multiple parties in parliament.

As Chapter 2 explains in more detail, the presence of several parties makes it difficult for a single party to win a majority of seats, and one would expect multiparty coalition governments to be common. Ideally, to parallel the work presented here on the EU-15, we would have data for the veto-player distance for each country. Yet, such data do not exist to date. A rough proxy is simply to look at how common multiparty coalition governments and/or minority governments are in practice. Yläoutinen (2005, 66) provides those data and compares the ten Central and Eastern European countries in terms of the type of government they typically have formed in the last decade. If one looks at the period for which we have budget data, that is, 1996–2002, his data indicate that only Bulgaria had a one-party majority government, and that government was in power only in 2001–2005. Yläoutinen also discusses the coalitions that formed in each country, and that discussion makes it clear that Hungary has also become an exception in practice over several elections. Two blocs, the Left led by the political party MSZP and the Right led by Fidesz, dominate the political landscape, and the common form of government is one large party of either bloc aligned with a small party closely affiliated with it (Benoit 2002; *Economist Country Report* 2007).

We therefore would predict that the contract form of fiscal governance would be most appropriate for all countries but Hungary, while Hungary should have delegation.[1]

The Gleich Index

While this comparison fits well with the first part of the book, a somewhat different index may be more useful for this set of countries for both a theoretical and a practical reason, and we will use it in the remainder of this chapter. In contrast to the incumbent EU countries, where the heads of state have largely ceremonial positions and there is no need to include them in an assessment of budgeting decisions, the heads of state can play a more active role in the budgeting process in the new member states. All Central and East European countries which have joined the EU have directly elected presidents, and some of them have formal budgetary competence.

Another difference between the new and the incumbent EU member states arises from the fact that the former adopted new constitutions after the end of communism. This is the relevance of constitutional clauses with fiscal relevance, such as debt limits and balanced budget requirements. Such clauses are less common in the EU-15, but they do occur in several of the new constitutions. Gleich's (2002) index of budgeting institutions in the Central and East European new member states, which otherwise is based on von Hagen (1992), includes the role of the president in the budget process and the importance of constitutional rules. We will use this index in the rest of this chapter. Importantly this group of countries had no multiannual targets of any kind at the time, so Gleich (2002) did not include any information on them in his index.[2]

---

[1] While we have no data on ideological distance, it is likely that the distance changes frequently in these countries, and that this change then makes it more difficult to develop fiscal contracts. Governments turn over frequently, even almost yearly, in the Baltic states. Reelection of incumbent governments is also a rare event. Chapter 5 found that increases in the standard deviation of ideological distance made it more difficult to institutionalize fiscal contracts in the EU-15, and the same phenomenon may be happening with this set of countries as well.

[2] The lack of multiannual targets when institutions are first formed, in fact, is informative. In order for such targets to be effective, one needs a fairly sophisticated technical capacity to make projections, understand their implications for expenditure for specific ministries, and have adequate reporting mechanisms that report information on the state of the budget. The basic technical capacity as well as some centralization of the budget process generally exist in the established democracies in the West but have to be created in these new democracies.

Table 6.1. *Index of Budgeting Institutions*

	Index		Index
Bulgaria	5.33	Lithuania[b]	6.95
Bulgaria[a]	6.08	Lithuania[c]	6.19
Czech Republic	6.43	Poland	5.43
Czech Republic[a]	7.42	Poland[a]	7.53
Czech Republic[c]	7.19	Poland[b]	7.78
Estonia	8.32	Romania	5.19
Hungary	5.32	Slovakia	6.62
Latvia	8.00	Slovenia	7.69
Lithuania	6.20		

Note: [a] indicates changes in 1998, [b] changes in 1999, and [c] changes in 2001.

Following earlier research in this area, Gleich's (2002) index of centralization of the budget process is based on information gathered through the study of relevant legal documents and questionnaires sent to finance ministry officials, central bank economists, and members of the legislature in 1998–2000. For details, see Appendix 1.

Table 6.1 reports the institutional index developed in this way. The index reflects the status of budgeting institutions in the countries indicated at the end of the 1990s. Note that for the Czech Republic, Lithuania, and Poland, we obtain more than one observation, reflecting changes in the legislation and procedures in these countries in 1998, 1999, or 2001.

As before, a larger value of the index indicates the existence of budgeting institutions which are more appropriate to centralize the budget process. The table indicates that Estonia and Latvia had the strongest budgeting institutions at the time, while Romania and Hungary had the weakest institutions in this group. Poland moved significantly from being among the countries with the weakest institutions to being among the leading countries in this group (more details on the Polish case appear at the end of the chapter). Bulgaria moved from a low to a middle position after making reforms at the same time it adopted a currency board in 1997. Both Lithuania and the Czech Republic made institutional reforms improving their budgeting institutions in the late 1990s but partly reversed these improvements with further reforms in 2001.[3]

---

[3] Gleich (2002) shows that the institutional index correlates positively with the degree of fiscal discipline achieved in the CEECs.

The institutional choices captured by the index are the results of decisions taken and implemented gradually over time. Hence, there exists no definite reference year that qualifies as the year of enactment (of the complete set) of budget institutions. For the purpose of this study, we use the index scores at two stages of the institutional reform process. The first version, INDEX_1, summarizes the initial institutional framework that evolved during the first half of the nineties, and in particular in the years close to 1995.[4] The second version, INDEX_2, represents institutional characteristics of the budget process as of 2001.

Institutional Choice

In this section we formulate a set of hypotheses about the choice of budgeting institutions in the new EU member countries. We pursue three main arguments. The first is that institutional rules can be regarded as substitutes for voluntary cooperation. The second is that institutional choice is driven by past experiences of fiscal crises. The third is that institutional choice is rewarded by external players such as international organizations.

The reasoning behind the first hypothesis starts from the idea that the players in the budget process are more willing to agree on institutional rules constraining their own behavior when they perceive that the alternative of fragmented decision making is very costly. In Chapter 2, we have argued that the budget process involves a common pool externality creating a prisoner's dilemma game among the players. An individual player would cooperate with the other players and adopt the collectively optimal spending level if the expected present value of the cooperative outcome is larger than the expected present value of the gain from choosing the individually optimal spending level. In a one-shot game, however, the latter is the dominant strategy and the collectively optimal budget is chosen only if the budget process is centralized adequately. In repeated games, the *folk theorem* implies that voluntary cooperation can be sustained in equilibrium if the expected payoffs from coordination in the long run outweigh the short-run benefits from noncooperation. Furthermore, field studies and laboratory experiments suggest that generalized norms of reciprocity,

---

[4] Note that two of the countries in the sample, the Czech Republic and Slovakia, became independent states only in 1993, and it was 1995/96 by the time most countries had established the basic legal framework of the budget process (public finance law, parliamentary rules of procedure).

fairness, and trust enhance the likelihood of cooperation and constitute important constraints against overusing common pool resources (e.g., Ostrom 1990; Ostrom, Gardner, and James Walker 1994).

This suggests that institutional rules centralizing the budget process are most important in environments where the conditions for voluntary cooperation are the weakest. In other words, the expected benefits from imposing institutional constraints should be larger where voluntary cooperation is less likely. While institutional rules impose a cost on policymakers by constraining their individual choices, rational policymakers should accept stronger constraints on their own choices if the expected benefit from having such constraints in place is larger. This is our first hypothesis.

Hypothesis 1. The weaker the conditions for voluntary cooperation, the stronger the incentive for adopting institutional rules for coordinating budgeting decisions. Thus, the institutional index should vary negatively with variables measuring the likelihood of voluntary cooperation.

A first variable we consider is *political fragmentation*. As Weingast, Shepsle, and Johnson (1981); Velasco (2000); and Perotti and Kontopolous (1999) suggest, the common pool problem of budgeting should worsen with the number of distinct groups that participate in decision making. Political fragmentation, that is, the existence of many small political constituencies with different preferences, may raise the benefit from imposing-strong institutional rules for coordination. To measure political fragmentation, we use variables accounting for the number and relative strength of the parties represented in parliament. The first is the (average) number of parties in parliament, NPP1 and NPP2. NPP1 is based on electoral results from the early 1990s, NPP2 on the results of later elections.[5]

---

[5] For NPP1, we use the following elections. Bulgaria: the National Assembly, 1994; Czech Republic: the Chamber of Deputies (lower house), 1992; Estonia: the Riigikogu, 1992 and 1995; Hungary: the Parliament, 1994; Latvia: the Saeima, 1993 and 1995; Lithuania: the Seimas, 1992; Poland: the Sejm (lower house), 1993; Romania: the Chamber of Deputies (lower house), 1992; Slovakia: the National Council, 1992 and 1994; Slovenia: the National Assembly, 1992. For NPP2, we use the following: Bulgaria: the National Assembly, 1994 and 1997; Czech Republic: the Chamber of Deputies (lower house), 1992, 1996 and 1998; Estonia: the Riigikogu, 1992, 1995 and 1999; Hungary: the Parliament, 1994 and 1998; Latvia: the Saeima, 1993, 1995 and 1998; Lithuania: the Seimas, 1992, 1996 and 2000; Poland: the Sejm (lower house), 1993 and 1997; Romania: the Chamber of Deputies (lower house), 1992, 1996 and 2000; Slovakia: the National Council, 1992, 1994 and 1998; Slovenia: the National Assembly, 1992, 1996 and 2000.

The second measure of political fragmentation is the "effective number of parties" in parliament, which takes into account the relative size of the parties in the legislature (Taagepera and Shugart 1989). It is constructed as the inverse of a Herfindahl-Hirschmann index:

$$ENPP = \left(\sum_{i=1}^{n} P_i^2 \right)^{-1},$$ (1)

where P_i stands for the share of seats in parliament of party i. Again, we calculate two variables, ENPP1 and ENPP2, representing averages of ENPP of one or more elections, using the same database as for computing the corresponding variables NPP1 and NPP2. From Hypothesis 1 (H1), we expect a positive correlation of these variables with the index on budget institutions.

Social and economic polarization is closely related to political fragmentation in our analysis. The larger the ethnic or economic divides within a population, the more difficult voluntary cooperation will be. We do not have data on political cleavages in these countries that would match Lijphart's (1999) study of established democracies, which tracks the active cleavages that proved useful in Chapter 5. We do, however, have data on the *potential* cleavages that may exist along four dimensions. The first is the ethnic fragmentation index (ETHNIC) (e.g., Easterly and Levine 1997; Knack and Keefer 1997; Glaeser et al. 2000). The index represents the probability that two legislators chosen at random belong to different ethnic groups. It is computed as follows:

$$ETHNIC = 1 - \sum_{i=1}^{n} G_i^2,$$ (2)

where G_i represents the share of ethnic group i in the total population. The index is increasing in the degree of ethnic diversity.

Many particularistic benefits are granted to specific sectors in the economy. Hence, the more diversified the economy, or the more relatively powerful and distinct sectors exist, the larger is the incentive of each occupational group to demand benefits at the expense of the population at large. To capture the effect of the fractionalization of the economy, we construct the following variable:

$$SECTORS = 1 - \sum_{i=1}^{n} E_i^2,$$ (3)

where E_i stands for the share of employment in sector i, whereas $i =$ {agriculture, industry, services}. SECTORS ranges from 0 to 2/3, with a higher value indicating that an economy is more heterogeneous.[6]

The degree of income inequality is another proxy for economic conflict (e.g., Alesina and La Ferrara 2000). We use two measures of income inequality. The first is the ratio of the percentage share of total household income earned by the 10% best-earning households to the percentage share of total household income earned by the 10% lowest-earning households (INCDIST). As a second measure of income inequality we compute the average value of the Gini coefficient (GINI) for the years 1991–1995.[7] Finally, the decision of a player to cooperate or not hinges on the discount factor employed to assess the intertemporal flow of benefits and costs. For the purposes of the present study, it is useful to interpret the discount factor as representing the probability that the game will terminate at the end of each period. Players expecting to interact frequently and repeatedly have a high discount factor, which should lead to a greater likelihood and duration of cooperation. Frequent changes in coalitions and turnover of government imply that players are uncertain about their participation in future governments and, therefore, less likely to play a cooperative strategy. In view of this, we use two measures of political stability to proxy the discount factors. The first variable is the number of prime ministers during the years 1990–1995 (NPM1), and during the period 1990–2000 (NPM2). A difficulty with this measure is that a country that experiences a short, turbulent time characterized by turnovers of prime ministers, followed by a longer period without changes in prime ministers, may have the same number of prime ministers as a country where prime minister turnovers occur frequently in regular intervals. Ideally, one would want to distinguish these cases. To do this, we also consider a measure that weighs the term length of the prime ministers, that is, the effective number of prime ministers:

$$ENPM = \left(\sum_{i=1}^{n} T_i^2 \right)^{-1} \tag{4}$$

where T_i stands for the term length of prime minister i, measured as the number of days a prime minister stayed in office divided by either the

---

[6] Data for employment by occupation are from the CIA *World Factbook*. Data for Slovenia are taken from the *Statistical Yearbook of the Republic of Slovenia* 1999.

[7] For some countries, time series data for the Gini coefficient start later than 1991. Data for the years after 1995 are not available.

number of days of the period 1990–1995 (ENPM1) or by the number of days of the period 1990–2000 (ENPM2). We expect a positive correlation between these measures of fragmentation and the institutional index.

Our second hypothesis derives from the reasoning explained in Chapter 5, namely, that governments may be willing to adopt new institutions that restrict their spending and/or borrowing activities in response to a fiscal crisis. This leads to our second hypothesis:

Hypothesis 2. Stronger coordination mechanisms should be expected in those Central and East European countries with the most serious budget situations in the initial transition phase.

The restoration of democracy is a true break from past patterns, so it is not appropriate to include "past" fiscal crises to determine whether a country is more likely to begin the period with fitter fiscal institutions. As an alternative, we include as explanatory variables the gross public debt-to-GDP ratio for 1993[8] (DEBT) and the average size of the general government budget balance-to-GDP ratio for the years 1989–1992 (BALANCE). A positive value of BALANCE indicates a budget surplus. We expect that actors are more likely to invest in strong coordination mechanisms, even if doing so curtails their moves, when the initial fiscal situations during the time of institution building are precarious, that is, in the case of transition countries when public debt ratios and/or budget deficit ratios were high in the early 1990s.

Our third hypothesis rests on the idea that domestic political choices may be influenced by pressures and rewards from external authorities. Thus, a collective action problem among the policymakers of a country could be solved by the presence of an external actor who imposes an appropriate incentive structure that facilitates cooperative outcomes among the actors involved in the budget process (Bates 1988; Ostrom 1990). This is our third hypothesis:

Hypothesis 3. Institutional choices respond to pressures and rewards from external actors.

---

[8] The first year for which public debt data for at least half of the countries in the sample are available is 1993. For Latvia, the debt ratios refer to 1994, for Romania to 1995, and for Estonia and Lithuania to 1997. We also considered the ratios of external debt to GDP as a substitute for (initial) public debt ratios to get a more comparable dataset on initial conditions, but since the availability of external debt data for the early 1990s is comparable with the availability of public debt data (in particular for the Baltic countries), the size of external debt does not seem to be a better proxy for initial fiscal stress than public debt figures (secondarily, the correlation between the public debt data described earlier and the earliest available external debt figures is very high; the correlation coefficient has the value 0.95).

Two external actors are particularly relevant in our context. The first is the International Monetary Fund (IMF), which has provided technical assistance and guidelines for fiscal policy and management to transition countries (Tanzi 1992; Thuma, Polackova, and Ferreira 1998; LeLoup et al. 1998, 2000; Potter and Diamond 2000). Furthermore, Letters of Intent (and their attached Memoranda on Economic Policy) written by governments in Central and East European Countries in the context of their request for financial support from the IMF frequently contain indications of the intention to undertake or to continue budgetary reforms. This suggests that institutional reforms in the fiscal sector may increase the likelihood of receiving financial support from the IMF. There is, however, an important alternative argument to be considered. This is that by granting financial support in times of crisis, the IMF reduces the pressure for domestic institutional reform on national governments.

The second external actor is the European Union. Given the strong intention of these countries to join the EU at the time, the annual preparations by the candidate countries of Preaccession Economic Programs since 2001, and the requirement that new member countries reach agreements on all chapters of the *acquis* (in particular Chapter 11, Economic and Monetary Union; Chapter 28, Financial Control; and Chapter 29, Finance and Budgetary Provisions), the European Union may have played an important role. That such a relation exists appears to be manifest in the case of Poland. The Polish constitution that took effect in 1997 states that the level of public debt may not exceed 60% of GDP, which is a clear reference to the fiscal criteria for entering the EMU established in the framework of the Maastricht Treaty. We conjecture that the earlier a country started negotiations with the EU on accession, the earlier it designed budget processes conducive to fiscal discipline.

We use two variables as gauges for the influence of the IMF and the EU. The power of the IMF should depend on the extent to which a country relies on financial support from the IMF. As proxy for the degree of financial dependence, we use the average value of a country's total loans and credits to the IMF outstanding, as a percentage of GDP, for the period 1991–1995 (IMF1), or for the years 1991–2000 (IMF2).[9] To see whether or

---

[9] We use the following data from the International Finance Statistics or from the IMF homepage www.imf.org to calculate IMF1 and IMF2: total loans and credits outstanding (end of period, in SDR), national currency units per SDR (end of period), and gross domestic product.

Table 6.2. *Correlation Coefficients*

	INDEX_1	INDEX_2
Fragmentation		
NPP	0.56**	0.08
ENPP	0.77**	0.61**
ETHNIC	0.76**	0.45**
SECTORS	−0.40	−0.26
INCDIST	0.33	0.53**
GINI	0.35	0.33
Political Instability		
NPM	−0.31	−0.14
ENPM	−0.24	0.22
Past Fiscal Crises		
DEBT	−0.64**	−0.35
BALANCE	−0.61**	−0.32
External Pressure		
IMF	−0.40	−0.44*
EU	0.16	0.39

Note: * indicates statistical significance at the 10% level, ** significance at the 5% level.

not the preconditions for joining the EU (and the EMU) have induced countries in the first group to start negotiations on EU accession to reform their budget institutions more quickly than others, we define a dummy variable (EU) that takes a value of 1 if the country is in the first group of countries with which the EU started negotiations (Czech Republic, Estonia, Hungary, Poland, Slovenia) and 0 if it is in the second group (Bulgaria, Latvia, Lithuania, Romania, Slovakia). We expect that countries in the first group might have invested more heavily in reforming budget institutions during the last decade in order to conform to EU standards.

Empirical Analysis

This section reports cross-country analyses to test the hypotheses formulated earlier. The empirical evidence of institutional choice is limited to the experiences of ten transition countries in the 1990s and the new millennium. The ten countries considered are Bulgaria, the Czech Republic, Estonia, Hungary, Latvia, Lithuania, Poland, Romania, Slovakia, and Slovenia. Data sources and descriptions of the explanatory variables appear in Appendix 2.

We begin with a simple correlation analysis. The first column of Table 6.2 reports the correlation coefficients between INDEX_1 and the explanatory variables discussed earlier. The variables measuring political fragmentation are positively and significantly correlated with the institutional index. The same is true for social polarization as measured by ethnic divides, but the correlations with our measures for economic polarization are insignificant and some have the wrong sign. The measures for political instability show no significant correlations with the index, and the signs are opposite from the expected. INDEX_1 is negatively correlated with the level of initial public debt-to-GDP ratios and the average size of the budget balance-to-GDP ratios of the period 1989–1992. Only the latter correlation coefficients are consistent with the argument that a fiscal crisis in the early years of the transition phase would have induced policymakers to choose decision-making structures that strengthen the coordination of budgeting decisions. Finally, INDEX_1 is inversely related to the ratio of total credit and loans to the IMF to GDP. The correlation between INDEX_1 and the measure of IMF involvement is negative and almost significant, suggesting that IMF involvement has weakened the domestic reform efforts in the CEEC. EU1 also has the expected sign, indicating that being in the first group of countries with which the EU started accession negotiation has a positive impact on the quality of budget institutions. However, the correlation coefficient is fairly low.

The correlation coefficients between INDEX_2 and the explanatory variables reported in the second column of Table 6.2 show qualitatively similar results. For this version of the index, the INCDIST measure of economic polarization shows a significant positive correlation. Furthermore, the variable measuring IMF involvement now has a negative correlation that is statistically significant; the correlation with the EU1 variable is almost statistically significant.

Table 6.3 shows the Spearman rank correlation coefficients between the different explanatory variables and the indexes representing the institutional quality of the budget process. The Spearman rank correlation coefficients are more suitable to assess the statistical significance of the correlations given the small sample size. Compared to Table 6.2, the correlation of INDEX_1 with our measure of sectoral fragmentation is now significant but negative, while the correlation with INCDIST is now almost significant and positive. The correlation between this variable and INDEX_2 is significant when measured by the rank correlation. Both versions of the index are negatively and significantly correlated with the

Empirical Analysis

Table 6.3. *Spearman Rank Correlation Coefficients*

	INDEX_1	INDEX_2
Fragmentation		
NPP	0.49**	0.30
ENPP	0.68**	0.66**
ETHNIC	0.72**	0.48*
SECTORS	−0.48**	−0.38
INCDIST	0.39	0.61**
GINI	0.27	0.37
Political Instability		
NPM	−0.13	−0.11
ENPM	−0.10	0.39
Past Fiscal Crisis		
DEBT	−0.58**	−0.50**
BALANCE	−0.51**	−0.38
External Pressure		
IMF	−0.43*	−0.45*
EU	0.17	0.38

Note: * indicates statistical significance at the 10% level, ** significance at the 5% level.

initial public debt-to-GDP ratios (DEBT), when rank correlations are considered.

Next, we turn to results obtained from regressing the indexes of budget institutions on a set of explanatory variables.[10] As a result of the scarcity of degrees of freedom, the number of control variables is constrained, and any results are necessarily to be regarded with some caution.

Table 6.4 presents the regressions using INDEX_1 as the dependent variable. We use OLS regressions and report heteroskedasticity-consistent standard errors. A first and strong result is that the degree of political and ethnic fragmentation has a positive and significant impact on the institutional index. This result remains when we take into account several other variables as controls. In line with Hypothesis 1, this suggests that policymakers in countries troubled with a very fragmented political system and significant ethnic divides chose better institutional designs of the national budget processes. This is consistent with the idea that policymakers choose

---

[10] Results from bivariate regressions of the budget institution indexes on each of the explanatory variables confirm the results from the Spearman rank correlation coefficients, and therefore are not reported here.

Table 6.4. *Cross-Country Regression Results*

	Dependent Variable: INDEX_1					
	(1)	(2)	(3)	(4)	(5)	(6)
Constant	4.479*** (0.92)	4.133*** (1.03)	4.445*** (1.04)	5.625*** (0.55)	5.511*** (0.51)	4.895*** (0.77)
ENPP	0.526*** (0.13)	0.563*** (0.16)	0.525*** (0.14)			
ETHNIC				5.950*** (0.82)	6.159** (0.99)	5.367*** (1.27)
DEBT	−0.006 (0.01)		−0.006 (0.01)	−0.002 (0.00)		−0.007 (0.005)
SURPLUS		0.049 (0.11)			0.014 (0.04)	
IMF1	−0.007 (0.17)	−0.012 (0.17)		−0.237** (0.09)	−0.249** (0.09)	
EU1			0.041 (0.58)			0.720 (0.46)
R^2	0.6298	0.6096	0.6299	0.8293	0.8250	0.7694
N	10	10	10	10	10	10

Note: Numbers in parentheses are heteroskedasticity-corrected (White) standard errors. *, **, *** indicate significance at the 10%, 5%, and 1% levels.

institutions rationally when they have the opportunity for institutional innovation.

Interestingly, and in contrast to the evidence presented in the previous chapter, the estimated effect of both DEBT and BALANCE is never significantly different from zero. Thus, we cannot detect any systematic role of initial fiscal conditions in influencing the design choice of budget processes. Hypothesis 2 is not supported here.

Being in the first group of countries with which the EU started negotiations on EU membership (EU1) apparently also has had no effects on the initial institutional structure of the budget process. This is not very surprising, however, given that decisions on accession negotiation were taken in the second half of the nineties. The coefficient on IMF1 is negative and significantly different from zero after controlling for ethnic fragmentation and initial fiscal conditions. This indicates that the countries that have relied more on financial support from the IMF have not established budget processes that are more suitable for achieving fiscal discipline. Thus, the data support Hypothesis 3 with the qualification that the expectation of financial assistance from the IMF has weakened pressure for internal political reforms strengthening the coordination of budgeting decisions.

Table 6.5 reports the results of regressing INDEX_2 on the explanatory variables. Again, it appears that the more the party structure in parliament is fragmented, as measured by the effective number of parties in parliament (ENPP), the stronger are the coordination mechanisms chosen. The coefficient estimates of the income inequality variable INCDIST indicate that more economically polarized societies establish stronger coordination mechanisms in the budget process. This evidence supports the view that greater fragmentation and higher polarization increase the willingness to establish explicit budget institutions for facilitating coordination and for achieving and sustaining cooperative outcomes.

In contrast to the results shown in Table 6.3, the regression estimate in column 3 of Table 6.5 reveals that the variable BALANCE now has a significant negative coefficient, suggesting that countries that exhibited large deficits in the early transition phase have created stronger budget institutions over the next decade. The coefficient loses significance when IMF involvement is controlled for; the IMF variable then is significant. This may be due to some correlation between these two variables, which is likely if IMF support went mainly to countries that initially had large deficits.

Table 6.5 also shows that being in the first group of the new member countries had a positive influence on the choice of budgeting institutions,

Table 6.5. *Cross-Country Regression Results*

			Dependent Variable: INDEX_2				
	(1)	(2)	(3)	(4)	(5)	(6)	(7)
Constant	3.058 (1.65)	3.358 (1.86)	0.412 (1.90)	5.215*** (1.18)	5.024*** (1.14)	5.164*** (1.13)	4.930** (1.38)
ENPP2	0.905** (0.32)	0.916** (0.36)	1.267** (0.40)				
INCDIST				0.310* (0.15)	0.331* (0.15)	0.307* (0.14)	0.289 (0.17)
DEBT	0.013 (0.01)			-0.003 (0.01)			-0.008 (0.01)
BALANCE		-0.161 (0.09)	-0.214** (0.08)	-0.128 (0.16)	-0.04 (0.08)	-0.166* (0.08)	
IMF	-0.231* (0.11)	-0.235* (0.11)			-0.201 (0.11)		
EU			1.139** (0.48)				0.632 (0.63)
R^2	0.6260	0.6454	0.7138	0.4701	0.4676	0.4553	0.4914
N	10	10	10	10	10	10	10

Note: Numbers in parentheses are heteroskedasticity-corrected (White) standard errors. *, **, *** indicate significance at the 10%, 5%, and 1% levels.

although the effect is not robust across specifications. The comparison between the impact of IMF involvement and EU accession is telling, nevertheless. If EU accession is perceived as a reward for good policy performance, it clearly raises the incentives for institutional reforms. Note also that the entire accession process focused on institutional reform in the transition countries, as accession could only happen after these countries had adopted the core institutional framework of the EU. In contrast, the IMF focuses more on macroeconomic outcomes and policies.

The differences between the two versions of our index stem from the institutional reforms in Bulgaria, Poland, Lithuania, and the Czech Republic in the late 1990s and 2000. Thus, the differences between Tables 6.4 and 6.5 can be interpreted in terms of these reforms. Table 6.5 then suggests that these reforms reflected the experience of early fiscal crises more than the institutions adopted during the first half of the 1990s. It also indicates that the expected payoff from EU accession became relevant only in the later years of our sample.

Next Steps – The Development of Fiscal Institutions in Poland

The first part of the chapter indicated that no country had institutions that fit well a "contract" form of fiscal governance, while the second part discussed why there has nevertheless been variation in the institutions that are in place. Poland provides a good case to connect the themes of the chapter and to consider the progress that is still needed in the new member states. On the Gleich index, it finished near the top of the group, falling behind only Estonia and Latvia. On the delegation index, which appears in Figure 6.1, Poland's institutions circa 2002 are weaker than in all EU-15 countries but the expected contract states of Belgium and the Netherlands. If one makes a comparison to the institutions in place in Poland in 2006, which is possible because of a recent study (Hallerberg and von Hagen 2006), Poland has a score of 0.43, which is lower than that of all EU-15 countries.

This finding is not a surprise. As Chapter 3 explains, one should not expect to find strong finance ministers in countries that have regular multi-party coalition governments and/or minority governments. Under such situations, there will be players in the budget process whose assent is required and who have different policy preferences than the finance minister, and they will refuse to delegate strong powers to the minister. Since the introduction of the new constitution in 1997, there has never been a one-party majority government.

It turns out, in fact, that Poland represents a prototypical case to illustrate the weakness of the finance minister when there are multiple parties needed to pass legislation. One simply has to examine the number of finance ministers who have been in office the past few years and the reasons for their departure. From 2000 to 2007, there were ten different finance ministers, suggesting little opportunity for such ministers to develop their authority. Moreover, several of these ministers left office after losing battles over fiscal policy. Jarosław Bauc repeatedly failed to induce his cabinet colleagues to agree to spending cuts when the economy slowed in 2001 under an AWS minority government, and despite his efforts his prime minister fired him for reportedly not making clear the fiscal mess early enough.[11] Under a three-party coalition (SLD-PSL-UP), Marek Belka resigned in July 2002 after the cabinet refused to stick to his proposed spending limits. Grzegorz Kolodko resigned a year later after Prime Minister Miller sided with his economics minister, Jerzy Hausner, over his finance minister on tax matters. For the remainder of the term under the coalition government that deteriorated into a minority government, Hausner's assent meant that the finance minister was not even the strongest minister on budgetary and economic matters. The first finance minister under the minority government formed in 2005, Teresa Lubińska, lasted less than three months in office, while Zyta Gilowska served twice within the same year under what has become a multiparty coalition government through 2007.

The point of this discussion is that a marked strengthening of the role of the finance minister in Poland is unlikely given the underlying political dynamics. The finance minister needs the prime minister's support in key internal battles in order for delegation to function effectively, and there has to be a sense that he or she is making sometimes painful decisions for the good of the government, and for the good of the party in power. The fact that some finance ministers, such as Zyta Gilowska and Grzegorz Kolodko before her, simultaneously held the position of Deputy Prime Minister did not guarantee that they would be able to set fiscal policy in the government.[12]

---

[11] *Business Week*, September 10, 2001.

[12] Poland is also a prototypical case of a widespread bias in the perception of the power of the finance minister especially (but not only) by the individual finance minister. As one former Polish finance minister repeatedly argued, "The Polish finance minister has a very strong position in the budget process ... as long as he or she is in office." That is, there can be a large difference between the formal and the effective power of a finance minister.

Given that Poland has had either coalition governments or minority governments (or both) since the passage of the new constitution in 1997, a fiscal contract approach would be the most appropriate way for Poland to centralize the budget process. Yet the experience to date with fiscal targets has not been positive. The SLD-PSL-UP coalition formed in 2001, for example, did negotiate what Zubek (2006) refers to as a "fiscal contract" when it assumed office, which included multiannual budget targets. Within months of setting these targets, however, the cabinet had decided to violate them. In 2006, Prime Minister Marcinkiewicz made a pledge to keep to a 30-billion-zloty deficit target in the coming years. There existed no subtargets to reach this goal. Moreover, one can question whether the goal itself was ambitious or whether it was set because it would be easy to reach.[13]

The question then is, which version of contracts should be put in place. The nature of the fiscal contract depends upon whether there are majority or minority governments, with legal, multiannual contracts suggested under minority governments. Indeed, such governments have been common in Poland. The past two began as majority governments but fell into minority, while the government that entered office in fall 2005 began life in minority. These governments did manage to survive, and to pass adequate budgets, largely as a result of idiosyncratic political conditions. After the AWS-UF coalition collapsed in mid-2000, Balcerowicz's Union of Freedom nevertheless continued to back the government on budget votes. Similarly, the SLD fell into minority as the number of independent members of parliament increased. Given that the electoral rule is based on the votes political parties receive, the independents would lose their positions after the next elections. If they blocked the budget, they were essentially pushing forward the time when they would lose their offices. The PiS government installed in 2005 used a similar tactic in the run-up to passage of the 2006 budget. Polls of how people would vote indicated that the two small parties that supported the PiS government on budget issues (and that later joined the PiS in a formal coalition) – the Polish Families League and Self-Defence – would lose seats if there were early elections while the PiS would gain seats, and this fact gave the PiS a strong negotiating position before passage of its government's first budget.

Nevertheless, the track record under minority governments is not good. While the SLD used the weak position of the independents to gain their

---

[13] The IMF (2005) commented after a November 2005 staff visit that the 30-billion-zloty target is not very ambitious.

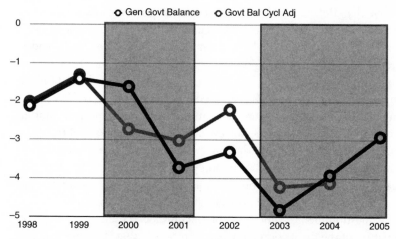

Figure 6.2 Budget Balance and Minority Governments in Poland. Figures from AMECO (2005) are represented as percentage of GDP and are in ESA 95 terms. The shaded areas represent the time when there was a minority government in office.

support without the need for budget concessions when passing the annual budget, it still had problems maintaining fiscal discipline in the run-up to the 2005 election because of its inability to stop private-member bills. Three episodes are both illuminating and troubling. In the first case, two private member bills from the government's own party and a citizen-submitted bill were the basis for granting early retirement benefits to miners in July 2005. The second case concerned the reimbursement of VAT for building materials. While two private-member bills provided the basis for the legislation, all parliamentarians present voted for the bill. The president then vetoed it, but the Sejm overrode the veto with all but three members supporting the bill. The president then signed it in August 2005. Finally, a private-member bill on the indexation of pensions passed 393 to 4 at about the same time.[14] These laws all had fiscal implications either immediately or in the near future.[15]

---

[14] The ease with which these amendments changed spending provides evidence to rebut a widely held belief that spending is too "rigid" in Poland to be changed quickly. See also Markiewicz and Siwinska-Gorzelak (2003), who argue that the rigidity hypothesis is a myth.

[15] The laws specified that these benefits became law at different times. The indexation of pensions began 14 days from the announcement, the reimbursement of VAT entered force in January 2006, and the law on early retirements took effect beginning in January 2007.

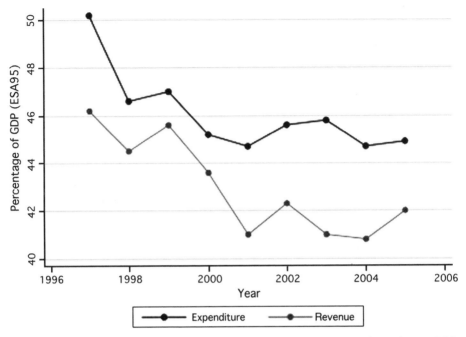

Figure 6.3 Levels of Expenditures and Revenue. Data for 1997–2004 from the AMECO database, European Commission; data for 2005 from the Convergence Program the Polish Government submitted in January 2006. All figures are in ESA 95 terms.

The aggregate evidence supports this impression that fiscal discipline has become lax, especially under minority governments. Figure 6.2 compares the general government balance and the cyclically adjusted balance since 1998. The shaded area indicates the period when there was a minority government in office in Poland. This graph suggests two issues about minority governments in Poland. First, the budget balance worsens noticeably at the beginning of such governments. Second, even taking into consideration cyclical factors, the balance remains stubbornly in negative territory.

Another way to examine these results is to look at the volatility of the components of the budget balance. Figure 6.3 compares expenditures and revenues as a percentage of GDP. Expenditures declined initially and have been relatively flat since 2000, remaining between 45% and 46% of GDP. Revenues experienced a similar pattern but with a steeper drop from 1999 to 2001, then more continuity from 2002 on as revenues

161

remained in the 41% to 42% range. The stability is fairly remarkable given the changes in economic fortunes over time. After falling to a rate of about 1%, real growth picked up to almost 4% in 2003 and over 5% in 2004. The budget aggregates did not change in any noticeable way to reflect that change in economic fortunes. Once again, we suspect that the minority governments in place were not able to make appropriate adjustments on both sides of the budget, expenditures and revenues.[16]

What kind of fiscal contract could be operational in Poland? Consistently with the broad themes we discuss in Chapter 2, the International Monetary Fund has recommended that the government adopt a Fiscal Responsibility Law that would include an expenditure rule to supplement the debt rule in its constitution.[17] The International Monetary Fund also suggests three-year rolling budget projections (IMF 2005a, 2005b). A more political solution arises from the underlying political dynamics of the system over a constitutional amendment. In Sweden, the government and one or more opposition parties agree to what amounts to a fiscal contract that they then write into law. In the Polish case, a "Stabilisation Pact for Fiscal Stability," the possibility of which was discussed in 2006, could play that role. This pact would be multiannual, preferably for three years, focused on expenditures, and enshrined into Polish law. If the pact fell apart because of differences among the parties, or if political parties began to splinter and party discipline weakened over the life of the government (as is common), it would still take a majority in parliament to change its terms.

This focus on institutions is in contrast to more traditional views of Polish public finances prevailing in the country and among Polish academics. These views focus on the importance of personalities, informal

---

[16] The clear structural break in the series in 2000–2001 has implications for the calculation of any elasticities of revenues and expenditures based on growth rates. Real growth is 4%–5% through 2000, and both revenues and expenditures as a percentage of GDP decline. Growth returns to the same level the past few years, yet expenditures and revenues hardly change.

[17] Poland's Public Finance Act establishes three rules to reinforce the constitutional limit. If the debt level is above 50% of GDP but not as high as 55%, the deficit may not be higher the following year. In particular, according to the Public Finance Act, the deficit to revenues ratio cannot increase. This applies to local governments as well. If the debt level is at least 55% but not 60% of GDP, the debt level the following year cannot be higher. Finally, if the debt level is 60% or greater, the government at all levels must have a balanced budget or surplus the following year. It should be noted that the definition of debt levels is a domestic one, and is not the same thing as the definition at the European level in the form of the ESA 95 accounting standard. So far, this rule has never been applied, so there is no experience with it in practice.

networks, and party systems more than we do (e.g., Dabrowski 1993).[18] It is important to think about the relationship between these explanations and the one provided here. Personalities are most relevant when institutions are weak and individual actions can have a comparatively big effect on the budget. Party systems matter, but they matter in the way discussed here – they affect whether delegation or fiscal contracts are more effective at centralizing the budget process.

Conclusion

This chapter studies the institutional structure of the budget process in the Central and East European countries that have joined the European Union by 2007. We find that the countries generally should have fiscal contracts in place, but no country did develop such a framework in the run-up to EU membership. At the same time, there was some variation in the institutions that these countries used, and we consider what factors account for the differences in the institutional framework. We explore the influence of features of the social and political structure, the initial fiscal situation, and the influence of external actors on the institutional design choices using a set of variables identified as proxies for these different possible institutional choice determinants. The main empirical finding is that countries with larger degrees of political fragmentation, as measured by the effective number of parties in parliament, and/or more social polarization, measured by either the degree of ethnic fragmentation or the degree of income inequality, are associated with budget institutions that are more conducive to fiscal discipline. Another interesting finding is that countries that have relied more heavily on financial support from the IMF have actually established less appropriate institutional structures of the budget process. This is consistent with the hypothesis that access to IMF support and the implied fiscal surveillance might weaken the need for domestic political reforms to establish appropriate institutions.

This finding of an effect of an important international institution, the IMF, on the choice of budgeting institutions in European countries begs the question of the effect the European Union has on fiscal governance in its member states. This is the subject of the next chapter.

---

[18] Bratkowski and Rostowski (2005) similarly focus on the importance of fiscal institutions in Poland.

Appendix 1: Characterization of CEEC Budgeting Institutions

Table 6A.1 lists the institutional elements used to construct the institutional index and the classification scheme used to translate the qualitative properties into numerical values for each of the stages of the budgeting process. For each institutional arrangement, a value on a scale of 0 to 4 is assigned; a high value indicates that the institutional characteristic should promote coordinated and cohesive decision making. Because of institutional changes during the sample period, the index scores of some countries show some variation over time.

A. Executive planning stage. In CEEC, the executive branch of government is responsible for the preparation of the budget draft. Participants in this stage include the prime minister, the finance minister, and the spending ministers. Four items represent the features of this stage. *Item 1* refers to the existence of permanent constraints on budgetary parameters such as legal limits on the size of budget deficits or government borrowing.

Item 2 assesses the use of fiscal targets and ceilings as elements that guide the budget preparation.

Given that the use of multiannual targets has started only very recently in CEECs, their potential impact on budget outcomes cannot be analyzed yet. Therefore, we concentrate on possible effects of annual spending and deficit targets only.

Item 3 refers to the power of the finance minister in the compilation of the draft budget. *Item 4* reflects the mode of conflict resolution in the executive. Following von Hagen (1992), we classify procedures where the whole cabinet is involved in the reconciliation as less centralized than procedures where senior cabinet committees discuss important matters before they are sent to the cabinet.

B. Legislative stage. We consider five variables quantifying the scope of amendments the parliament and the national president can make to the executive's budget proposal and the fragmentation of the legislative decision making process. *Item 5* reflects the distribution of budgetary powers between the houses of parliament. *Item 6* considers the existence of formal amendment constraints. *Item 7* refers to the sequence of decision making during the parliamentary budget deliberation and investigates whether a decision is made on the size of budget totals before the work on the details of the budget starts. We suggest that a process in which the budget totals are fixed first is less fragmented than one that does not set any ceilings for total spending or the deficit. *Item 8* summarizes the relative

Conclusion

Table 6A.1. *Construction of the Index: Institutional Arrangements and Their Index Parameters*

Institutional Characteristics	Weighting Factors			Numerical Coding
	Index	Subindex	Item	
A. Preparation	0.33			
1. Existence of statutorily mandated fiscal rules		0.25		
a. Balanced budget rule				4.00
b. Limits on public borrowing				2.00
c. No legal limits on borrowing				0.00
2. Sequence of budgetary decision making		0.25		
a. MF sets forth aggregate and specific budget targets in initial budget circular				4.00
b. MF proposes, cabinet decides on targets for budget aggregates and spending limits are assigned to each ministry before spending ministries develop budget requests				3.00
c. MF proposes, cabinet decides on targets for budget aggregates before spending ministries develop budget requests				2.00
d. Budgetary targets are set on the basis of preliminary budget requests				1.00
e. No budget targets are determined				0.00
3. Compilation of the draft budget		0.25		
a. Finance ministry holds bilateral negotiations with each spending ministry				4.00
b. Finance ministry only collects budget requests and compiles summary for cabinet session				0.00
4. Members of executive responsible for reconciling conflicts over budget bids		0.25		
a. MF or PM can veto or overrule cabinet decision				4.00
b. Senior cabinet committee, then whole council of ministers or cabinet				2.00
c. Executive collectively (e.g., council of ministers or cabinet)				0.00

(continued)

Table 6A.1 *(continued)*

Institutional Characteristics	Weighting Factors			Numerical Coding
	Index	Subindex	Item	
B. Legislation	0.33			
5. Relative power of the upper house vis-à-vis the lower house		0.20		
a. No budgetary power vested in upper house or unicameral parliament				4.00
b. Lower house has prerogatives				2.00
c. Both houses have equal rights (e.g., joint sittings)				0.00
6. Constraints on the legislature to amend the government's draft budget		0.20		
a. Deficit provided in the draft budget cannot be exceeded, or individual amendments have to indicate offsetting changes				4.00
b. No restrictions				0.00
7. Sequence of votes		0.20		
a. Initial vote on total budget revenues, expenditures, and the deficit				4.00
b. Final vote on budget aggregates				0.00
8. Relative power of the executive vis-à-vis the parliament		0.20		
a. Cabinet can combine a vote of confidence with a vote on the budget			0.33	4.00
b. Draft budget is executed if parliament fails to adopt the budget before the start of the fiscal year			0.33	4.00
c. Parliament can be dissolved if it fails to adopt the budget in due time			0.33	4.00
9. Authority of the national president in the budget procedure		0.20		
a. No special authority				4.00
b. President has veto right (president elected by parliament)				2.67
c. President has veto right (president directly elected by citizens)				1.33
d. President has veto right (qualified majority required to override veto)				0.00

Institutional Characteristics	Weighting Factors			Numerical Coding
	Index	Subindex	Item	
C. Implementation	0.33			
10. Flexibility to change budget aggregates during execution		0.25		
a. Any increase in total revenues, expenditures, and the deficit needs to be approved by the parliament in a supplementary budget				4.00
b. Revenue windfalls can be used to increase expenditure without the approval of the parliament as long as the deficit is not increased				2.67
c. Simultaneous changes in revenues and expenditures allowed without approval of parliament if budget balance is not changed				1.33
d. At discretion of government				0.00
11. Transfers of expenditures between chapters (i.e., ministries' budgets)		0.25		
a. Require approval of parliament				4.00
b. MF or cabinet can authorize transfers between chapters				2.67
c. Limited				1.33
d. Unrestricted				0.00
12. Carryover of unused funds to next fiscal year		0.25		
a. Not permitted				4.00
b. Only if provided for in initial budget or with finance ministry approval				2.67
c. Limited				1.33
d. Unlimited				0.00
13. Procedure to react to a deterioration of the budget deficit (due to unforeseen revenue shortfalls or expenditure increases)		0.25		
a. MF can block expenditures				4.00
b. The cabinet can block expenditures				2.67
c. Approval of the parliament necessary to block expenditures				1.33
d. No action is taken				0.00

power of the executive and the legislature in three dimensions. The budget process is considered to be more centralized if institutional arrangements favor the executive. The first issue relates to the government's ability to call for a vote of confidence in connection with the vote on the budget. The other two issues concern institutional arrangements applied in cases when the parliament does not approve the budget within a certain time frame. *Item 9* captures the power of the president in the budget process.

C. Executive implementation stage. There are two major forces that may undermine fiscal discipline at this stage. The first concerns the extent by which the budget law binds the execution of spending during the year. In this vein, *item 10* considers the flexibility of changing budget aggregates during the fiscal year. *Item 11* considers the flexibility of transfers of budgetary appropriations among different parts of the budget. *Item 12* looks at the possibilities of carrying funds forward or backward into or from the next fiscal year. The second force concerns the degree of flexibility to react to unforeseen revenue shortfalls or expenditure increases. *Item 13* regards the procedures for fiscal adjustments to changing economic circumstances.

D. Aggregation. To combine the institutional elements covered in Table 6A.1 into a comprehensive description of the budget process, we aggregate the numerical codes to an index for each country. The table shows the weights used to aggregate the variables into the overall index and the three subindexes:

$$INDED = \frac{1}{4}\sum_{j=1}^{4} v_{jit} + \cdot\frac{1}{5}\sum_{j=5}^{9} v_{jit} + \cdot\frac{1}{4}\sum_{j=10}^{13} v_{jit}, \tag{A1}$$

where v_{jit} is the score of country i on item j in period t.

Appendix 2: Data

Table 6A.2. *Definition and Sources of Explanatory Variables*

INDEX	Definition and Source
NPP[a]	(Average of) the number of parties in parliament after elections. *Source:* Berglund, Hellén, and Aarebrot (1998), the Parline Database of the Inter-Parliamentary Union (www.ipu.org), and various country reports in the December editions of the *European Journal of Political Research*.

INDEX	Definition and Source
ENPP[a]	(Average of) the effective number of parties in parliament after elections. $ENPP = \left(\sum_{i=1}^{n} P_i^2\right)^{-1}$, where P_i stands for the share of seats in parliament of party i. *Source:* Berglund, Hellén, and Aarebrot (1998), the Parline Database of the Inter-Parliamentary Union (www.ipu.org), and various country reports in the December editions of the *European Journal of Political Research*.
NPM[a]	Number of prime ministers over the period specified in the text. *Source:* Zárates Political Collection (http://www.terra.es/personal2/monolith/).
ENPM[a]	Effective number of prime ministers. $ENPM = \left(\sum_{i=1}^{n} T_i^2\right)^{-1}$, with T_i equal to the ratio of the number of days prime minister i held office to the total number of days of the period specified in the text (1990–1995 or 1990–2000). *Source:* Zárates Political Collection (http://www.terra.es/personal2/monolith/).
ETHNIC	Ethnic fragmentation index. $ETHNIC = 1 - \sum_{i=1}^{n} G_i^2$, where G_i stands for the share of ethnic group i in the total population. *Source:* National statistical yearbooks, *Encyclopædia Britannica*.
SECTORS	Index of heterogeneity of economic structure. $SECTORS = 1 - \sum_{i=1}^{n} E_i^2$, with E_i the share of employment in sector i = {agriculture, industry, services}. *Source: The World Factbook* 2001 (CIA), *Statistical Yearbook of Slovenia* 1999.
INCDIST	$$INCDIST = \frac{Share\ of\ household\ income\ or\ consumption,\ decile\ X}{Share\ of\ household\ income\ or\ consumption,\ decile\ I}.$$ Indicator of income inequality. *Source: The World Factbook* 2001 (CIA)
GINI	Gini coefficient of household income inequality (average over 1991 or earliest available to 1995). *Source:* TransMONEE database 2000 (UNICEF).
DEBT	Gross public debt-to-GDP for 1993 (or earliest available, see note 12). *Source:* EBRD *Transition Report* 2001 Update.
DEFICIT	Average general government budget surplus of the years 1989–1992. *Source:* EBRD *Transition Report* 1994.
IMF[a]	Total credit and loans to the IMF outstanding (in percentage of GDP). *Source: International Finance Statistics* (IMF) various issues, and www.imf.org.
EU1	Dummy variable, EU1 = 1 if country in first group with which the EU started accession negotiations, and 0 otherwise.

[a] Two variables are calculated on the basis of data for two distinct subperiods: (a) the initial years until 1995 and (b) the first decade after the collapse of the communist regime. For details on periods, see the text.

7

EMU and Fiscal Governance in Europe

The European Monetary Union (EMU) includes a new framework for the fiscal policies of its member states. The need to create a genuine institutional framework to deal with public finances in EMU was recognized already in the Delors Report (1989), which called for institutional safeguards of fiscal discipline in the monetary union and argued that a lack of fiscal discipline might undermine the stability of the new currency. The fear that high and rising public debts would undermine the central bank's ability to deliver price stability has left its mark on all important documents and political decisions on the way to EMU.

In terms of technical economic analysis, fiscal policy and monetary policy are indeed linked through the "intertemporal budget constraint," the requirement that, in the long run, the discounted sum of a government's expected expenditures cannot exceed the discounted sum of its expected revenues.[1] Given an expected stream of expenditures, governments in EMU must adjust taxes to assure that the intertemporal budget constraint holds, since they cannot use the printing press freely to monetize their debts. Otherwise, they will be forced at some point to default on their debts. A fiscal crisis would arise, and pressures would rise on the European Central Bank to bail out the troubled government.[2]

This reasoning leads to the conclusion that EMU needs a fiscal framework preventing the national governments from running up excessive levels

---

[1] See e.g., Sargent and Wallace (1981).

[2] Note that while the ECB cannot legally bail out a government in fiscal difficulties by buying its debt directly in the primary market, it might still do so indirectly. A bailout could be *ex post*, with the central bank buying up large amounts of government debt in the secondary market, or ex ante, with the central bank holding down interest rates to reduce the government's interest payments. However, financial market intervention and interest rate setting would have to be fully justifiable with the maintenance of price stability, and not with an intended bailout for the euro area.

of debt that could threaten the common good of EMU, that is, price stability. The tricky question is how to translate this conclusion into a framework that guides and constrains the governments' fiscal policies in the short run. Since the governments' intertemporal budget constraint pertains to the long run, it has no strong implications for today's budgetary policies and fiscal flows.[3] Excessively tight restrictions on fiscal policies in the short run would seem unjustifiable, because they might force governments under some circumstances to adopt policies that would seem unreasonable or even damaging for their own countries. But too loose restrictions would not have any binding effects on government policies and, therefore, fail to achieve the goal of sustainable public finances. Either way, the framework would lack credibility.

An important distinction exists between sustainable public finances and optimal public finances. Optimal public finances are the outcome of an optimization problem which consists of a set of policy goals, political preferences regarding policy outcomes, resource constraints, and (assumptions about) the laws describing the functioning of the economy. Designing optimal policies is, therefore, by nature a political task. Sustainability is just one of the constraints that must be fulfilled in this task: that is, all optimal policies are sustainable, but not all sustainable policies are optimal. This distinction reveals the nature of the policy problem of designing a fiscal framework for EMU: the more the rules meant to achieve sustainability constrain short-term fiscal policies, the more likely they are to get in the way of optimal policy choices in the short run, and the more the governments will try to get around these rules. Focusing the framework too much on annual fiscal performance, therefore, has the result of politicizing the framework for sustainability to an unnecessary extent and could be self-defeating. The proper response, therefore, is to design a framework that combines guidelines for short-run budgetary policies with proper judgment about current and future developments.

The Fiscal Framework of EMU

The Excessive Deficit Procedure and the Stability and Growth Pact

The cornerstone of the fiscal framework of the European Union is the *Excessive Deficit Procedure* (EDP) according to Article 104 of the Treaty

---

[3] This is best seen in the fact that governments can always promise future actions to collect more revenues to compensate for today's deficits. See Perotti et al. (1998) for a more detailed discussion.

on European Union (TEU). The EDP unconditionally obliges the EU member states to avoid "excessive deficits" and sets up a procedure for monitoring their fiscal performance and, if necessary, penalizing profligate behavior. The TEU charges the European Commission with the task of monitoring budgetary developments and the stock of public sector debt of the member states, checking in particular their compliance with two *reference values*, one for the ratio of the deficit to GDP, and one for the ratio of public debt to GDP. A protocol on the EDP added to the TEU sets these reference values at 3% and 60%, respectively. If a member state does not comply with these reference values, the European Commission is obliged to write a report to the ECOFIN about the matter, unless the deficit and the debt are approaching their reference values in a satisfactory way, or the excess of the deficit over the limit is exceptional and temporary. The Commission's report is to take into account whether the deficit exceeds public investment spending and "all other relevant factors, including the medium term economic and budgetary position" (Art. 104(3)) of the country concerned.[4]

If the Commission considers that an excessive deficit exists, it makes a recommendation to ECOFIN to decide that this is indeed the case. ECOFIN is the European Council in its *rendition* as the assembly of the ministers of finance of the member states.[5] ECOFIN votes on this recommendation by qualified majority after taking into account any observations the country concerned may make and the opinion of the Economic and Financial Committee (EFC), which advises the ECOFIN in these matters (Art. 114, TEU) and includes representatives of the European Commission and the European Central Bank in addition to those of the member states. Thus, the decision whether or not an excessive deficit indeed exists is ultimately left to the ECOFIN, that is, the governments of the member states.

If ECOFIN decides that an excessive deficit indeed prevails, it makes confidential recommendations to the country concerned how to correct the situation within a given period. If the country does not take appropriate

---

[4] According to Art. 104(3) the commission may also prepare a report if a member state complies with the criteria but the commission sees the risk of an excessive deficit nevertheless.

[5] In the EU framework, the European Council is the body representing the member states and taking the main political decisions in the EU. The European Council meets in a variety of compositions depending on the different policy areas. Among these, the European Council of Foreign Ministers and ECOFIN are the two most important ones. The European Council of the Heads of State decides on the general direction of EU policies.

action and does not respond to these recommendations in a satisfactory way, ECOFIN may make its views and recommendations public, ask the government concerned to take specific corrective actions, and, ultimately, impose a financial fine on the country. In that case, the country would first be required to make a non-interest-bearing deposit with the European Community. If the excessive deficit persists, this deposit can be turned into a fine paid to the Community.[6] ECOFIN can abrogate its decisions under the EDP at any stage of the process upon a recommendation from the Commission. All council decisions in this context are made by qualified majority; once a country has been found to have an excessive deficit, its votes are not counted in these decisions.

To assure that the functioning of the EDP would not be undermined by creative accounting and data manipulation, all EU member states had to adopt unified public sector accounting rules and standards. During the run-up to EMU before 1999, EU member states were obliged to submit *Convergence Reports* to the European Commission explaining how they intended to achieve the targets or maintain their deficits and debts below the critical values.

The EDP is an attempt to balance the advantages of simple constraints on budgetary aggregates with the need for sound economic judgment accounting for specific economic circumstances. The numerical constraints on deficits and debts only serve as triggers for an assessment prepared by the European Commission and made by the European Council. Since they do not themselves define what an excessive deficit is and breaching them does not imply any sanctions per se, there is no need to make these criteria responsive to economic circumstances, for example, by redefining them to exclude interest spending or cyclical effects on spending and revenues. The Commission's analysis, the EFC's opinion, the observations of the country concerned, and, ultimately, ECOFIN's judgment can take these and other circumstances into account.

To become members of EMU, countries had to stay below the limits for general government deficits and debts defined by the EDP. The threat of not qualifying for EMU gave the fiscal rules considerable power between 1992 and 1998. By 1994, ECOFIN had declared all EU member states except Luxembourg as having excessive deficits. These declarations were revoked by 1997. The decision of which countries qualified for EMU was taken in 1998 on the basis of 1997 fiscal data.

---

[6] Note that neither the deposit nor its conversion into a fine affects the budget of the country in question as both are financial transactions.

The Stability and Growth Pact

The Stability and Growth Pact (SGP) was adopted by the European Council in 1997 to develop the fiscal framework of EMU further.[7] The SGP modifies the EDP in several ways. First, it sets up an early warning system strengthening the surveillance of the public finances of the member states. Under the SGP, EMU member states submit annual Stability Programs to the European Commission and ECOFIN explaining their intended fiscal policies and, in particular, what they plan to do to keep the budget close to the new and stricter medium-term objective of "close to balance or in surplus." Implementation of these programs is subject to ECOFIN's scrutiny. On the basis of information and assessments by the Commission and the EFC, ECOFIN can issue early warnings to countries that risk significant deviations from the fiscal targets set out in their Stability Programs. The goal of the Stability Programs is to strengthen the "preventive arm" of the fiscal rule, that is, to reduce the risk that countries exceed the 3% deficit constraint.

Second, the SGP gives more specific content to the vague notions of "exceptional" and "temporary" breaches of the 3% limit, defines the rules for financial penalties, and it speeds up the process by setting specific deadlines for the individual steps. Third, the SGP gives political guidance to the parties involved in the EDP, calling on them to implement the rules of the EDP effectively and in a timely manner. It commits the Commission in particular to using its right of initiative under the EDP "in a manner that facilitates the strict, timely, and effective functioning of the SGP." The rules of the SGP were further developed in a set of ECOFIN decisions regarding the format and content of the Stability Programs.[8] In October 1998, ECOFIN endorsed a Monetary Committee (the precursor of the Economic and Financial Committee) opinion, the "code of conduct," specifying criteria to be observed in the assessment of a country's medium-term budgetary position and data standards and requirements for the programs. In October 1999, ECOFIN recommended stricter compliance with and timelier updating of the programs. In July 2001 ECOFIN endorsed an appended code of conduct refining the format and the use of data in the stability programs, including the use of a common set of assumptions about economic developments outside the EMU. The Commission (2000) has

---

[7] For an account of the genesis of the SGP see Stark (2001).
[8] See European Commission (2002, 23).

produced a detailed framework of interpretation of divergences from the targets set in the stability programs.

Compared to the original EDP, the main impact of the SGP has been to reduce the weight of economic judgment and to raise the importance of the numerical criteria in the fiscal framework, thus making it more akin to a rigid numerical rule. In practice, this rule has focused more on the annual deficit than the debt ratio, partly because many EMU member states exceeded the debt limit anyway, and partly because debt ratios are difficult to change and to control by annual budgetary policies. In line with this increasing focus on the annual deficit, the ECOFIN adopted a decision in 2003 that countries exceeding the 3% constraint should achieve annual reductions in their structural deficits by at least 0.5% of GDP annually.

Stability Pact Crisis and Reform

Somewhat ironically, Germany, the very country that had pushed for tighter fiscal rules in EMU in the mid-1990s, was the second EMU member country and the first of the large member countries to violate the fiscal rules. In early 2002, the Commission noted that the country had missed its Stability Program targets by a significant margin and was approaching a deficit of 3% of GDP. In view of this, the Commission proposed that ECOFIN issue an early warning to Germany under the procedures of the SGP. To avoid that shortly before the national elections scheduled for the fall of the same year, the German government struck a deal in ECOFIN by which Germany promised to balance the budget by 2004 in return for not receiving an early warning. After its reelection in September, however, the German government revealed that the country was going to exceed the 3% deficit ratio by a large margin in 2002 and 2003. In January 2003, ECOFIN declared that Germany had an excessive deficit. But, already in May 2003, the Commission found that the German government had made sufficient efforts to reach budget balance and that there was no need to consider financial fines. It turned out later that Germany did not lower its deficit below 3% of GDP in 2003; nor did it do so in 2004 or 2005.

Also in spring 2002, the newly appointed French government announced its intention to postpone balancing the budget until 2007, three years later than its commitments from the previous Stability Program. France had a deficit ratio in excess of 3% in 2002, yet the French finance minister did not respond to the Commission's request for an adjustment program. In summer 2002, the Italian government also stated that it intended to postpone the budget balance required under the SGP. ECOFIN issued an early warning to the French government in January 2003 and declared that France had an excessive deficit in June 2003. In June and July 2004, ECOFIN declared that the Netherlands and Greece had excessive deficits. In July 2004, ECOFIN also found that several of the new member states that entered the EU in May of the year had excessive deficits: the Czech Republic, Cyprus, Hungary, Malta, Poland, and the Slovak Republic.

Meanwhile, the governments of Germany, France, and other countries had started pushing for a reform of the SGP, asking for more "flexibility."[9] For example, Germany wanted to have its large net contribution to the EU budget and the fiscal costs of German unification recognized as excuses for running large deficits. The European Commission admitted that the SGP was too rigid when, in a remarkable statement, its president, Romano Prodi, publicly called the SGP "stupid." In December 2004, ECOFIN decided to suspend the ongoing EDP procedures until after a reform of the SGP. The European Council adopted a reform of the SGP in March 2005. Its main points were as follows: (1) The medium-term objective for national budgetary positions to be "close to balance or in surplus" can now be differentiated according to national circumstances, allowing for room for more budgetary maneuver, taking into account the need for public investment and taking into account the fiscal consequences of structural reforms. (2) A clarification of the term "exceptional; and temporary" excess of the deficit over the reference value of 3% of GDP, considering "as exceptional an excess over the reference value which results from a negative growth rate or from the accumulated loss of output during a protracted period of very low growth relative to potential growth" (p. 33). (3) A clarification of the term "all other relevant factors" in the assessment of a country's deficit, taking into account the fiscal consequences of structural reforms and "financial contributions to fostering international solidarity and to achieving European policy goals, notably the unification of Europe" (p. 34). The latter would allow Germany to use German unification as a convenient excuse for its lack of fiscal discipline.[10] Notice the prominence of the terms "structural reforms" and "potential output growth," which are wide open for interpretation. In view of the huge uncertainty of any estimates of the fiscal consequences of structural reforms[11] and potential

---

[9] See Fatas et al. (2003) for a review of the reform debate and proposals.

[10] Sims and Miller (2005).

[11] See Beetsma and Debrun (2004) and IMF (2004) for a discussion.

output growth, national governments will be able to specify whatever they wish as excuses for large deficits.

Clearly, the governments' request for more flexibility in the EDP and the SGP was odd, because the procedures contained a lot of room for judgment from the beginning and the numerical criteria were never meant to be binding thresholds. While many economists participating in the public debate affirmed the need to take into account cyclical conditions, public investment, and the quality of economic policies, they overlooked the simple fact that judgments of this kind were already possible under the existing rules.[12] Notably for the themes of this book, one part of the overall reform is that ECOFIN has placed more stress on the importance of domestic fiscal institutions. Those institutions are supposed to be complementary to member state commitments under the Stability and Growth Pact, with stability and convergence programs to include a section on the "institutional features of public finances."

Fiscal Performance under the EMU Fiscal Rules

Government Debt, Deficits, and Spending

We now turn to fiscal performance in the EU. Table 7.1 shows the evolution of general government debt in the EU since 1992. Between

Table 7.1. *Government Debt since 1992*

	Change in Debt Ratio (percentage)			
Period	All EU States	Large States	Intermediate States	Small States
1992–1997	15.8	18.8	4.1	3.3
1998–2003	–4.7	–4.9	–10.5	–7.1

Source: European Economy Statistical Appendix Spring 2002, Fall 2003.

---

[12] For example, the Commission (2002) and Buti and van den Noord (2003) propose to focus on structural balances rather than the actual deficit, a suggestion that was already incorporated in the 2001 Code of Conduct. Blanchard and Giavazzi (2004) call for a "golden rule" excluding investment spending from the budget, which the EDP rules hint at. Coeuré and Pisani-Ferry (2003) recommend that the emphasis should be shifted to the debt ratio.

1992 and 1997, the average debt ratio of the EU member states increased by almost 16%. It peaked at 75.2% in 1996, up from about 60% in 1991. In 1997, fiscal data from which was used as the basis for the May 1998 decision on which countries could enter the monetary union, it still stood at 75%. Between 1998 and 2003, the average debt ratio fell by 4.7%. Considering that this period was one of strong economic growth, this is no great achievement. In most recent years, the debt ratio has started to increase again. Judged from average performance, therefore, EMU countries did not reduce their debt ratios over the past thirteen years and the data suggest that the process for fiscal consolidation that started with the Maastricht Treaty was rather unsuccessful.

Behind this average performance, however, are very different patterns for individual countries. A few countries already managed to reduce their debt ratios during the second half of the 1980s: Denmark, Ireland, Luxembourg, Portugal, Sweden, and the United Kingdom. Table 7.1 shows that the debt ratio of the large states, Germany, France, Spain, and the United Kingdom, rose by almost 19% between 1992 and 1997. In contrast, it rose by only very small amounts in the intermediate and small states. After 1998, it fell by only 5% in the large states, but much more substantially in the intermediate and small states. In fact, the debt ratios of France, Germany, and Portugal rose over the five years from 1999 to 2003, while Belgium, Denmark, Spain, Italy, the Netherlands, Sweden, and the United Kingdom achieved further, significant reductions. Thus, the fiscal rule imposed by the Maastricht Treaty seems to have done very little to stabilize the debt ratio on average and its effectiveness seems to vary strongly across countries.

All EU countries except Greece and Austria already saw improvements in their budget balances in the second half of the 1980s, when economic growth had improved in Europe compared to the late 1970s and early 1980s. Ireland, Belgium, Portugal, and Sweden saw the strongest improvements comparing the averages of 1986–1991 with those of 1980–1985. In contrast, comparing the average surplus ratios from 1992–1998 with those from 1986–1991 reveals that only five states achieved improvements after the adoption of the Maastricht Treaty, Belgium, Greece, Ireland, Italy, and the Netherlands. The larger states, Germany, France, Spain, and the United Kingdom, all had increasing deficits relative to GDP during this period. Average deficits generally improved after 1998, but this may have been due to the strong economic growth during 1999–2000. As the European economies moved into a recession, surplus ratios began to fall again in most EU countries.

Discretionary Fiscal Policy

Fiscal outcomes such as deficit ratios are determined by both fiscal policy and endogenous economic developments; for a general discussion of the role of discretionary fiscal policy and automatic stabilizers under EMU, see, among others, Stark and Manzke (2002). As noted by Blöndal (2003, p. 8), annual economic growth rates are the most important determinants of fiscal performance in the short run. It is, therefore, necessary to separate the effects of policy from the effects of economic growth to see how much of the observed developments can be attributed to government policy as opposed to windfall gains and losses from strong economic growth and recessions. In this section, we use the growth-accounting approach proposed in Hughes Hallett et al. (2001) for that purpose. Separating the effects of growth and policy requires some assumption about the relationship of economic growth to changes in this ratio. To do this, we start from the observed primary surplus ratio, s, for a given year:

$$s_t = \frac{R_t - G_t}{Y_t} = (r_t - g_t), \tag{1}$$

where R denotes government revenues, G noninterest government spending, Y GDP, $r = R/Y$, and $g = G/Y$. The annual change in this ratio is

$$\Delta s_t = \frac{\Delta R_t - \Delta G_t}{Y_{t-1}} - \frac{\Delta Y_t}{Y_{t-1}}(r_t - g_t). \tag{2}$$

We define a "neutral" fiscal policy as one that keeps the average tax rate and the volume of government spending unchanged over the previous year, that is, $r_t = r_{t-1}$ and $\Delta G_t = 0$.[13] With this definition, the contribution of economic growth to the change in the surplus ratio is

$$\Delta s_t^g = \left(\frac{\Delta Y_t}{Y_{t-1}}\right) g_t. \tag{3}$$

---

[13] The assumption of a constant tax ratio is in line with empirical estimates of macroeconomic tax functions in OECD countries and does not contradict the fact that income taxes are progressive at the individual level.

Using this definition, we obtain the policy-induced change in the surplus ratio or the fiscal impulse as

$$\Delta s_t^P = \Delta s_t - \Delta s_t^g. \tag{4}$$

This definition attributes any change in the average tax rate and all changes in government spending to discretionary fiscal policy.[14] We use this part as our indicator of discretionary fiscal policy, since it measures the active contribution of any policy actions to observed changes in the deficit ratio. Note that a positive value indicates a discretionary fiscal contraction, while a negative value indicates a discretionary fiscal expansion.

Table 7.2 reports the averages and standard deviations of the fiscal impulses for the EU countries from 1981 to 2003. The table bears a number of interesting observations. First, we note that in three EU countries, Belgium, Denmark, and Germany, the volatility of fiscal impulses was smaller after 1991 than before. In these countries, the Maastricht fiscal rule seems to have induced a smoother course of fiscal policy over time. For the remaining countries, however, we could not reject the hypothesis of equal variances.

Second, we find that the average fiscal impulse was larger in six EU countries in 1992–2003 than in 1981–1991, and smaller in the other eight EU countries, indicating a less expansionary discretionary fiscal policy in the first and a more expansionary policy in the second group. Only in Ireland, however, is the difference in means statistically significant, and there, policy became more expansionary. This suggests that to the extent that some EU countries achieved reductions in their deficit ratios in the 1990s, they benefited from the effects of economic growth rather than discretionary fiscal contractions. We also tested for differences in the means between 1981–1985 and 1986–1991, but the results were not significant.

Third, we find that the average fiscal impulse in 1999–2003 was more expansionary than the 1992–2003 average in all EU countries except Austria and Portugal. Thus, fiscal policy has become more expansionary in all EU countries except Austria and Portugal since the start of EMU in

---

[14] Alternatively, one might use the cyclically adjusted budget balances as published by the European Commission or the OECD and used in Chapter 4. These estimates, however, are based on past data and policies. If the introduction of fiscal rules induced changes in the comovements of cyclical output and budget balances, they could be quite misleading. Buti and van den Noord (2003, 2004b) use a similar approach and reach similar conclusions regarding fiscal policy in the early years of EMU.

Table 7.2. *Fiscal Impulses in the EU*

Country	Standard Deviation 81–03	Average 81–91	Average 92–03	p-value (a)	Average 99–03	p-value (b)
BE	1.44 0.76 (0.02)	–0.25	–0.67	0.41	–1.10	0.05
DK	2.13 1.06 (0.02)	–0.28	–1.22	0.12	–1.28	0.17
D	2.16 0.61 (0.00)	–1.28	–0.62	0.17	–0.98	0.08
GR	2.76	–0.37	–0.89	0.34	–2.28	0.00
E	0.98	–0.87	–0.75	0.38	–0.81	0.41
F	0.81	–1.12	–1.05	0.85	–1.48	0.10
IE	1.93	–0.20	–2.70	0.00	–3.17	0.20
I	1.32	–0.59	–0.38	0.36	–1.01	0.08
L	1.86	. . .	–2.00	. . .	–2.44	0.05
NL	1.42	–0.69	–1.34	0.14	–1.58	0.58
AT	1.23	–1.03	–0.98	0.46	–0.77	0.45
P	1.96	–0.24	–0.92	0.21	–0.71	0.36
SF	1.93	–1.51	–1.03	0.29	–1.54	0.19
S	2.21	–0.72	–1.39	0.24	–2.58	0.07
UK	1.40	–0.99	–1.18	0.38	–2.04	0.06

Note: For Belgium, Denmark, and Germany we report sample standard deviations for 1981–1991 (upper entry), 1992–2003 (lower entry), and the *p*-value of an F-test for equal variances. For all other countries, the F-test for equal variances did not reject the nullhypothesis. The *p*-value (a) is the *p*-value of a t-test for equal means (one-sided test) between 1981–1991 and 1992–2003, accounting for unequal variances where necessary. The *p*-value (b) is the corresponding one-sided test for the mean of 1991–1998 being larger than the mean of 1999–2003.

1999. The changes are significant in eight EU countries: Belgium, Germany, Greece, France, Italy, Luxembourg, Sweden, and the United Kingdom. Note that this group includes all large countries except Spain. This is significant, as the threat of not making it into EMU as a result of lax fiscal policies was no longer looming over the European countries once EMU had started. Elsewhere, we have dubbed this observation "consolidation fatigue" (von Hagen and Harden 1994). EU governments used the first chance to relax fiscal policy.

To gain some further insights into the conduct of fiscal policy in the EU, we pool the fiscal impulses of all member states in a regression model. The data exclude Luxembourg, for which we do not have the fiscal data for all years of the 1980s. Table 7.3 reports the results for the period from 1981 to 1991. Our baseline model projects the annual fiscal impulse on a constant, its own lag, the growth rate of real GDP, and the lagged ratio of government debt to GDP. We also include a "crisis" dummy

Table 7.3. *Empirical Models of Fiscal Impulses in the EU, 1981–1991*

	Dependent Variable: Fiscal Impulse		
	Model 1	Model 2	Model 3
Constant	−0.72	−0.94	−0.70
p-value	0.053	0.02	0.035
Lagged Fiscal Impulse	−0.28		
p-value	0.73		
Crisis Dummy	−6.31	−5.82	−5.17
p-value	0.00	0.000	0.0005
Lagged Debt Ratio	0.013	0.013	0.014
p-value	0.008	0.008	0.004
Real GDP Growth Rate	−0.27	−0.21	−0.21
p-value	0.0004	0.003	0.003
Election Dummy			−0.89
p-value			0.002
R^2	0.21	0.17	0.22
F-test (*p*-value)	0.000	0.000	0.000
Number of Observations	141	154	154

accounting for the fiscal effects of the Swedish and Finnish crises in 1991. Country fixed effects were not significant and were dropped from the model.

The table reveals some interesting properties of fiscal policy in the EU. First, the coefficient on the lagged fiscal impulse is negative, indicating that governments tend to reverse part of a given fiscal impulse in the following year. However, the coefficient is not statistically significant and we drop the lag from the model. Second, the coefficient on the lagged debt ratio is positive, indicating that discretionary policy reacts with a fiscal contraction to an increase in public debt relative to GDP. This can be regarded as a necessary condition for fiscal sustainability, as the debt ratio would be unbounded without such a reaction. The result also confirms the finding in Hughes Hallett et al. (2002) that the likelihood of fiscal consolidations in EU and OECD member states during the period from 1960 to 1999 rises when the debt ratio increases. Third, the coefficient on real GDP growth is significantly negative, indicating that discretionary fiscal policy tightens when output slows and eases when output growth rises. This procyclical pattern of discretionary fiscal policy in Europe is consistent with previous results.[15] It suggests that governments systematically counteract automatic stabilizers built into the tax system. Finally, we add a dummy "election" to our model, which is 1 in election years and 0 in all other years.[16] The result is reported as Model 3 in Table 7.3. The election dummy has a coefficient of (–0.89), which is statistically highly significant. EU governments in the 1980s undertook discretionary fiscal expansions during election years.

Table 7.4 presents a similar analysis for the 1990s. Again, we start by regressing fiscal impulses on an own lag, the lagged debt–GDP ratio and the real GDP growth rate. As in the 1980s, fiscal impulses are not persistent over time. Thus, we drop the lagged fiscal impulse in Model 2. As before, the lagged debt ratio appears with a significant, positive coefficient: that is, the sufficient condition for sustainability continues to hold. Note that the coefficients on the lagged debt ratio are very similar in the 1980s and 1990s and are not statistically different from each other. Thus, the fiscal rules of the 1990s did not affect the governments' adjustment to a buildup of government debt. Finally, the fiscal impulses remained procyclical in the 1990s.

Next, we add an "EMU" dummy to the model, which is 0 for all years from 1991 to 1998 and 1 starting in 1999. Table 7.4 shows that this dummy has a coefficient of (–0.73), which is statistically significant. This confirms the hypothesis of *consolidation fatigue*: once the threat of not making it into EMU because of excessive deficits was relieved, fiscal policy became more expansionary in the EU. Note that given the procyclicality of discretionary fiscal policy observed before, this fiscal expansion cannot be explained by the weak economic performance of the EU economies after the year 2000.

---

[15] See e.g., Brunila and Martinez-Mongay (2002), IMF (2001a), Fonseca Marinheiro (2005). Buti and van den Noord (2004b) find that their measure of the fiscal impulse is counter-cyclical, but they use output gaps rather than growth rates to measure cyclical effects. We also estimated fiscal impulses corrected for the trend in the ratio of government spending to GDP, approximating the trend by five-year moving averages. We did this to account for the fact that spending ratios generally trended downward in the 1980s and 1990s in many EU countries. The interpretation then is that the trend is not part of annual discretionary fiscal policy. The main difference in the results compared to those that are not detrended is that the lagged debt ratio no longer appears with a positive coefficient. That is, the negative trend in the spending ratio reflects the governments' reaction to the positive trend in the debt ratios.

[16] The election dates from 1981 to 1991 are taken from Lijphart's Elections Archive (www.dodgson.ucsc.edu/lij) and from the reports on "National Elections" in various issues of *Electoral Studies*. Post-1991 election dates are taken from www.cnn.com/world/election. watch.

Table 7.4. *Empirical Model of Fiscal Impulses in the EU, 1992–2003*

	Model 1	Model 2	Model 3	Model 4
Constant	−1.24	−1.26	−0.83	−0.93
p-value	0.002	0.001	0.038	0.023
Lagged Fiscal Impulse	0.016			
p-value	0.85			
Lagged Debt Ratio	0.0097	0.0099	0.008	0.008
p-value	0.048	0.042	0.089	0.089
Real GDP Growth Rate	−0.19	−0.20	−0.19	−0.20
p-value	0.001	0.001	0.0009	0.0004
EMU Dummy			−0.73	−0.42
p-value			0.004	0.15
Election Dummy				0.54
p-value				0.16
(Election Dummy)*(EMU Dummy)				−1.21
p-value				0.037
R^2	0.08	0.09	0.13	0.15
F-test (p-value)	0.02	0.0006	0.0004	0.00005
Number of Observations	168	168	168	168

Note, also, that the intercept of Model 3 is smaller in absolute value than the intercept of Model 2 in Table 7.4. This suggests that discretionary fiscal policy was less expansionary than in the 1980s before the start of EMU. Hence, the fiscal rules seem to have had some effect in the desired direction between 1991 and 1998, when the penalty for exceeding the deficit limits was large. Finally, we note that including the EMU dummy raises the p-value of the lagged debt ratio somewhat.[17]

Next, we include the election dummy in the model. Since our previous results indicate that the EU fiscal rules lost bite after 1998, we interact this dummy with the EMU dummy. Thus, the coefficient on the election dummy picks up any election-year effect on discretionary fiscal policy between 1992 and 1998, while the sum of the coefficients on the election dummy and the interactive dummy picks up the effect of elections on

[17] We also estimated a model interacting the EMU dummy with the lagged debt ratio and the real GDP growth rate. Neither interactive term had a significant coefficient. Nevertheless, the coefficient on the interacted lagged debt ratio was positive and the coefficient on the lagged debt ratio itself was 0.011 with a p-value of 0.06.

discretionary fiscal policy since the start of EMU. Model 4 in Table 7.4 has the results. The coefficient on the election dummy has a positive sign, but it is not statistically significant. In contrast, the coefficient on the interactive dummy has a negative sign and is statistically significant. This suggests that since EMU started, governments have systematically run fiscal expansions during elections years. This result is consistent with similar findings in Buti and van den Noord (2004b).[18] The electoral effect is not present, however, in the run-up to Stage III of EMU.

The empirical results are consistent with the career-concern model of the political business cycle, if one assumes that voters put a high priority on joining EMU during the 1990s. As long as EMU membership was not secured, voters rewarded signals of fiscal discipline as the latter would increase the chance of getting into the monetary union. Governments, therefore, had an incentive to undertake discretionary fiscal contractions in election years in order to look tough, and they did. Once EMU membership was secured, the old pattern of political budget cycles reemerged.

This result indicates that the fiscal rules of the EMU framework affected government behavior as long as voters put a high priority on fiscal discipline. This suggests that the electoral process is critical in enforcing fiscal rules at the national level. For fiscal rules to be effective, voters must be aware of the rules and perceive that violating them would carry a significant cost. Thus, the framework setting up the rules must have sufficient visibility and breaking the rules must have consequences voters care about. This seems not to be the case in the EU after the start of the monetary union.

EMU Fiscal Rules and the Budget Process

We can now consider the link between fiscal rules and budgeting institutions. Two aspects of this arise. First, the EU fiscal rules (EDP), with their emphasis on numerical limits for the budget deficit and general government debt, and annual stability programs (SGP) setting targets for deficits and governments spending closely resemble the contract approach to centralization of the budget process. Table 7.5 pursues this similarity in more detail, using the

---

[18] Preliminary results reported in von Hagen (2003) using data up to 2001 suggested that the election effects are stronger in preelection years than in election years. Controlling for election-year effects, we do not find preelection year effects in our sample. This, too, is consistent with Buti and van den Noord (2004b).

Table 7.5. *Fiscal Rules Index, EU Countries*

Country	Horizon	Commit-ment	Coalition	Stability Program	Shock Rules	MF Implementation	Fiscal Rule Index
Countries Following Contracts Approach							
B	4	4	4	2	4	1	15.0
DK	3	2	0	0	4	2	9.3
Ei	2	2	4	3	0	3	11.3
L	4	4	4	3	4	2	17.0
NL	3	4	4	3	4	1	15.3
P	2	4	0	0.5	4	2	10.5
SF	3	3	4	1	0	1	8.7
SW	2	4	2	1.5	0	0	6.8
Countries Following Delegation Approach							
A	2	3	0	1.5	0	4	8.8
D	3	3	0	1.5	0	2	7.5
E	3	2	0	1.5	0	3	7.8
F	2	3	0	1.5	0	4	8.8
Gr	2	2	0	0.5	0	4	7.2
I	3	2	0	1.5	0	3	7.8
UK	2	3	0	3.5	4	4	14.8

Note: Fiscal Rule Index = 2*(Horizon + Commitment + Coalition)/3 + Stability Program + Shock Rules + MF Execution.

institutional data from 2001. The upper half of the table lists the countries expected to apply the contracts approach: Belgium, Denmark, Finland, Ireland, Luxembourg, the Netherlands, Portugal, and Sweden. The lower half of the table lists the countries expected to follow the delegation approach: Austria, Germany, Spain, France, Greece, Italy, and the United Kingdom.

Hallerberg et al. (2001) provide institutional data about the budgeting practices in the EU countries regarding specifically the governments' commitment to fiscal rules and the connectedness with the European fiscal regime. Some of those items appear in Chapter 3, but there is also information about the connection between national- and European Union–level fiscal plans that appear in the 2001 report that is useful here.[19] We look at the following aspects: the time horizon of a government's multi-annual fiscal program, the degree of commitment to annual fiscal targets, the anchoring of the fiscal targets in the coalition agreement, the connection between the national budget and the national stability program, the existence of clear rules for dealing with shocks to expenditures or revenues during the fiscal year, and the strength of the finance minister to enforce the budget law during the implementation phase of the budget. We use the numerical coding of the institutional data to construct a "fiscal rules index." A large value on this index indicates the following: a relatively long time horizon of the multiannual fiscal program, a strong political commitment to the annual fiscal targets, fiscal targets being written into the coalition agreement, a close connection between the fiscal targets embedded in the budget and those expressed in the stability program and between the annual budget process and the process of writing and updating the stability programs, the prevalence of rules for dealing with unexpected spending or revenue developments, and a relatively strong finance minister during the implementation phase. A low value on this index indicates a short time horizon or the nonexistence of a multiannual fiscal program, the interpretation of fiscal targets as being merely indicative, no mention of fiscal targets in the coalition agreement, only a loose connection between the fiscal targets spelled out in the budget and those of the stability program and between the annual budget process and the process of writing and updating the stability program, no rules for dealing with revenue or expenditure shocks, and a weak position of the finance minister in the implementation phase of the budget.

---

[19] The focus of Chapter 3 is on the evolution of fiscal institutions over two decades, so we include material on fiscal institutions that are relevant only in the EMU period in this chapter.

The last row of Table 7.5 reports the fiscal rule index. The table shows that Luxembourg has the strongest fiscal rule in the EU, followed by the Netherlands, Belgium, the United Kingdom, Ireland, Portugal, and Denmark. The median fiscal rule index among the EU countries is 8.8. The table shows that countries expected to follow the contracts approach generally have stronger fiscal rules than expected delegation countries. Sweden and Finland are the only two expected contracts countries with a rules index below the median, while the United Kingdom is the only expected delegation country with an index strictly above the median. The difference between the two groups is statistically significant (a chi-square test has the value $X^2 = 5.53$, $p = 0.019$). This shows that there is a significant, positive correlation between the expected contracts and hard fiscal rules, as well as between expected delegation and soft fiscal rules. The evidence thus suggests that countries expected to adopt fiscal contracts used the framework and pressure of the Maastricht process to develop strong fiscal rules. The expected delegation countries except the United Kingdom did not follow the same pattern.

Considering the individual items, Table 7.5 shows that the fiscal programs in expected contract states generally have longer time horizons than in expected delegation states, that the degree of commitment is stronger than in expected delegation states, and that the fiscal targets in all expected contract states but in no expected delegation state are anchored in coalition agreements. Furthermore, a majority of the expected contract states have explicit rules for dealing with revenue or expenditure shocks. The United Kingdom is the only expected delegation state where that is true.

The correlation between the fiscal rule index and the budget surplus ratios across the EU states is not statistically different from zero. As we suggest earlier in this book, the reason is that states with good budgeting institutions under a delegation form of fiscal governance achieved a high degree of fiscal discipline similar to that of states with strong fiscal rules. However, if we take the five states with a fiscal rules index above the EU average of 10.9, we see that a hard fiscal rule does make a difference. These states are Belgium, Ireland, Luxembourg, the Netherlands, and the United Kingdom. All five experienced a negative annual growth rate of the debt-GDP ratio since the start of EMU. For the states with soft fiscal rules (i.e., an index below the mean) this is true for five out of ten. A chi-square test indicates that the difference in performance is statistically significant ($X^2 = 3.75$, $p = 0.052$). If we define the medium-term goal of "close to balance" under the SGP as an average surplus ratio above (–1.0) since the start of EMU, all five states with hard fiscal rules fulfill that condition, but only four out of six states with soft rules ($X^2 = 5.0, p = 0.025$). Finally, since the start of EMU, all five states with hard fiscal rules had an average expenditure ratio of at least 2% below the 1992–1998 average. For the states with soft rules, this is true only for six out of 10 ($X^2 = 2.73, p = 0.098$). Thus states with hard fiscal rules have shown a better average fiscal performance since the start of EMU – an example for Schick's (2003, 8) verdict that "fiscal rules are effective only if they are supported by other changes in budgeting."

Projections and Compliance under EMU

Another way to consider this issue is to look at the compliance with projections in the stability and convergence programs. In Chapter 4, we presented evidence on forecasting errors. We suggested that there were three reasons why there would be errors – unexpected economic developments, governmental nonadherence to preannounced targets, and an intentional, cautionary bias that reduced the likelihood of unexpected deficits. The beginning of Stage III of EMU included the requirement that all states make forecasts for five years (or $t - 1$ to $t + 3$). This means that expected delegation states must make the same forecasts as contract states even though those forecasts do not play the same domestic role as they do in contract states. Our expectation is that delegation states therefore are less likely to respect their future forecasts.

To measure how well a given state sticks to its forecasts, we would like to separate out the discretionary action of a government from growth effects. This means that a measure like the difference between the average projected change and actual changes in the budgetary balance is not sufficient because it includes changes due to economic growth and the operation of automatic stabilizers. We try to control for the growth forecast error to get at the discretionary element. To do this, we use again the measures of the fiscal stance already introduced in Chapter 4.

Table 7.6 presents the results for this discrepancy between the envisaged consolidation and actual outcomes for different sample periods and using interaction effects. The first three columns refer to simple changes in budgetary balances as share of GDP. Looking at the first two columns, a negative significant coefficient is found for delegation states for the programs released from 1998 onward. In the third column we differentiate between the period before and the period from 1998 onward using

Table 7.6. *Forecast Error in Projected Fiscal Stance (OLS Regression)*

	Balance			Fiscal Stance (Constant Growth)		
	1991–2004	1998–2004	1991–2004	1991–2004	1998–2004	1991–2004
Constant	−0.17 (0.27)	0.30 (0.49)	−0.08 (0.25)	−0.09 (0.28)	−0.67* (0.39)	0.01 (0.23)
Output Gap	−0.09* (0.04)	−0.03 (0.09)	−0.07 (0.05)	−0.09* (0.05)	−0.07 (0.10)	−0.08 (0.06)
Output Volatility	−0.04 (0.07)	−0.20 (0.16)	−0.07 (0.07)	−0.01 (0.08)	−0.15 (0.13)	−0.05 (0.07)
Convergence Need	0.03 (0.04)	−0.04 (0.12)	0.04 (0.03)	0.05 (0.04)	0.06 (0.09)	0.07** (0.03)
Election	0.03 (0.19)	0.29 (0.25)	0.03 (0.19)	0.16 (0.15)	0.32 (0.26)	0.15 (0.14)
Veto-player	−0.05 (0.39)	−0.77 (0.67)	0.03 (0.41)	0.07 (0.35)	−0.58 (0.61)	0.13 (0.37)
Delegation	−0.21 (0.22)	−0.70** (0.25)		−0.18 (0.23)	−0.87*** (0.20)	
Contract	0.31 (0.24)	0.28 (0.29)		0.12 (0.23)	−0.17 (0.21)	
Delegation (pre-1997)			0.18 (0.20)			0.20 (0.23)
Delegation (post-1997)			−0.38 (0.22)			−0.35 (0.23)
Contract (pre-1997)			0.32 (0.27)			0.10 (0.25)
Contract (post-1997)			0.25 (0.25)			0.07 (0.24)
F-test Delegation (pre) = delegation (post)			15.21***			7.17***
F-test Contract (pre) = contract (post)			0.16			0.02
Test Delegation (post) = contract (post)			8.47***			5.45**
Ad. R^2	0.16	0.17	0.20	0.13	0.17	0.17
F-test	11.96***	4.32***	13.03***	8.88***	5.20***	11.11***
Nobs	139	90	139	138	90	138

Note: Asterisks indicate significance at a 1% (***), 5% (**), and 10% (*) level.

time dummies and interacting them with the governance dummies. The results indicate that the coefficient estimated for the period from 1998 onward is significantly smaller than for the earlier subsample. There is no clear difference for contract states. In the post-1997 period, the coefficient for delegation regimes is smaller than the one obtained for contract states. This result holds at a 1% significance level. Columns 4 to 6 report the results of the same exercise using the fiscal stance as a dependent variable. Qualitatively the results are identical although the coefficients for the contract form of governance are somewhat smaller and therefore not all results attain the same significance level. Interestingly, the coefficient for the convergence need carries a positive coefficient, which is, however, generally not different from 0 at standard significance levels.

Preserving Sustainable Public Finances: A Sustainability Council for EMU

The experience recounted previously and the institutional considerations discussed in the first section of the chapter indicate that the fiscal framework of EMU needs improvements in two directions: less focus on short-run fiscal flows and stronger surveillance and monitoring procedures. At the heart of the proposal that follows is the idea to replace the rigid rules by a judgmental assessment of the fiscal situation and outlook of each euro-area member state and to entrust the judgment of sustainability to an independent institution, the European Sustainability Council. This would solve the basic credibility problem of the current framework. The proper link between the EMU's long-run interest in sustainability and short-run constraints and exigencies on fiscal policy would be preserved by the independence of the Sustainability Council from short-term political pressures.[20] Since the council would strictly focus on sustainability and it would have no operational powers in fiscal policy setting, there would no risk that it might undermine the independence of the ECB. The council would support the functioning of monetary policy by exerting political pressure on governments to align their fiscal policies with the long-term sustainability requirement.

---

[20] Our proposal builds on work originally presented in von Hagen and Harden (1994, 1995), further elaborated in Eichengreen, Hausmann, and von Hagen (1999). Wyplosz (2002) presents a proposal based on these ideas.

The Sustainability Council would be legally set up by the European Parliament, which would also provide its resources. Its members should be individuals of high public reputation as experts on public finance or public finance management. Membership in the Sustainability Council need not be a full-time activity for all members, although the chair and the vice chair should have full-time professional appointments. The Sustainability Council should have a small staff and secretariat and should have guaranteed access to all relevant information at the national and Community levels. The Sustainability Council should have the right to use the services of the European Commission and of the national government accounting courts to support its work.

The idea of creating yet another institution at the European level may seem unattractive to some. After all, the current European structure with its network of overlapping policy processes and its opaque institutional setup seems to call for fewer rather than more policymaking bodies. Yet the Sustainability Council would improve the transparency and visibility of the current institutional framework for public finances in EMU without interfering with the independence of the ECB. Anticipating another criticism, some may find the idea of delegating some authority over public finances – historically the core of parliamentary rights – to an independent body as incompatible with modern democracy. Yet, as we will argue, a properly designed Sustainability Council can improve the functioning of democratic government rather than limit it (von Hagen and Harden 1994). The delimitation of the Sustainability Council's authorities and competences is the key issue here. In fact, several countries in the EU have already moved in this direction in recent years.

Mandate

The Sustainability Council would have the sole statutory task of safeguarding the sustainability of public finances in the euro area. While this is the counterpart of the ECB's principal task of maintaining price stability, the Sustainability Council has no need of a secondary objective – supporting the general economic policies in the euro area – since it would have no *operative* role in fiscal policy. The use of the instruments of fiscal policy would be left entirely to the national governments. Within the EMU framework, the function of the Sustainability Council would be to make the implications of the governments' intertemporal budget constraint explicit. To fulfill its task, the Sustainability Council must assess the financial position of a government in all relevant aspects, produce forecasts of future financial developments, and, on this basis, evaluate the risk of future fiscal crises.

Like "price stability," the empirical content of the concept of sustainability of public finances has to be made operational. An important part of the Sustainability Council's task is, therefore, to develop a framework for the assessment of public finances and for making forecasts and judgments. This, again, is similar to the task of the ECB. Yet, it is unlikely that the Sustainability Council will settle on a unique number in this definition as the ECB did for price stability. In fact, there is no need to do that, since, in contrast to the ECB's case, the Sustainability Council is not charged with the implementation of sustainability and, therefore, its definition of sustainability is not needed to hold it accountable for its actions in the short run. Thus, the Sustainability Council is free to develop an empirical concept of sustainability that overcomes the basic problem, that is, that general numerical limits are not meaningful in this context.

The fact that the Sustainability Council would not have the authority to set taxes or expenditures for a country is key for its democratic legitimacy. The Sustainability Council's mandate would be to make the limits that monetary union imposes on national fiscal policy choices explicit. This is a legitimate interest of the union, and it can be assumed that national parliaments and governments, by agreeing to enter into a monetary union dedicated to price stability, agreed to accept those limits. Thus, the creation of a Sustainability Council does not take away further sovereignty from national governments compared to what is implied already by entering EMU.

Nevertheless, the Sustainability Council could hardly judge the sustainability of a country's public finances without taking into account a view of the proper size and structure of the public sector in that country. While the assessment of a country's fiscal situation and outlook may contain recommendations regarding the total volume and distribution of public spending and revenues, fixing these volumes would be beyond the mandate of the Sustainability Council. Thus, the Sustainability Council may find itself in disagreement with national governments, precisely because the latter desire an increase in the public sector. Governments could improve the process and ensure that the Sustainability Council's decisions were linked to democratic political choice by announcing, on their part, multiannual targets for the size and structure of the public sector. Such targets, if announced by a government upon taking office, would most likely become part of each political party's electoral platform and, thereby, improve the democratic accountability of the governments in public finances.

Method of Operation

The national governments would submit their annual and medium-term fiscal plans to the Sustainability Council, which would judge the compatibility of the implied change in general government debt with sustainability. The Sustainability Council would make its judgment and the underlying reasoning public in a written report to the European Parliament and propose adjustments from the national governments.

Note the substantial difference between the change in general government debt, the main focus of the Sustainability Council, and the reference values of the Maastricht Treaty. The treaty defines a deficit on an accruals basis, implying that some items are excluded that the Sustainability Council would cover in its limit, such as privatization receipts, capital ("below-the-line") transactions, or changes in the value of foreign-currency-denominated debt. The Sustainability Council would, therefore, take a more encompassing view and judgment. Furthermore, the change in general government debt considered by the Sustainability Council would set an unambiguous limit on government borrowing. In contrast to the EDP, there would be neither room nor need for judgment once this had been established.

The Sustainability Council could have procedures that allow for involvement with different degrees of intensity for different countries. For example, the Sustainability Council could apply a simple first test using some rather broad-brushed analysis and turn to a more intensive investigation only in cases where the first test is failed. The 3% and 60% criteria of the Excessive Deficit Procedure are examples for such a first test. This would likely reduce the number of countries investigated intensively each year and, therefore, allow for a smaller administration.

To fulfill its task, the Sustainability Council would produce an annual report on the sustainability of public finances in each member state and submit it to the European Parliament. In the preparation of the report, the Sustainability Council would, without prejudice to its independence, allow for participation of the national governments and other institutions such as the ECB in the process, for instance, by holding hearings with experts and representatives of the relevant bodies. The Sustainability Council should use all relevant information for its tasks and be able to obtain that information.

As a general rule, the Sustainability Council would present its report in the capital of the country concerned. This is important, because a general

European public still does not exist in the EU. Since its effectiveness relies on the Sustainability Council's ability to mobilize public opinion and debate, it is critical for the council to talk directly to the media and the public, especially when it has reasons to criticize government policies. A voice from Brussels would hardly be heard in the individual countries. Furthermore, the Sustainability Council should seek opportunities to talk directly to the parliaments of countries where the sustainability of public finances is questionable. Where similar institutions exist at the national level, such as the High Council of Public Finances in Belgium, it would be natural and useful for the Sustainability Council to talk to these institutions both in the preparation of its report and when the report is presented in public.

Enforcement

Under the European Treaty, member states of EMU have the unconditional obligation to safeguard the sustainability of public finances. If the Sustainability Council has the mandate of defining and operationalizing what sustainability means and implies for national fiscal policies in the short run, this obligation implies that national governments are committed to implementing the Sustainability Council's judgments and prescriptions.

The question remains, how can this commitment be enforced? The current framework of public finances in EMU relies on two enforcement mechanisms, peer pressure and the possibility to impose financial fines on countries with persistent excessive deficits. But the effectiveness of these enforcement mechanisms remains very much in doubt. While peer pressure has not worked with the large states, Germany, France, and Italy in particular, the effectiveness of the threat of financial fines remains to be tested in the EMU framework. But the lenience with which Germany's fiscal developments were treated in 2002 and 2003 suggests that the European Commission and the council wish to avoid that test.

It is clear that the Sustainability Council can rely neither on peer pressure nor on financial fines. As a Community institution, it does not talk to the national governments in the same way as ECOFIN does. At the same time, the council could not impose penalties on national governments, because its role is different from the role of the Community's European Court of Justice. Therefore, the Sustainability Council would have to rely primarily on political pressures generated through public to enforce its judgments. To do so, the council must have the right to make its judgments and recommendations fully public in a timely manner. This includes the right to make press declarations on individual cases and to educate the public though public statements about the importance and the proper interpretation and implementation of sustainability. It also includes the right to talk to the European Parliament and to national parliaments. The Sustainability Council must have the right to make differentiated judgments on the fiscal situation of each member state in public, pointing to risks and problems as it sees fit. Finally, in order to create clear competences and preclude political haggling, the Sustainability Council should have the sole right to recommend to the ECOFIN Council the imposition of financial fines under the Excessive Deficit Procedure of the European Treaty, and the ECOFIN Council should be required to take a vote on that proposal.

Enforcement in this way can only work if the public regards the Sustainability Council as an authority on this matter. A council making unreasonable judgments or posing unreasonable demands on national governments frequently would soon lose attention in the public debate, as would a council basing its judgments on shaky analysis and questionable assumptions. The need to rely on public opinion, therefore, creates a strong incentive for the Sustainability Council to exert good judgment, to use its public role carefully, and to refrain from making public announcements and hinting at impending fiscal crises unless the situation is truly severe.

Finally, governments in EMU should have an opportunity to prepare a response in reasonable time and not be taken completely by surprise by announcements of the Sustainability Council. This can be achieved by demanding that the Sustainability Council forward its assessment of a country to the relevant government a few days before it is made public.

Independence, Accountability, and Transparency

To fulfill its role properly and make unbiased judgments, the Sustainability Council must enjoy full political independence of the national governments of the member states and of other Community institutions such as the European Commission. Like the independence of the European Central Bank, the independence of the Sustainability Council is determined in four statutory rules: first, a rule stating that the Sustainability Council does not take any directives from any national government of EU member states, from other national institutions of EU member states, nor from any Community institution; second, a rule stating that the Sustainability

Council has the right to develop its own framework of analysis and its own operational concept of sustainability.

The third rule determines the resources available to the Sustainability Council. This rule should fix the Sustainability Council's budget for a medium-term horizon, say, five years, and should be amendable only by a qualified majority of the votes in the European Parliament. Such a rule would shield the Sustainability Council from short-sighted attempts of politicians to make it ineffective by draining it from resources.

Fourth, the members of the Sustainability Council should be personally independent of political pressures. Following the example of the European Central Bank, personal independence can be assured by giving the council members fixed-term, nonrenewable appointments of sufficient length, say, eight years, to acquire the necessary expertise and standing in the public debate. Appointments should be staggered to assure that the Sustainability Council does not change entirely at the end of a given year, thus assuring continuity in its views and judgments. It should be impossible to dismiss members of the Sustainability Council except for severe faults of unethical or unprofessional behavior to assure that they cannot be threatened to be removed from their positions if they take decisions which are unpopular with the governments. Salaries of Sustainability Council members should be determined by a formula specified by the council's statutes and linked to the salaries of comparable EU offices.

The independence from political pressure should be balanced by appropriate mechanisms of accountability. As indicated earlier, the Sustainability Council should report to the European Parliament. The European Parliament should have the right to call the chair of the Sustainability Council for hearings and the right to dismiss the Sustainability Council in toto by qualified majority. Given the wide publicity that such an action would have, the European Parliament would do that only in cases of severe misperformance of the Sustainability Council.

The independence of the Sustainability Council should also be balanced by a high degree of transparency of operation. Limited transparency would only reduce the effectiveness of the Sustainability Council's public announcements, as it might raise doubts about the competence and unbiasedness of its deliberations and judgments. This calls for the publication of all materials relevant for a decision by the Sustainability Council as well as the minutes of its meetings. However, there is no need to do this immediately after the meeting or decision, a requirement that might affect the Sustainability Council's ability to obtain and process all relevant information. The Sustainability Council could choose a publication lag of, say, six to twelve months, within which all relevant information is published.

Apart from that, all members of the Sustainability Council should be free to express their views on the sustainability of the public finances of individual countries. This would promote open and public debate about the relevant issues in member states where sustainability is indeed at risk and, therefore, raise public pressures on the governments to correct the situation.

Appointments, Composition, and Resources

In the context of fiscal policy, the role of the Sustainability Council would be a fairly technical albeit important one. Its members should have sufficient experience in the public sector. In some member states of the EU, academics with the necessary expertise would probably be regarded as appropriate candidates, while in other member states, such candidates would count as irrelevant and the public prefer individuals with careers in international institutions such as the IMF. Since the appointment of the members would be by the European Parliament, the members of parliament could take care of such national differences in preferences through the nomination procedure. For a European institution, the question of country representation naturally arises. Since the role of the Sustainability Council is not to make policy choices, representation of all countries at all times would not be important for its legitimacy.

By decision of the European Parliament, the Sustainability Council should be vested with the resources necessary to fulfill its task. This includes a staff for producing the necessary analysis and a small secretariat. EMU member states must be required to give the Sustainability Council full and timely access to all information requested.

8

Conclusion

This book has developed a theory of fiscal governance. By "governance" we mean the package of rules, norms, and institutions that structure the way governments make a budget. We argue that the way governments decide on budgets affects the content of the budgets that are implemented. Decentralized fiscal governance, which we refer to as *fiefdom*, leads to more spending and larger budget deficits than the decision makers themselves want. The reason for this is the existence of a common pool resource problem. When such a problem exists, policymakers consider the full benefits of their spending decisions but only part of the tax burden. Centralization of the decision-making process reduces the size of the common pool resource problem.

We indicate that there are two ideal forms of fiscal governance that can provide this budget centralization. *Delegation* occurs when decision makers delegate power to one central player in the budget process who has the responsibility to consider the full tax burden. In practice, this person is usually the finance minister. Our study indicates that delegation is especially strong in countries such as the United Kingdom and France. Fiscal contracts occur when the political parties that form the government commit themselves to targets that are intended to last the life of the coalition. Such contracts are especially strong in the Netherlands and Finland.

The choice between these forms of fiscal governance depends upon the underlying political structures of a given country. There is a potential principal-agent game that affects how a form of fiscal governance functions. If there is no ideological conflict among the cabinet members, then there is no risk of agency loss when strategic powers are delegated to a finance minister. As differences among the "principals" increase, however, they no longer want to give one central player the same power. Fiscal contracts represent a viable alternative. The terms of the agreement as well as what constitutes a violation of that agreement are clear to the actors.

Our empirical work indicates that countries had better fiscal performance if they had sets of fiscal rules, institutions, and norms consistent with their expected form of fiscal governance. Those states that had one-party governments so that the ideological distance among cabinet members was small maintained fiscal discipline when they had strong finance ministers. Similarly, states that had multiparty coalition governments implying that there was a greater ideological distance among cabinet members did best when they had more complete fiscal contracts.[1] In Chapter 5, we consider why states adopt the fiscal institutions that they do. Consistently with the better policy outcomes reported earlier in the book, countries are more likely to adopt fiscal institutions that are consistent with their expected form of fiscal governance. If governments are usually one-party majority, they are more likely to have institutions that reinforce the powers of the finance minister, while countries with regular multiparty governments generally have more extensive multiannual fiscal frameworks. In addition to this more functionalist view, previous experience with the consequences of decentralized fiscal institutions also mattered; countries with a history of severe fiscal crises have more centralized fiscal institutions today.

While the first part of the book focuses on the domestic institutions of the EU-15, or the countries that composed the European Union when the euro was introduced in 1999, the last two chapters extend the scope of the discussion. Noting that a series of studies have indicated that centralization of the budget process leads to better fiscal performance in the Central and East European countries that joined the European Union in 2004 and 2007, we consider why those countries chose the fiscal institutions that they did. We find that the most divided societies, both politically and ethnically, made the greatest efforts to centralize their budget process. Given that such countries are more likely to suffer severe common pool resource problems (actors have more incentives to consider a smaller portion of the overall tax burden), the threat of a serious fiscal crisis seems to make a difference. At the same time, we also find that the overall set of rules,

---

[1] We also consider the effects of preelectoral pacts in Chapter 2 on the basis of data from Nadenicheck-Golder (2006), with the expectation that parties that are able to form them would also be able to delegate to a strong finance minister. For the sample of countries we have for ideological distance and preelectoral pacts, however, the overlap is exact: that is, coalitions with high ideological distance do not have parties signing preelectoral pacts. We focus in this Conclusion only on ideological distance.

norms, and institutions is still relatively weak in all countries. Given the prevalence of coalitions with great ideological differences among the ruling parties in all countries but Hungary, more institutional strengthening along the "fiscal contracts" mode are needed.

Our last chapter explores the relationship between domestic forms of fiscal governance and the framework of rules on fiscal policy at the European Union level. We consider the performance of countries both after the Maastricht Treaty and after the beginning of Stage III of Economic and Monetary Union, and we find that fiscal policy was generally more expansionary under EMU. While we conclude that the EU framework has not had the desired effect, we did see a role for a new Europe-wide institution. We propose in particular the creation of a Sustainability Council. Its job would be to monitor the development of general government debt in the European Union and to produce an annual report on the sustainability of public finances in each country. Its intended audience would be domestic publics, and the recommendations of the report would be announced initially in the relevant member state capital.

Contributions to Policy Debates

There are several contributions this book makes to the current literature. The first concerns fiscal rules, such as balanced budget requirements, parliamentary procedures, debt brakes, and/or multiannual fiscal planning (e.g., Feld and Kirchgässner 2004; Alt and Lowery 1994). The assumption is that the existence of a debt brake or deficit target will be sufficient to improve fiscal discipline in a given country. The discussion also appears at the European level. Recently, the European Commission (2006) issued a nuanced study about the role of numerical fiscal rules in European countries in its annual *Public Finances in EMU* report. It focused in particular on the effects of those rules on procyclicality. One concern of the report was that "hard" rules that can maintain fiscal discipline may lead to procyclicality in the budget. This could be a problem especially during "good" times. For example, consider a government with a target of a balanced budget that is experiencing an economic boom in a given year. Tax receipts go up while the demand for expenditure items such as social insurance go down. Governments in these situations could simply stick to the "rules" and spend any additional amount over a given target. This behavior would then leave the country more vulnerable when the economy weakens. The report concluded that the design of balance budget and expenditure rules is crucial – rules designed to be applied over the cycle and multiannual expenditure caps can reduce procyclicality. Nevertheless, "a certain trade-off could emerge between fiscal rules for fiscal discipline and stabilisation in good times" (200).

We have no qualms with the particulars of the Commission's analysis about procyclicality. We also find encouraging the discussion of the utility of "fiscal councils" at the domestic level that appears in the report. As we suggested with our proposal for a Fiscal Sustainability Council at the European level in Chapter 7, such councils can play an important role in increasing the transparency and operation of fiscal policy in *all* countries. We do, however, want to be careful about the overall message concerning the efficacy of fiscal rules. Our work suggests that the effectiveness of such rules depends very much on the underlying political environment. Detailed multiannual expenditure targets work well under multiparty coalition governments, but they may be almost irrelevant under one-party majority governments, that is, in situations when the ideological conflict (or distance) among cabinet members is small. The reason is that the necessary, and sufficient, institutional device to centralize the budget process involves delegation to a strong finance minister. In the absence of such a minister, the ministries are unlikely to stick to whatever targets are imposed on the government. In the presence of a strong finance minister, such targets may prove useful to such a central player (as they sometimes have been for Chancellor Gordon Brown in the United Kingdom), but they are neither necessary nor sufficient to maintain fiscal discipline. Similarly, "strengthening" a finance minister will have little effect in a country with real ideological differences in the cabinet. Finance ministers can play an important role in monitoring the execution of the budget in such countries and in providing technical guidance, so they remain vital parts of government. But in the absence of fiscal contracts among the political parties that are necessary to pass the budget, the "strengthening" will not suffice to ensure fiscal discipline. Our empirical work in Chapter 4 provides the evidence for this argument – given the same set of fiscal institutions, their ability to maintain fiscal discipline varied depending upon the ideological distance of the government. In an expected delegation country such as France, for example, fiscal discipline was maintained when ideological distance was small, but it deteriorated under the same framework meant to reinforce the finance minister as ideological distance increased. Our message is clear – the appropriate form of fiscal governance depends crucially on the potential for ideological conflict among the parties necessary to pass the budget. In terms of policy, this suggests that a major weakness of the European framework today is the one-size-fits-all approach of the Stability and Growth Pact.

The book has implications for other work on institutions. A growing body of literature focuses on the economic effects of electoral systems, and in particular on the distinction between proportional representation and plurality. In terms of budgetary outcomes, some contend that proportional systems should have more redistribution and larger public sectors (Iversen and Soskice 2006), while others insist that such systems should have higher budget deficits (Persson and Tabellini 2000, 2003). A problem for the literature on electoral systems is that the exact causal chain is not consistent across studies. Why is it exactly, for example, that proportional representation systems have larger public sectors than countries with plurality? Is it because proportional representation affects party incentives, so that parties focus on distinct groups in society, such as pensioners, rather than the population more broadly under this system (e.g., Milesi-Ferretti, Perotti, and Rostagno 2002)? Or is the general finding due to the effects on cabinet, that is, that there are more parties in government on average under proportional representation, and large parties are more likely to internalize externalities than small parties because they represent more groups (Bawn and Rosenbluth 2006)? Relatedly, do multiparty governments have difficulty making any tough decisions, with the result that expenditures ratchet upward over time (e.g., Alesina and Perotti 1995)?

In this book, electoral systems are critical because they affect the party system. Plurality electoral systems make it likely that there will be a two-party system, with one-party majority governments being the rule. This outcome in terms of government composition then means that plurality systems should adopt delegation. Proportional representation systems, however, are somewhat more nuanced. More often than not, such systems lead to regular multiparty coalition governments where fiscal contracts should be effective (e.g., Netherlands, Finland). But the correspondence between proportional representation and regular multiparty coalition governments is not exact. Some have government types that either change over different elections (e.g., Austria) or tend to produce either one-party governments or governments where the ideological distance among coalition partners is low (e.g., Greece and Spain). Electoral systems therefore serve as an important predictor of the long-run fiscal governance equilibrium, with plurality usually leading to one-party government while proportional representation has more variance but is more likely on average to have multiparty coalition governments.

Finally, there is also a clear empirical contribution of this book. We make available an unprecedented dataset of fiscal institutions that spans the period 1985–2004. As attention in the academic and policy communities has turned increasingly to institutions, international organizations have begun to set up databases to collect all sorts of information on how countries make budgets. Our book suggests a systematic way in which different institutions fit together, and how they *should* fit together. Moreover, an unavoidable problem with new datasets is that they do not have many years of data. Our work allows other scholars to explore arguments they may have longitudinally as well as laterally.

Contribution to Theoretical Debates

As we indicated in Chapter 1, there are increasingly sophisticated arguments that suggest that some institutions complement one another. Those complementaries may exist to reinforce the likelihood of a given political outcome. For Lijphart (1999), institutions like plurality electoral systems, two-party legislatures, and one-party majority government combine with weak "checks and balances" institutions like weak courts, strong lower levels of government (or federalism), and weak central banks to enable a majority to rule the country. The contrasting case combines proportional representation electoral systems, multiparty legislature, and multiparty coalition governments with strong "checks and balances" institutions to encourage a consensual form of decision making.

Lijphart (1999) also has a prescription for the design of institutions. He suggests that countries with multiple cleavages in a society should opt for a consensual form of democracy. If societies become more sophisticated, that is, if they move beyond a standard economic Left-Right cleavage to include cleavages based on religion, ethnicity, and attitudes toward environmental stability (among others), they should make concomitant changes to their political systems so that they fit better the ideal of a "consensual" democracy.

We do not disagree with the core message, but our work indicates that one should consider the implications of such changes for fiscal governance. Consider changes in one of Lijphart's (1994) classic cases, New Zealand. It introduced a German-style two-ballot system in the early 1990s, which led in turn to multiparty coalition governments. To the extent that those parties differed significantly on ideology, one would expect a move to fiscal contracts within the government. Similarly, there has been a trend to greater fiscal decentralization that one observes around the world in the 1990s (e.g., Rodden, Eskelund, and Litvack 2003). For Lijphart, these trends represent more consensual government. According to our analysis, a simple move to more decentralized fiscal decision making may be problematic unless fiscal discipline is "hardwired" in fiscal rules – the common pool resource problem may be increased if new powers to spend money at the subnational level are not matched with institutions that encourage subnational governments to consider the full tax implications of their spending decisions. Changes in one set of institutions have concrete implications for the design of other institutions.

The same holds for the varieties of capitalism literature (e.g., Hall and Soskice 2001). There is an indisputable interaction between the areas of corporate governance and labor relations, on the one hand, and public finances, on the other hand. For example, Estevez-Abe, Iversen, and Soskice (2001) and Mares (2003) indicate that social protection helps to overcome market failures in skill formation. Similarly, the link between social protection and wage bargaining is well established in the political economy literature.[2] Our approach leads one to ask under which conditions such welfare policies lead to fiscal sustainability problems and what determines governments' ability and willingness to rein in these problems. In this respect, it adds to the knowledge about complementarities across institutional arrangements and spheres of policymaking.[3]

A good example is provided by Germany, the prototypical coordinated market economy in the varieties of capitalism literature. With reunification, the fiscal strains built into the system in reacting to exogenous shocks became increasingly visible under these extraordinary circumstances. The transfer of the West German social security system to the New Länder was the necessary condition of the employment-destroying wage policies during the initial years. At the same time, private firms and investors were temporarily shielded from the immediate effects of market pressures through the substantive subsidies to capital channeled though the Treuhand system. This led to a fiscally and economically unsustainable state of high social security contributions, high unemployment in the new Länder, and continuous transfer payments adding to the government deficit. On the

---

[2] See e.g., Layard, Nickell, and Jackman (2005).
[3] See Crouch et al. (2005) for a discussion addressing different dimensions of complementarity.

firm and labor market side, the result was a decline in the importance of coordinated wage bargaining in the new Länder and wage moderation. On the fiscal side, however, consecutive governments had troubles in coping with the consequences and squaring the circle between regaining fiscal sustainability and reducing taxes.[4]

Our approach explains institutional mechanisms behind the fiscal deterioration. During the initial period, the expansion of social spending in parallel with the prevalence of extrabudgetary funds and a weakening of the position of the minister of finance in the cabinet undermined the delegation system in place. Later on, changes in the party system and the growing ideological difference among the parties in government, already starting with the coalition of the Greens with the Social Democrats in 1998, weakened the usefulness of a delegation form of governance. After the 2005 elections, a coalition between the Christian and Social Democrats, which would have made a contract approach more suitable to maintain fiscal discipline, was formed. However, the coalition partners failed to take that step.

Streek (2007), when looking at the fiscal crisis of the German welfare state, which is an integral part of its coordinated market economy, ponders whether the persistent failure of reform reflects an "inner logic" of the modern state. Our approach provides a conceptual framework and the international empirical evidence showing that the fiscal crisis is rather the result of weak budgetary institutions failing to contain spending pressures. In fact, the success of Swedish governments in refurbishing their public finances after a severe crisis and a restructuring of the budget process in the 1990s is a telling counterexample, as explained in detail in Chapter 5.

A more intriguing issue is the mutual impact of party representation and the organization of workers and firms. The point can best be illustrated when looking at "hard times," which may lead to institutional change. Economic crises and government weakness or electoral uncertainty have regularly given rise to social pacts between social partners and the government in a number of European countries (e.g., Hassel 2006). In some economically successful cases, such as the 1987 pact in Ireland and the 1982 Wassenaar agreement, the wage moderation agreed in the pact went

---

[4] See von Hagen and Strauch (1999) and von Hagen, Strauch, and Wolff (2002) for a detailed analysis of the postreunification fiscal developments and the related institutional changes. For the changes to the welfare state and the corporate governance and wage setting system see Hall (2007) and Streek (2007).

hand in hand with a commitment to reduce labor taxes and social security contributions on the side of the government.[5] Governments lived up to this commitment and simultaneously consolidated the budget balance. In both cases, budgetary consolidation was accompanied by a centralization of the budget process (Hallerberg 2004).

Hamann and Kelly (2006) and Baccaro (2006) suggest that governments tend to engage in social pacts when they are "weak" and face a high degree of electoral uncertainty. Government weakness reflects the lack of clear parliamentary majority. The situation of electoral uncertainty corresponds to the factors identified by our approach that are conducive to the formation of a fiscal contract. Baccaro (2006) argues additionally that the support of union and employer organizations is a crucial element in the formation and continuation of a social pact. Governments must be able to rally both social partners behind a policy package and maintain the consensus.

The existence of a social pact thus changes the political economy that parties have to face. On the one hand, it may reduce the exit option of a coalition partner since mobilizing organized interests behind a deviating party platform may be more complicated. This disciplining effect is likely to dominate in the short run and may have indeed been a condition supporting the centralization of the budget process which helped to engineer a fiscal adjustment. On the other hand, it may change the ideological stance of parties and increase the competitiveness of the system by enlarging the space of possible coalitions. Such a change in the political landscape is likely to emerge over the medium run with the evolution of labor market institutions. The type of rapprochement Wassenaar represents provides a more conducive environment for fiscal contracts because it subsequently made the Dutch party system more competitive. The Dutch Liberal Party (VVD) had not participated in a coalition government with the Dutch Social Democrats (PvdA) at any time in the postwar period. This meant that the Christian Democrats (CDA), who occupied the center on a strict Left-Right economic scale, were always in government. One can speculate that as the institutions of a coordinated market economy were strengthened by the Wassenaar agreement, capital and labor worked productively with each other on some (though obviously not all) issues. The political parties that provided rough proxies of representation of these groups, the Dutch Liberal Party and the Social Democrats, in turn were able to reduce the animosity they had felt toward each other, and a coalition between the two became at least

---

[5] See Annett (2007).

a possibility; in fact, the PvdA and VVD eventually formed their first coalition in 1994. This increase in party competition increased the punishment a given party in government would face if it defected from the fiscal contract. While the CDA could not be replaced if it ignored the terms of a contract through the early 1980s, any party could be replaced in the period that followed.

Before moving on to future research opportunities, we would also like to comment on what contribution our work makes to the political business cycle literature. There is mixed evidence that incumbent governments try to influence the macroeconomy before elections with the aim of convincing voters that the incumbent has managed the economy well (e.g., Nordhaus 1975). Schuknecht (1999) as well as Clark (2003) build upon a Mundell-Fleming framework to predict that fiscal cycles should be especially prevalent with fixed exchange rates and open capital. The move to EMU represents an increase in the number of states with fixed exchange rates, with twelve of fifteen irrevocably fixed to one another in the eurozone and another, Denmark, essentially fixed under ERM II. Capital is also mobile across European Union countries, so the prediction based on Schuknecht (1999) and Clark (2003) would be a greater prevalence of fiscal political cycles. Chapter 7 presents evidence consistent with this view on fixed exchange rates and elections, namely, a pronounced fiscal loosening prior to elections in the EMU period.

Our argument also adds an interesting twist to the political business cycle literature that focused on domestic institutions instead of capital mobility and the exchange rate. As Clark and Hallerberg (2000) first suggested, one would expect fiscal business cycles to be stronger in states with delegation than in states with fiscal contracts. As we explain in Chapter 2, under delegation the parties in government run together in future elections. The benefit from the reelection of the "incumbent" benefits them all. Under fiscal contracts, however, the parties generally run against each other in successive elections. Any "benefit" from a short-term manipulation of the economy may accrue to one's political opponent, and government parties will not want the fiscal boost in the first place. Chapter 4 presents compelling evidence that supports this argument. Table 4.1 indicates that in the regression that includes all states, there is some fiscal loosening if there is an upcoming election. Once one separates the states into expected delegation and expected contracts, the coefficient doubles for expected delegation states but is statistically indistinguishable from zero in the expected contract states. The form of fiscal governance in place has a strong effect on the intensity of political business cycles before a given election.

Future Research

The elaboration of our causal mechanisms also suggests some limitations of the current study. Electoral systems matter because they determine the ideological spread of the parties needed to pass the budget. So long as there is a majority government in office, the main action at the formation stage of the budget happens in the cabinet. The reason is that there is generally strong party discipline in West European countries. It is rare that parties reach an agreement in cabinet and then face rebellion among the rank and file of the different parties. Moreover, to the extent that there are temptations to change the government's budget, there are often rules in parliament that make changes to that budget difficult. As we indicated in Chapter 2, countries with electoral systems that encourage parliamentarians to think about a small slice of the total burden, such as the plurality systems in France and in the United Kingdom, have some of the most strict rules on what parliament can do to the proposed budget.

If one extends the study to non-European cases, one will soon discover that party discipline varies much more than it does in our sample. The fact that a president cuts a deal with the majority leader in Congress does not guarantee that the budget will pass through the legislature. Moreover, as this example indicates, there may be more actors involved in the process than in the countries we consider, such as an elected president.

Some comments are in order to translate our framework to other cases. A crucial part of what makes both delegation and fiscal contracts work is the punishment mechanism. In the former case, the key punishment is the dismissal of defecting ministers. In the latter case, it is the end of the coalition, with new elections the result if a new coalition cannot be formed. In presidential systems, dismissal of offending ministers is up to the executive, while dissolution of the coalition has a different meaning when it cannot lead to new elections that can rebalance the distribution of parties in the legislature. In particular, only the electorate can dismiss the executive in most cases.[6] This would presumably lead to two implications. The first is that delegation should be more effective than contracts because of the stronger punishment mechanism in presidential systems; presidents can dismiss defecting ministers

---

[6] Impeachment proceedings can lead to the dismissal of a president. As Perez-Línan (2007) indicates, impeachments have become increasingly common in Latin America since the restoration of democracy. Nevertheless, there is a difference between parliamentary and presidential systems that remains. While prime ministers may relinquish office if they lose a vote on their budget that is also a confidence vote at the same time, impeachment proceedings do not begin as an immediate consequence of a president's losing specific votes.

as they see fit. Yet our work also indicates that increasing ideological distance will undermine the effectiveness of the president; note that it is the ideological distance of the number of parties needed to pass legislation, not simply the distance among members of the cabinet. This suggests that the ability of the president to maintain discipline will break down as the number of parties in the legislature needed to pass legislation multiplies.

An excellent recent paper (Cheibub 2006) explores some of these themes. He examines the budgetary performance of all democracies from 1946 through 2002. He finds that presidential democracies as a whole have higher budget balances. The reason, he argues, is that voters can identify a player to hold accountable for poor performance, and presidents therefore champion fiscal discipline. Moreover, fiscal rules that reinforce the powers of the president have a clear effect on the ability of presidents to promote fiscal discipline. Crucially, the "rules" he considers are restrictive. He looks at presidential power to initiate legislation, whether the legislature can amend the president's budget, and the default position that is the outcome if the legislature does not pass a budget (with the president's budget then adopted the rule that strengthens both the president and increases fiscal discipline). In countries where these rules and procedures strengthen the hand of the president, fiscal discipline is generally higher.

Our findings for the Central and East European countries provide a useful contrast to Cheibub's argument. As we indicated in Chapter 5, some basic level of centralization along the same lines Cheibub describes is desirable. Yet the "government" is not so neatly separated from parliament; though these countries have elected presidents and though there are some differences in what presidents can do, strictly speaking none of the systems in our study are "presidential." Parliaments elect prime ministers, and through votes of confidence parliaments can remove presidents. Following Gleich (2002), in fact, we had the opposite prediction from Cheibub's, namely, that stronger presidents undermine the government's budget. Given the sense that the president owes specific constituencies for their support in elections in Central and East European countries, this additional actor could, in theory, champion those interests rather than consider the best interests of the country as a whole.[7] This

---

[7] As Yläoutinen (2005) indicates, the president's role in these countries has been circumscribed so that this worry has not really arisen (or been tested). While most countries do allow the president to veto the state budget, through 2005 there was no case of a president using this veto, and presidents have generally stayed out of the budget process.

discussion suggests that there may be fundamental differences in the effectiveness of fiscal institutions in parliamentary and presidential democracies, and any application of this study to a broader set of cases should account for these differences.

More work should also consider the effects international organizations may have in reinforcing domestic fiscal rules. Chapter 7 called for the creation of a Sustainability Council at the European Union level. In a broader context, one of the coauthors of this study has argued separately that such councils would serve an important function in a Latin America setting but at the national level (Eichengreen, Hausmann, and von Hagen 1996, 1999). In non-European settings where there is neither a single currency nor a European-level institutional framework to support it, the most obvious international actor is the International Monetary Fund. This organization negotiates programs with countries that often include fiscal stipulations for what the country receiving the loan must do. While we do not have hard data to confirm this, our sense is that the IMF negotiates what look like fiscal contracts, but it does so mostly with finance ministries. This suggests a mismatch between the type of fiscal governance the IMF presumes, which is delegation centered on the finance ministry, and the type of fiscal governance that exists in practice, which can be more varied. In particular, negotiations that include all of the major spending resorts are probably more effective for both parties concerned (the IMF and the country receiving the loan). Future work should consider how these interactions play out in practice.

Finally, there are some theoretical arguments that could fruitfully be applied to other policy settings. At a more abstract level, we consider what types of institutions can address common pool resource problems in the presence of a principal-agent relationship. That is, the solution varies depending upon how close are the preferences of the principals. Moreover, an important point is that a solution is possible even when ideal preferences among the principals vary a lot. The question then turns to the punishment mechanism again. For coalition governments, the fall of the government can be an effective deterrent to cheating on the contract. The punishment mechanism may be difficult to put in place in other settings. For example, if one applies this model to a treaty on the environment that includes carbon targets for future years despite the fact that ideal preferences on this issue diverge, how can one be sure that countries will stick by them?

These are all possible topics for future research that would build on the current book. As it stands now, our work does have concrete policy implications for countries. It is important to centralize the budget process. *What* types of institutions will serve this function, however, will depends upon the underlying politics.

Bibliography

Alesina, Alberto, Ricardo Hausmann, Rudolf Hommes, and Ernesto Stein. 1999. Budget Institutions and Fiscal Performance in Latin America. *Journal of Development Economics* **59**(2): 253–273.

Alesina, Alberto, and Eliana La Ferrara. 2000. Who Trusts Others? CEPR Discussion Paper no. 2646. London: Center for Economic Policy Research.

Alesina, Alberto, and Roberto Perotti. 1995. Fiscal Expansions and Adjustments in OECD Countries. *Economic Policy* **10**(2): 207–248.

Alesina, Alberto, and Roberto Perotti. 1997. Fiscal Adjustments in OECD Countries: Composition and Macro-Economic Effects. *IMF Staff Papers* **44**: 210–248.

Alt, James, and David Dryer Lassen. 2006a. Fiscal Transparency, Political Parties and Debt. *European Economic Review* 530–550.

Alt, James, and David Dryer Lassen. 2006b. Transparency, Political Polarization, and Political Budget Cycles in OECD Countries. *American Journal of Political Science* **50**(3): 530.

Alt, James E., and Robert C. Lowry. 1994. Divided Government, Fiscal Institutions, and Budget Deficits: Evidence from the States. *American Political Science Review* **88**(4): 811–828.

Annett, Anthony. 2000. Social Fractionalization, Political Instability, and the Size of Government. IMF Working Paper no. 00/82. Washington, D.C.: IMF.

Annett, Anthony. 2007. Lessons from Successful Labor Market Reformers in Europe. IMF Policy Discussion Paper PDP/07/01. Washington, D.C.: IMF.

Annual Macroeconomic Database (AMECO) 1999. European Commission. Luxembourg: Eurostat.

Artis, Michael, and Massimilano Marcellino. 2001. Fiscal Forecasting: The Track Record of the IMF, OECD and EC. *Econometrics Journal* **4**: S20–S36.

Baccaro, Lucio. 2006. The Political Economy of Social Concertation. Mimeo. Available at web.mit.edu/baccaro/www/papers/pol-econ-12-06.pdf.

Balassone, Fabrizio, Daniele Franco, and Stefania Zotteri. 2006. EMU Fiscal Indicators: A Misleading Compass? *Empirica* **33**: 63–87.

Balls, Ed, and Gus O'Donnell, eds. 2002. *Reforming Britain's Economic and Financial Policy: Towards Greater Economic Stability*. Basingstoke, UK: Palgrave.

Baltagi, Badi H. 2005. *Econometric Analysis of Panel Data*. New York: Wiley.

Barro, Robert F. 1979. On the Determination of Public Debt. *Journal of Political Economy* **87**: 940–971.

Bates, Robert H. 1988. Contra Contractarianism: Some Reflections on the New Institutionalism. *Politics and Society* **16**: 387–401.

Bawn, Kathleen, and Frances Rosenbluth. 2006. Short versus Long Coalitions: Electoral Accountability and the Size of the Public Sector. *American Journal of Political Science* **50**(2): 251–65.

Beetsma, Roel and Xavier Debrun. 2004. Reconciling Stability and Growth: Smart Pacts and Structural Reforms. *IMF Staff Papers* **51**(3): 431–456.

Berglund, Sten, Tomas Hellén, and Frank H. Aarebrot. 1998. *The Handbook of Political Change in Eastern Europe*. Cheltenham, UK, and Northampton, Mass.: Edward Elgar.

Blanchard, Olivier J., and Francesco Giavazzi. 2004. Improving the SGP Through a Proper Accounting of Public Investment. Centre for Economic Policy Research Working Paper No. 4220. London: CEPR.

Blöndal, Jon. 2003. Budget Reform in OECD Member Countries: Common Trends. *OECD Journal of Budgeting* **2**(4): 7–25.

Bouthevillain, Carine, et al. 2001. Cyclically Adjusted Budget Balances: An Alternative Approach. ECB Working Paper No. 77. Frankfurt: European Central Bank.

Bratkowski, Andrzej, and Jacek Rostowski. 2005. *What Institutional Changes Are Needed to Improve Fiscal Discipline in Poland?* Warsaw: Ius et Lex.

Brunila, Anne, and Carlos Martinez-Mongay. 2002. The Challenge for Fiscal Policy in the Early Years of EMU. In Marco Buti and Andre Sapir, eds., *EMU and Economic Policy in Europe: The Challenge of the Early Years*. Northampton, Mass.: Edward Elgar.

Budge, Ian, Hans-Dieter Klingemann, Andrea Volkens, Judith Bara, and Eric Tanenbaum. 2001. *Mapping Policy Preferences: Estimates for Parties, Electors, and Governments 1945–1998*. New York: Oxford University Press.

Buiter, Willem. 2003. Ten Commandments for a Fiscal Rule in E(M)U. *Oxford Review of Economic Policy* **19**(1): 84–99.

Bulgaria, Government of. 1998. Memorandum on Economic Policies, September 9, 1998. Available at http://www.imf.org/external/NP/LOI/090998.htm.

Buti, Marco, and Gabriele Giudice. 2002. Maastricht's Fiscal Rules at 10: An Assessment. Mimeo, European Commission, March 25. Available at http://www.econ.upf.es/crei/activities/sc_conferences/14/buti2.pdf.

Buti, Marco, and Paul van den Noord. 2003. Discretionary Fiscal Policy and Elections: The Experience of the Early Years of EMU. OECD Economics Department Working Paper 351, Paris: OECD.

Buti, Marco, and Paul van den Noord. 2004a. Fiscal Policy in EMU: Rules, Discretion, and Political Incentives. Economic Papers 206, Brussels: European Commission.

214

Bibliography

Buti, Marco, and Paul van den Noord. 2004b. Fiscal Discretion and Elections in the Early Years of EMU. *Journal of Common Market Studies* **42**(4): 737–756.

Calvert, Randall L. 1995. Rational Actors, Equilibrium, and Social Institutions. In Jack Knight and Itai Seneds, eds., *Explaining Social Institutions*. Ann Arbor: University of Michigan Press. 95–120.

Canova, Fabio, and Evi Pappa. 2004. The Elusive Costs and Immaterial Gains of Fiscal Constraints. Working Paper, Bocconi University.

Castles, Francis, and Peter Mair. 1984. Left-Right Political Scales: Some Expert Judgments. *European Journal of Political Research* **12**: 73–88.

Cheibub, José Antonio. 2006. Presidentialism, Electoral Identifiability, and Budget Balance in Democratic Systems. *American Political Science Review*. **100**(3): 353–368.

Claeys, Peter. 2005. Policy Mix and Debt Sustainability: Evidence from Fiscal Policy Rules. CESifo Working Paper 1406, Munich: CESifo.

Clark, William Roberts. 2003. *Capitalism, Not Globalism: Capital Mobility, Central Bank Independence, and the Political Control of the Economy*. Ann Arbor: University of Michigan Press.

Clark, William Roberts, and Mark Hallerberg. 2000. Strategic Interaction between Monetary and Fiscal Actors under Full Capital Mobility. *American Political Science Review* **94**(2): 323–346.

Codogno, Lorenzo, Carlo Favero, and Alessandro Missale. 2003. Yield Spreads on EMU Government Bonds. *Economic Policy* **37**: 505–532.

Coeuré, Benoît, and Jean Pisani-Ferry. 2003. A Sustainability Pact for the Eurozone. Manuscript. Available at http://www.pisani-ferry.net/base/papiers/re-03-keynes-subtainability.pdf.

Cox, Gary. 1997. *Making Votes Count: Strategic Coordination in the World's Electoral Systems*. New York: Cambridge University Press.

Crouch, Colin, Wolfgang Streek, Robert Boyer, Bruce Amable, Peter A. Hall, and Gregory Jackson. 2005. Dialogue on Institutional Complementarity and Political Economy. *Socio-Economic Review* **3**: 359–382.

Daban, Teresa, Enrica Detragiache, Gian Maria Milesi Ferretti, and Steven Symansky. 2001. Rules-Based Fiscal Policy and the Fiscal Framework in France, Germany, Italy, and Spain. Mimeo. Washington D.C.: IMF.

Dabrowski, Marek. 1993. Metody opracowania budżetu państwa. *Rozwiązania polskie a systemy innych państw demokratycznych*. Warszawa: Center for Social and Economic Research.

Dafflon, Bernard, and Sergio Rossi. 1999. Public Accounting Fudges towards EMU: A First Empirical Survey and Some Public Choice Considerations. *Public Choice* **101**: 59–84.

De Haan, Jakob, and Jan-Egbert Sturm. 1994. Political and Institutional Determinants of Fiscal Policy in the European Community. *Public Choice* **80**: 157–172.

De Haan, Jakob, and Jan-Egbert Sturm. 1997. Political and Economic Determinants of OECD Budget Deficits and Government Expenditures: A Reinvestigation. *European Journal of Political Economy* **13**: 739–750.

Delors Report (Committee for the Study of Economic and Monetary Union). 1989. *Report on Economic and Monetary Union in the European Community*. Luxembourg: Office for Official Publications of the EC.

Diebold, Francis. 2000. *Elements of Forecasting*. Cincinnati: South-Western Thomson Learning.

Dore, Osmon, and Paul R. Masson. 2002. Experience with Budgetary Convergence in the WAEMU. Working Paper 02/108. Washington D.C.: International Monetary Fund.

Duverger, Maurice. 1954. *Political Parties. Their Organization and Activity in the Modern State*. New York: Wiley.

Duverger, Maurice. 1980. A New Political System Model: Semi-Presidential Government. *European Journal of Political Research* 8(2): 165–187.

Easterly, William, and Ross Levine. 1997. Africa's Growth Tragedy: Policies and Ethnic Divisions. *The Quarterly Journal of Economics* 112: 1203–1250.

Edin, Per-Anders, and Henry Ohlsson. 1991. Political Determinants of Budget Deficits: Coalition Effects versus Minority Effects. *European Economic Review* 35: 1597–1603.

Eichengreen, Barry. 1990. One Money for Europe? Lessons from the U.S. Currency Union. *Economic Policy* 5(10): 117–187.

Eichengreen, Barry, Ricardo Hausmann, and Jürgen von Hagen. 1996. Reforming Budgetary Institutions in Latin America: The Case for a National Fiscal Council. Working Paper. Washington D.C.: Interamerican Development Bank.

Eichengreen, Barry, Ricardo Hausmann, and Jürgen von Hagen. 1999. Reforming Budgetary Institutions in Latin America: The Case for a National Fiscal Council. *Open Economies Review* 10(4): 415–442.

Eichengreen, Barry, and Jürgen von Hagen. 1996. Federalism, Fiscal Restraints, and European Monetary Union. *American Economic Review*. 86(2): 134–138.

Elliott, Graham, Ivana Komunjer, and Allan Timmermann. 2003. Estimating Loss Function Parameters, CEPR Discussion Paper No. 3821.

Emmerson, Carl, and Chris Frayne. 2002. The Government's Fiscal Rules. *Institute for Fiscal Studies Briefing Notes* 16. Available at http://www.ifs.org.uk/wps/bn161.pdf.

Estevez-Abe, Margarita, Torben Iversen, and David Soskice. 2001. Social Protection and the Formation of Skills: A Reinterpretation of the Welfare State. In Peter Hall and David Soskice, eds., *Varieties of Capitalism: The Institutional Foundations of Comparative Advantage*. Oxford: Oxford University Press. 145–183.

European Commission. 2002. Coordination of Economic Policies in the EU: A Presentation of the Key Features of the Main Procedures. *Euro Paper 45*.

European Commission. 2004. *Public Finances in EMU*. Brussels: Directorate-General for Economic and Financial Affairs.

European Commission. 2006. *Public Finances in EMU*. Brussels: Directorate-General for Economic and Financial Affairs.

Fabrizio, Stefania, and Ashoka Mody. 2006. Can Budget Institutions Counteract Political Indiscipline? *Economic Policy* 21(48): 689–739.

Bibliography

Fatas, Antonio, Andrew Hughes Hallett, Ann Siebert, Rolf R. Strauch, and Jürgen von Hagen. 2003. *Stability and Growth in Europe: Towards a Better Pact*. Monitoring European Integration 13. London: CEPR.

Favero, Carlo A., Francesco Giavazzi and Luigi Spaventa. 1997. High Yields: The Spread on German Interest Rates. *The Economic Journal* **107**: 956–85.

Feld, Lars P., and Gebhard Kirchgässner. 2004. On the Effectiveness of Debt Brakes: The Swiss Experience. Paper presented at the CESifo-LBI Conference on Sustainability of Public Debt, Munich, October 22, 2004.

Ferejohn, John, and Keith Krehbiel. 1987. The Budget Process and the Size of the Budget. *American Journal of Political Science* **31**: 296–320.

Fleming, J. Marcus. 1962. Domestic Financial Policies under Fixed and Floating Exchange Rates. *IMF Staff Papers* **9**: 369–380.

Filc, Gabriel, and Carlos Scartascini. 2006. Budget Institutions and Fiscal Outcomes: Ten Years of Inquiry on Fiscal Matters at the Research Department. *International Journal of Public Budget* **59**: 81–138.

Fonseca Marinheiro, Carlos Jose. 2005. Has the Stability and Growth Pact Stabilized? *Evidence from a Panel of 12 European Countries and Some Implications for Reform of the Stability and Growth Pact*. CESifo Working Paper 1411, Munich: CESifo.

Franzese, Robert John. 2002. *Macroeconomic Policies of Developed Democracies*. Ann Arbor: University of Michigan Press.

Frohlich, Norman, and Joe A. Oppenheimer. 1978. *Modern Political Economy*. Englewood Cliffs, N.J.: Prentice-Hall.

Fudenberg, Drew, and Jean Tirole. 1998. *Game Theory*. Cambridge, Mass.: MIT Press.

Gali, Jordi, and Roberto Perotti. 2003. Fiscal Policy and Monetary Integration in Europe. *Economic Policy* **18**(37): 533–572.

Gallagher, Michael, Michael Laver, and Peter Mair. 1992. *Representative Government in Western Europe*. New York: McGraw Hill.

Gardner, Roy, and Jürgen von Hagen. 1996. Sequencing and the Size of the Budget. In Werner Güth, Wulf Albers, Benny Moldovanu, and Eric van Damme, eds., *Understanding Strategic Interaction: Essays in Honor of Reinhard Selten*. Heidelberg: Springer.

Glaeser, Edward L., David I. Laibson, José A. Scheinkam, and Christine L. Soutter. 2000. Measuring Trust. *Quarterly Journal of Economics* August: 811–846.

Gleich, Holger. 2002. The Evolution of Budget Institutions in Central and East European Countries. Ph.D. Diss., University of Bonn.

Gleich, Holger. 2003. Budget Institutions and Fiscal Performance in Central and Eastern European Countries. ECB Working Paper No. 215. Frankfurt: European Central Bank.

Grilli, Vittorio, Donato Masciandaro, and Guido Tabellini. 1991. Institutions and Policies. *Economic Policy* **6**: 341–391.

Grimes, William. 2001. *Unmaking the Japanese Miracle*. Ithaca, N.Y.: Cornell University Press.

Hahm, Sung Deuk. 1994. The Political Economy of Deficit Spending: A Cross Comparison of Industrialized Democracies, 1955–1990. Manuscript.

Hahm, Sung Deuk, Mark S. Kamlet, and David C. Mowery. 1996. The Political Economy of Deficit Spending in Nine Industrialized Parliamentary Democracies: The Role of Fiscal Institutions. *Comparative Political Studies* **29**(1): 52–77.

Hall, Peter A. 2007. *The Evolution of Varieties of Capitalism in Europe.* Harvard University, mimeo.

Hall, Peter A., and David Soskice, eds. 2001. *Varieties of Capitalism.* Oxford: Oxford University Press.

Hallerberg, Mark. 2004. *Domestic Budgets in a United Europe: Fiscal Governance from the End of Bretton Woods to EMU.* Ithaca, N.Y.: Cornell University Press.

Hallerberg, Mark, and Patrik Marier. 2004. Executive Authority, the Personal Vote, and Budget Discipline in Latin American and Caribbean Countries. *American Journal of Political Science* **48**(3): 571–587.

Hallerberg, Mark, Rolf R. Strauch, and Jürgen von Hagen. 2001. The Use and Effectiveness of Budgetary Rules and Norms in EU Member States. Working Paper, Dutch Ministry of Finance.

Hallerberg, Mark, Rolf R. Strauch, and Jürgen von Hagen. 2004. Budgeting in Europe after Maastricht: Patterns of Reform and Their Effectiveness. *Hacienda Publica Española* **167**: 201–225.

Hallerberg, Mark, Rolf Strauch, and Jürgen von Hagen. 2007. The Design of Fiscal Rules and Forms of Governance in European Union Countries. *European Journal of Political Economy* **23**: 338–359.

Hallerberg, Mark, and Jürgen von Hagen. 1997. Electoral Institutions and the Budget Process. OECD-IADB Conference paper, Paris.

Hallerberg, Mark, and Jürgen von Hagen. 2006. *Fiscal Institutions in Poland.* Warsaw: Ernst & Young.

Hamann, Kerstin, and John Kelly. 2006. Voters, Parties and Social Pacts in Western Europe. Paper for delivery at the 5th International Conference of the Council for European Studies, Chicago, March 29–April 2, 2006.

Hassel, Anke. 2006. *Wage Setting, Social Pacts and the Euro: A New Role for the State.* Amsterdam: University of Amsterdam Press.

Hemming, Richard, and Michael Kell. 2001. Promoting Fiscal Responsibility – Transparency, Rules, and Independent Fiscal Authorities. Paper presented at the Banca D'Italia Third Workshop on Fiscal Rules, Perugia, February 1–3, 2001.

Huber, John D. 1996. *Rationalizing Parliament: Legislative Institutions and Party Politics in France.* Cambridge: Cambridge University Press.

Hughes Hallett, Andrew, Rolf R. Strauch, and Jürgen von Hagen. 2001. *Budgetary Consolidations in EMU.* European Commission Economic Papers 148, Brussels: European Commission.

Inman, Robert. 1993. Presidential Leadership and the Reform of Fiscal Policy: Learning from Reagan's Role in TRA 86. NBER Working Paper 4395, Cambridge, Mass.

Bibliography

Inman, Robert, and Michael A. Fitts. 1990. Political Institutions and Fiscal Policy: Evidence from the U.S. Historical Record. *Journal of Law, Economics, and Organization* **6**: 79–131.

Inter-American Development Bank. 1997. *Latin America after a Decade of Reforms*. Washington, D.C.: Johns Hopkins University Press.

International Monetary Fund. 2001. Cyclical Fiscal Policy Behavior in EU Countries. Selected Issues Paper.

International Monetary Fund. 2005a. Article IV Consultation – Staff Report; Staff Supplement; Public Information Notice on the Executive Board Discussion; and Statement by the Executive Director for the Republic of Poland. IMF Country Report No. 05/263, July.

International Monetary Fund. 2005b. Republic of Poland: Selected Issues. IMF Country Report No. 05/264, July.

International Monetary Fund. 2005c. Poland – Concluding Statement after the IMF Staff Visit, November 21, 2005.

Iversen, Torbin, and David Soskice. 2006. Electoral Institutions, Parties and the Politics of Class: Why Some Democracies Distribute More Than Others. *American Political Science Review* **100**(2): 165–181.

Katz, Richard. 1980. *A Theory of Parties and Electoral Systems*. Baltimore and London: Johns Hopkins University Press.

Kennedy, Suzanne, and Janine Robbins. 2001. The Role of Fiscal Rules in Determining Fiscal Performance. Department of Finance Canada Working Paper 2001-16.

Keser, Claudia, and Roy Gardner. 1999. Strategic Behavior of Experienced Subjects in a Common Pool Resource Game. *International Journal of Game Theory* **28**: 241–252.

Kiewiet, D. Roderick, and Kristin Szakaly. 1996. Constitutional Limits on Borrowing: An Analysis of State Bonded Indebtedness. *Journal of Law, Economics and Organization* **12**: 62–97.

Knack, Stephen, and Philip Keefer. 1997. Does Social Capital Have an Economic Payoff? A Cross-Country Investigation. *Quarterly Journal of Economics* November: 1251–1288.

Kneebone, Ronald D., and Kenneth J. McKenzie. 2000. A Case Study of Institutional Endogeneity? A Study of the Budgetary Reforms of the Government of Alberta, Canada. In Rolf Strauch and Jürgen von Hagen, eds., *Institutions, Politics and Fiscal Policy*. Boston/Dordrecht/London: Kluwer. 235–262.

Kopits, George, and Steven Symansky. 1998. Fiscal Policy Rules. Occasional Paper 162, Washington, D.C.: IMF.

Krogstrup, Signe, and Charles Wyplosz. 2006. A Common Pool Theory of Deficit Bias Correction. Working Paper, Graduate School of International Affairs, Geneva, August 21, 2006.

Kydland, Finn E., and Edward C. Prescott. 1977. Rules Rather Than Discretion: The Inconsistency of Optimal Plans. *Journal of Political Economy* **85**(3): 473–492.

Lao-Araya, Kanokpan. 1997a. The Effect of Budget Structure on Fiscal Performance: A Study of Selected Asian Countries. IMF Working Paper, Washington, D.C.

Lao-Araya, Kanokpan. 1997b. The Fiscal Constitution of a Developing Country: The Case of Thailand. Ph.D. Thesis, Bloomington: Indiana University.

La Porta, Rafael, Florencio Lopez-de-Silanes, Andrei Shleifer, and Robert W. Vishny. 1997. Trust in Large Organizations. *American Economic Review, Papers and Proceedings* **87**: 333–338.

Laver, Michael, and W. Ben Hunt. 1992. *Policy and Party Competition.* New York: Routledge, Chapman, & Hall.

Laver, Michael, and Norman Schofield. 1990. Multiparty Government. In *Comparative European Politics.* Oxford: Oxford University Press.

Laver, Michael, and Kenneth A. Shepsle. 1994. Cabinet Ministers and Government Formation in Parliamentary Democracies. In Michael Laver and Kenneth A. Shepsle, eds., *Cabinet Ministers and Parliamentary Government.* Cambridge: Cambridge University Press. 3–14.

Laver, Michael, and Kenneth A. Shepsle. 1996. *Making and Breaking Governments.* Cambridge: Cambridge University Press.

Layard, Richard, Stephen Nickell, and Richard Jackman. 2005. *Unemployment: Macroeconomic Performance and the Labour Market.* Oxford: Oxford University Press.

Ledyard, John. 1995. Public Goods: A Survey of Experimental Research. In John Kagel and Alvin Roth, eds., *Handbook of Experimental Economics.* Princeton, N.J.: Princeton University Press. 111–194.

Lee, Young, Changyong Rhee, and Taeyoon Sung. 2006. Fiscal Policy in Korea: Before and after the Financial Crisis. *International Tax and Public Finance* **13**(4): 509–531.

LeLoup, Lance, Andrea Dietz, Mihaly Hogye, Zoltan Papai, Laszlo Urban, and Laszlo Varadi. 1998. Budgeting in Hungary during the Democratic Transition. *Journal of Public Budgeting, Accounting & Financial Management* **10**: 89–120.

LeLoup, Lance, Bogomil Ferfila, and Christian Herzog. 2000. Budgeting in Slovenia during the Democratic Transition. *Public Budgeting & Finance,* Fall: 51–79.

Lijphart, Arend. 1984. *Democracies: Patterns of Majoritarian and Consensus Government in Twenty-One Countries.* New Haven, Conn.: Yale University Press.

Lijphart, Arend. 1994. *Electoral Systems and Party Systems: A Study of Twenty-Seven Democracies 1945–1990.* Oxford: Oxford University Press.

Lijphart, Arend. 1999. *Patterns of Democracy: Government Forms and Performance in Thirty-Six Countries.* New Haven, Conn.: Yale University Press.

Lithuania, Government of. 2000. Memorandum of Economic Policy, February 22, 2000. Available at http://www.imf.org/external/NP/LOI/2000/ltu/01/INDEX.htm.

Lupia, Arthur, and Mathew D. McCubbins. 1994. Who Controls? Information and the Structure of Legislative Decision Making. *Legislative Studies Quarterly* **19**(3): 361–384.

Bibliography

Mackie, Thomas T., and Richard Rose. 1991. *The International Almanac of Electoral History*. Third Edition. London: MacMillan.

MacRae, Duncan. 1977. A Political Model of the Business Cycle. *Journal of Political Economy*. **95**: 239–263.

Mares, Isabela. 2003. The Sources of Business Interest in Social Insurance: Sectoral versus National Differences. *World Politics* **55**: 229–258.

Markiewicz, Magorzata, and Joanna Siwińska-Gorzelak. 2003. Wydatki Sztywne Budzetu Panstwa. *CASE Studies and Analyses* 249.

Mattson, Ingvar, and Kaare Strøm. 1995. Parliamentary Committees. In Herbert Döring, ed., *Parliaments and Majority Rule in Western Europe*. New York: St. Martin's. 249–307.

McCubbins, Mathew D. 1991. Party Governance and U.S. Budget Deficits: Divided Government and Fiscal Stalemate. In Alberto Alesina and Geoffrey Carliner, eds., *Politics and Economics in the Eighties*. Chicago: University of Chicago Press. 83–122.

Milesi-Ferretti, Gian-Maria. 2004. Good, Bad, or Ugly? On the Effects of Fiscal Rules with Creative Accounting. *Journal of Public Economics* **88**: 377–394.

Milesi-Ferretti, Gian-Maria, Roberto Perotti, and Massimo Rostagno. 2002. Electoral Systems and Public Spending. *Quarterly Journal of Economics* **117**(2): 609–657.

Millar, Jonathan. 1997. The Effect of Budget Rules on Fiscal Performance and Macroeconomic Stabilization. Bank of Canada Working Paper 97–15. Ottawa: Bank of Canada.

Molander, Per. 2000. Reforming Budgetary Institutions: Swedish Experiences. In Rolf Strauch and Jürgen von Hagen, eds., *Institutions, Politics and Fiscal Policy*. Boston: Kluwer Academic. 191–214.

Morris, Richard, Hedwig Ongena, and Ludger Schuknecht. 2006. *The Reform and Implementation of the Stability and Growth Pact*. European Central Bank Occasional Paper No. 47. Frankfurt: European Central Bank.

Mulas Granados, Carlos. 2003. *The Political Economy of Fiscal Adjustments in the European Union*. Madrid: Juan March Institute.

Müller, Wolfgang, and Kaare Strøm. 1999. *Policy, Office, or Votes? How Political Parties in Western Europe Make Hard Decisions*. Cambridge: Cambridge University Press.

Mundell, Robert A. 1963. Capital Mobility and Stabilization Policy under Fixed and Flexible Exchange Rates. *Canadian Journal of Economics and Political Science* **29**: 475–485.

Nadenichek-Golder, Sona. 2006. Pre-Electoral Coalition Formation in Parliamentary Democracies. *British Journal of Political Science* **36**(2): 193–212.

Nordhaus, William D. 1975. The Political Business Cycle. *Review of Economic Studies* **42**: 169–190.

OECD. 2002. The OECD Budgeting Database. *OECD Journal of Budgeting* **2**(4): 155–171.

Olson, Mancur. 1965. *The Logic of Collective Action*. Cambridge, Mass.: Harvard University Press.

Ostrom, Elinor. 1990. *Governing the Commons*. Cambridge: Cambridge University Press.

Ostrom, Elinor, Roy Gardner, and James Walker. 1994. *Rules, Games, and Common Pool Resources*. Ann Arbor: University of Michigan Press.

Peach, Richard. 2001. The Evolution of the Federal Budget and Fiscal Rules. Paper presented at the Banca D'Italia Third Workshop on Fiscal Rules, Perugia, February 1–3.

Perez-Línan, Anibal. 2007. *Presidential Impeachment and the New Political Instability in Latin America*. Cambridge: Cambridge University Press.

Perotti, Roberto, and Yianos Kontopoulos. 1999. Government Fragmentation and Fiscal Policy Outcomes: Evidence from OECD Countries. In James Poterba and Jürgen von Hagen, eds., *Fiscal Institutions and Fiscal Performance*. Chicago: University of Chicago Press. 81–102.

Perotti, Roberto, Rolf Strauch, and Jürgen von Hagen. 1998. Sustainable Public Finances. London: CEPR/ZEI.

Persson, Torsten, and Lars Svensson. 1989. Why a Stubborn Conservative Would Run a Deficit: Policy with Time Inconsistent Preferences. *Quarterly Journal of Economics* **104**(2): 325–345.

Persson, Torsten, Gerard Roland, and Guido Tabellini. 2006. *Electoral Rules and Government Spending in Parliamentary Democracies*. Manuscript, Bocconi University.

Persson, Torsten, and Guido Tabellini. 2004. Constitutional Rules and Fiscal Policy Outcomes. *American Economic Review* **94**(1): 25–45.

Persson, Torsten, and Guido Tabellini. 2003. *The Economic Effect of Constitutions: What Do the Data Say?* Cambridge, Mass.: MIT Press.

Persson, Torsten, and Guido Tabelllini. 2000. *Political Economics: Explaining Economic Policy*. Cambridge, Mass.: MIT Press.

Poterba, James M. 1994. State Responses to Fiscal Crises: The Effects of Budgetary Institutions and Politics. *Journal of Political Economy* **102**(4): 799–821.

Poterba, James M. 1996a. Budget Institutions and Fiscal Policy in the U.S. States. *American Economic Review, Papers and Proceedings* **86**: 395–400.

Poterba, James M. 1996b. *Do Budget Rules Work?* NBER Working Paper No. 5550. Cambridge, Mass.: National Bureau of Economic Research.

Poterba, James, and Kim Rueben. 2001. Fiscal News, State Budget Rules, and Tax-Exempt Bond Yields. *Journal of Urban Economics* **50**: 537–562.

Potter, Barry H., and Jack Diamond. 2000. *Setting Up Treasuries in the Baltics, Russia, and Other Countries of the Former Soviet Union*. Occasional Paper 198. Washington, D.C.: International Monetary Fund.

Rodden, Jonathan. 2006. *Hamilton's Paradox: The Promise and Peril of Fiscal Federalism*. Cambridge: Cambridge University Press.

Rodden, Jonathan, Gunnar S. Eskeland, and Jennie Litvack, eds. 2003. *Fiscal Decentralization and the Challenge of Hard Budget Constraints*. Cambridge, Mass.: MIT Press.

Rodrik, Dani. 1999. Where Did All the Growth Go? External Shocks, Social Conflict, and Growth Collapses. *Journal of Economic Growth* **4**: 385–412.

Bibliography

Rogoff, Kenneth. 1990. Equilibrium Political Budget Cycles. *The American Economic Review* **80**(1): 21–36.

Rogoff, Kenneth, and Anne Sibert. 1988. Elections and Macroeconomic Policy. *Review of Economic Studies* **55**: 1–16.

Roubini, Nouriel, and Jeffrey D. Sachs. 1989. Political and Economic Determinants of Budget Deficits in the Industrial Democracies. *European Economic Review* **33**: 903–938.

Rubin, Irene. 1990. *The Politics of Public Budgeting: Getting and Spending, Borrowing and Balancing.* Chatham, N.J.: Chatham House.

Sargent, Thomas, and Neill Wallace. 1981. Some Unpleasant Monetarist Arithmetic. *Federal Reserve Bank of Minneapolis Economic Review*, Fall.

Savage, James D. 2005. *Making the EMU: The Politics of Budgetary Surveillance and the Enforcement of Maastricht.* Oxford: Oxford University Press.

Schick, Allen. 1993. Government versus Budget Deficits. In R. Kent Rockman and Bert A. Weaver, *Do Institutions Matter?* Washington, D.C.: Brookings Institution. 187–236.

Schick, Allen. 2003. The Role of Fiscal Rules in Budgeting. *OECD Journal on Budgeting* **3**(3): 7–34.

Schmidt, David, Robert Shupp, James Walker, T.K. Ahn, and Elinor Ostrom. 2001. Dilemma Games: Game Parameters and Matching Protocols. *Journal of Economic Behavior & Organization* **46**: 357–377.

Schuknecht, Ludger. 1999. Fiscal Policy Cycles and the Exchange Rate Regime in Developing Countries. *European Journal of Political Economy* **15**: 569–580.

Schumpeter, Joseph. 1942. *Capitalism, Socialism, and Democracy.* New York: Harper and Brothers.

Shi, Min, and Jacob Svensson. 2002. *Conditional Political Budget Cycles.* CEPR Discussion Paper 3352. London: CEPR.

Sims, G. Thomas, and John Miller. 2005. EU Deficit Loopholes Cause Worry; Higher Rates, Less Growth May Result If Budget Gaps in Euro Zone Grow Wider. *Wall Street Journal* March 22: 2.

Skilling, David. 2001. Policy Coordination, Political Structure, and Public Debt: The Political Economy of Public Debt Accumulation in OECD Countries since 1960. Ph.D. diss., Harvard University.

Stark, Jürgen. 2001. Genesis of a Pact. In: Anne Brunila, Marco Buti and Daniele Franco, eds., *The Stability and Growth Pact.* Houndmills, UK: Palgrave. 77–105.

Stark, Jürgen, and Bernhard Manzke. 2002. Which Role Should Budgetary Policy Play in Response to Cyclical Developments? In Ministry of Finance, ed., *Budgetary Policy in E(M)U: Design and Challenges.* The Hague: Ministry of Finance. 103–111.

Stein, Ernesto, Ernesto Talvi, and Alejandro Grisanti. 1997. Institutional Arrangements and Fiscal Performance: The Latin American Experience. Paper Presented at the Conference on Budgeting Institutions and Fiscal Performance: Perspectives for EMU, Bonn, Germany, June 27–29.

Stein, Ernesto, Ernesto Talvi, and Alejandro Grisanti. 1999. Institutional Arrangements and Fiscal Performance: The Latin American Experience. In James Poterba and Jürgen von Hagen, eds., *Fiscal Institutions and Fiscal Performance*. Chicago: University of Chicago Press. 103–133.

Stienlet, Georges. 2000. Institutional Reforms and Belgian Fiscal Policy in the 90s. In Rolf Strauch and Jürgen von Hagen, eds., *Institutions, Politics and Fiscal Policy*. Boston/Dordrecht/London: Kluwer. 215–234.

Strauch, Rolf R. 1998. Budget Processes and Fiscal Discipline: Evidence from the U.S. States. Working Paper, Zentrum für Europäische Integrationsforschung, Bonn.

Streek, Wolfgang. 2007. Endgame? The Fiscal Crisis of the German State. MPIfG Discussion Paper 07/7. Cologne: MPIfG.

Strøm, Kaare. 1990. *Minority Governments and Majority Rule*. Cambridge: Cambridge University Press.

Sturm, Roland. 1997. Recent Problems of Budgetary Policymaking in Germany. University of Birmingham Institute for German Studies, Working Paper IGS97/12.

Taagepera, Rein, and Matthew Soberg Shugart. 1989. *Seats and Votes: The Effects and Determinants of Electoral Systems*. New Haven, Conn.: Yale University Press.

Taagepera, Rein, and Matthew Soberg Shugart. 1993. Predicting the Number of Parties: A Quantitative Model of Duverger's Mechanical Effect. *American Political Science Review* 87(2): 455–464.

Tabellini, Guido, and Alberto Alesina. 1990. Voting on the Budget Deficit. *The American Economic Review* 80(1): 37–49.

Tanzi, Vito. 1992. Introduction. In Vito Tanzi, ed., *Fiscal Policies in Economics in Transition*. Washington, D.C.: International Monetary Fund. 1–7.

Tanzi, Vito, and Ludger Schuknecht. 2000. *Public Spending in the 20th Century*. Cambridge: Cambridge University Press.

Thuma, József, Hana Polackova, and Carlos Ferreira. 1998. Reforms in Public Finance Management. In Lajos Bokros and Jean-Jacques Dethier, eds., *Public Finance Reform during the Transition: The Experience of Hungary*. Washington, D.C.: International Bank for Reconstruction and Development/World Bank. 377–398.

Tilly, Charles. 1984. *Big Structures, Large Processes and Huge Comparisons*. New York: Russell Sage Foundation.

Tommasi, Mariano, Mark P. Jones, and Pablo Sanguinetti. 1999. Politics, Institutions and Public Sector Spending in the Argentine Provinces. In James Poterba and Jürgen von Hagen, eds., *Fiscal Institutions and Fiscal Performance*. 135–150.

Tsebelis, George. 1995. Decision Making in Political Systems: Veto Players in Presidentialism, Parliamentarism, Multicameralism and Multipartyism. *British Journal of Political Science* 25: 289–325.

Tsebelis, George. 2002. *Veto Players: How Political Institutions Work*. Princeton, N.J.: Princeton University Press.

Bibliography

Velasco, Andrés. 1999. A Model of Endogenous Fiscal Deficits and Delayed Fiscal Reforms. In James Poterba and Jürgen von Hagen, eds., *Fiscal Institutions and Fiscal Performance*. Chicago: University of Chicago Press. 37–57.

Velasco, Andrés. 2000. Debts and Deficits with Fragmented Fiscal Policymaking. *Journal of Public Economics* 76: 105–125.

Visser, Jelle, and Anton Hemerijck. 1997. *A Dutch Miracle – Job Growth, Welfare Reform and Corporatism in the Netherlands*. Amsterdam: University Press.

van den Noord, Paul. 2000. The Size and Role of Automatic Stabilizers in the 1990s and Beyond. OECD Economic Department Working Paper No. 230. Paris: OECD.

von Hagen, Jürgen. 1991. A Note on the Empirical Effectiveness of Formal Fiscal Restraints. *Journal of Public Economics* 44: 199–210.

von Hagen, Jürgen. 1992. Budgeting Procedures and Fiscal Performance in the European Communities. *Economic Papers* 96.

von Hagen, Jürgen. 1997. The Economics of Kinship. In Padma Desai, ed., *Going Global: Transition from Plan to Market in the World Economy*. Cambridge, Mass.: MIT Press.

von Hagen, Jürgen. 2002. Fiscal Rules, Fiscal Institutions, and Fiscal Performance. *Economic and Social Review* 33(3): 263–284.

von Hagen, Jürgen. 2003. Fiscal Sustainability in EMU: From the Stability and Growth Pact to a Sustainability Council for EMU. Manuscript, University of Bonn and Indiana University.

von Hagen, Jürgen. 2004. Political Economy of Fiscal Institutions. In Barry Weingast and Donald Wittman, eds., *Oxford Handbook of Political Economy*, Oxford: Oxford University Press. 464–478.

von Hagen, Jürgen, and Barry Eichengreen. 1996. Federalism, Fiscal Restraints, and European Monetary Union. *American Economic Review* 86: 134–138.

von Hagen, Jürgen, Mark Hallerberg, and Rolf R. Strauch. 2004. The Design of Fiscal Rules and Forms of Governance in EU Countries. Mimeo, ZEI University of Bonn.

von Hagen, Jürgen, and Ian Harden. 1994. National Budget Processes and Fiscal Performance: European Economy. *Reports and Studies* 3: 315–418.

von Hagen, Jürgen, and Ian Harden. 1995. Budget Processes and Commitment to Fiscal Discipline. *European Economic Review* 39: 771–779.

von Hagen, Jürgen, and Ian Harden. 1996. Budget Processes and Commitment to Fiscal Discipline. IMF Working Paper No. 96/78.

von Hagen, Jürgen, Andrew Hughes Hallett, and Rolf Strauch. 2002. Budgetary Consolidation in Europe: Quality, Economic Conditions and Persistence. *Journal of the Japanese and International Economics* 16(4): 512–535.

von Hagen, Jürgen, and Rolf Strauch. 1999. Tumbling Giant: Germany's Fiscal Experience with the Maastricht Criteria. In David Cobham and Georges Zis, eds., *From EMS to EMU*. London: Macmillan. 70–93.

von Hagen, Jürgen, and Rolf Strauch. 2001. Fiscal Consolidation: Quality, Economic Conditions and Success. *Public Choice* 109: 327–347.

von Hagen, Jürgen, Rolf Strauch, and Guntram Wolff. 2002. *East Germany: Transition with Unification, Experiments and Experiences*. ZEI Working Paper B02-19. Bonn: ZEI

von Hagen, Jürgen, and Guntram Wolff. 2006. What Do Deficits Tell Us about Debt? Empirical Evidence on Creative Accounting with Fiscal Rules in the EU. *Journal of Banking and Finance* **30**(12): 3259–3279.

Walker, James, and Roy Gardner. 1992. Probabalistic Destruction of Common-Pool Resources: Experimental Evidence. *Economic Journal* **102**: 1149–1161.

Walker, James, Roy Gardner, and Elinor Ostrom. 1990. Rent Dissipation in a Limited-Access Common-Pool Resource: Experimental Evidence. *Journal of Environmental Economics and Management* **19**: 203–211.

Warwick, Paul. 1994. *Government Survival in Western European Parliamentary Democracies*. New York: Cambridge University Press.

Weaver, R. Kent. 1986. The Politics of Blame Avoidance. *Journal of Public Policy* **6**: 71–98.

Wehner, Joachim. 2007. Budget Reform and Legislative Control in Sweden. *Journal of European Public Policy* **14**(2): 313–332.

Weingast, Barry R., Kenneth A. Shepsle, and Christopher Johnson. 1981. The Political Economy of Benefits and Costs: A Neoclassical Approach to Distributive Politics. *Journal of Political Economy* **89**: 642–664.

Wildavsky, Aaron. 1975. *Budgeting*. Oxford: Transaction Publishers.

Wildavsky, Aaron. 1986. *Budgeting: A Comparative Theory of Budgeting Processes*. Oxford: Transaction Publishers.

Woldendorp, Keman, and Ian Budge. 1993. Political Data 1945–1990. *European Journal of Political Research* **24**: 1–120.

Wooldridge, Jeffrey. 2002. *Economic Analysis of Cross Section and Panel Data*. Cambridge, Masss.: MIT Press.

Wyplosz, Charles. 2002. Fiscal Discipline in EMU: Rules or Institutions? Working Paper, Graduate Institute for International Studies, Geneva, April.

Wyplosz, Charles. 2005. Fiscal Policy: Institutions versus Rules. *National Institute Economic Review* **191**(1): 64–78.

Yläoutinen, Sami. 2005. Development and Functioning of Fiscal Frameworks in the Central and Eastern European Countries. Ph.D. Diss., University of Jyväskylä.

Zubek, Radoslaw. 2006. Poland: Unbalanced Domestic Leadership in Negotiating Fit. In Kenneth Dyson, ed., *Enlarging the Euro-Zone: The Euro and the Transformation of East Central Europe*. Oxford: Oxford University Press.

Index

Index